Approaches to Teaching
Hugo's *Les Misérables*

Approaches to Teaching Hugo's *Les Misérables*

Edited by

Michal P. Ginsburg

and

Bradley Stephens

The Modern Language Association of America
New York   2018

MLA and the MODERN LANGUAGE ASSOCIATION are trademarks
owned by the Modern Language Association of America.
For information about obtaining permission to reprint material from
MLA book publications, send your request by mail (see address below)
or e-mail (permissions@mla.org).

Library of Congress Cataloging-in-Publication Data is available from the
Library of Congress.
ISBN 978-1-60329-335-8 (cloth)
ISBN 978-1-60329-336-5 (paper)
ISBN 978-1-60329-337-2 (EPUB)
ISBN 978-1-60329-338-9 (Kindle)

Approaches to Teaching World Literature 150
ISSN 1059-1133

Cover illustration of the paperback and electronic editions:
Jean Victor Schnetz, *Fighting at the Hotel de Ville, 28 July 1830*, 1833,
oil on canvas. Musée de la Ville de Paris, Musée du Petit-Palais,
France / Bridgeman Images.

Published by The Modern Language Association of America
85 Broad Street, suite 500, New York, New York 10004-2434
www.mla.org

CONTENTS

Introduction

Michal P. Ginsburg and Bradley Stephens

Victor Hugo, one of France's foremost *grands hommes*, looms large over nineteenth-century French literature and indeed over the entire French literary landscape. His standing as the most imposing French poet of his time is evident from the need felt by the poets who followed him to "not repeat Hugo," or "faire autre chose que Hugo," as Paul Valéry put it.[1] His reputation as the leading writer for the theater was established early on, in the famous "battle" over his play *Hernani* (1830) that led to a resounding triumph for the Romantic movement. His status as a novelist is no less certain but is more complicated. His early novels, from *Han d'Islande* (1823) to *Notre-Dame de Paris* (1831), were in complete accord with the literary innovations and aesthetics of the period; when *Notre-Dame de Paris* appeared, Alphonse de Lamartine hailed Hugo as the Shakespeare of the novel in a letter dated 1 July 1831 (370–71). But his later novels, beginning with *Les Misérables*, were out of sync with both aesthetic and political trends. This "belatedness" accounts for much of the hostile criticism with which *Les Misérables* met when it appeared in 1862, and which was made all the more conspicuous by the novel's sensational popularity. But it also marks Hugo's specific, if not unique, position in the post-1848 social, political, and cultural arena: whereas for other writers of his time the repression of the workers' uprising of June 1848 meant loss of faith in the values of the Enlightenment and the revolution, it is precisely after the June Days that Hugo becomes a committed, militant republican. His interventions as an elected member of the Assemblée Législative on key questions such as poverty and press censorship signaled that he was increasingly embracing democratic values, as would be confirmed by his self-exile after Louis-Napoleon's coup d'état of December 1851.

Les Misérables (whose writing was interrupted by the 1848 revolution and completed thirteen years later) casts a retrospective view on the failure of the insurrection of 1832 and affirms, from a post-1848 standpoint, the need to envisage and fight for a more just social world—despite Hugo's awareness that achieving this goal would be far from simple. Hugo thus asserts the necessity of striving for social change as well as the role that literature—writing, reading, teaching it—can play in keeping this goal in view. As he put it in the short preface to *Les Misérables*, as long as misery exists, books like his own "pourront ne pas être inutiles" 'may not be useless.' Hugo's obsessive repetition in that preface of "tant que" 'as long as' suggests he was fully aware that the abolition of misery would not happen overnight, would not be brought about in one revolutionary event, which is why books such as his would remain important. His force of vision and unwavering conviction in the transformative power of humanity captivated readers across the world, then as now.

Hugo's unique sociopolitical standpoint cannot be separated from his belief in the indeterminate nature of the world, his faith in an enigmatic divine, his aversion toward systematic or categorical thinking, and his view of the artist as a "lighthouse" that guides his fellow human beings. These in turn are inseparable from the aesthetics of his novel. Ignoring the strictures of the reigning realist aesthetics (*Madame Bovary* was published five years before *Les Misérables*) while his Romantic worldview evolved, Hugo created characters that are larger than life and a plot that has little to do with the everyday existence of average people. The many discursive digressions, with topics ranging from French history to spoken slang, and the mélanges of different genres (tragedy, epic, romance, and so on) defy any formal conception of the novel and are integral to the novel's goal of representing those whom society excludes and ignores.

The novel's vast number of adaptations and multiple translations demonstrate that *Les Misérables* has lost neither its popular appeal nor its sociopolitical significance. Before the phenomenon of the famous stage musical began in the commercially electric and politically charged 1980s, Hugo's novel had already been repeatedly adapted. Generations around the world found a means of self-expression through the story, including during the Great Depression of the 1930s and the social unrest of the 1970s. The musical has helped ensure that *Les Misérables* remains inscribed upon the hearts and minds of the early twenty-first century. In the light of this extensive legacy, the novel's powerful preface is strikingly prophetic since Hugo's story continues to assert its relevance over a century and a half after it first appeared.

Figures such as Jean Valjean, Fantine, and Gavroche can and do resonate in our contemporary world, where social inequality persists, violence and discrimination against women is rife, and every second child on the planet is born into poverty. The spirit of Hugo's student revolutionaries has been stirring in the new millennium against the self-interest and repressive instincts of powerful elites, be it in the heart of the Occupy Wall Street movement, among the tents of Turkey's Gezi Park protests, or on Hong Kong's streets during the "Umbrella Revolution," and will continue to do so in the foreseeable future. In Hugo's own country, the "Nuit debout" 'Up All Night' movement launched in spring 2016 to resist labor reforms and austerity measures served as yet another reminder that the hardships and the indignation inherent in Hugo's portrait of nineteenth-century France are not confined to the past. Hugo continues to prompt our consciences and encourage our aspirations, as the actress Anne Hathaway implied when accepting the Academy Award in 2013 for her portrayal of Fantine in Tom Hooper's film musical version: "Here's hoping that someday in the not too distant future the misfortunes of Fantine will only be found in stories and never in real life."

However, a number of adaptations and translations have simplified Hugo's vision and sentimentalized it, offering readings that appropriate the story for commercial and ideological purposes without necessarily replicating its critical edge and crucial scope. It is therefore as important as ever to come back to the original novel, read what it tells us, and teach students how to read it—not a simple task. The novel's length, its refusal to limit itself to a linear plot, the many discursive passages where the plot is set aside, and its exorbitant language all make reading and teaching it challenging. Furthermore, the historical events and ideological conflicts essential to understanding the novel (often erased from anglophone adaptations) are neither easily accessible nor of obvious interest to most American students.

Our goal in assembling this volume of essays is to offer tools that will make the task of teaching *Les Misérables* less daunting and more rewarding. Part 1, "Materials," discusses the wide array of materials available to instructors. Besides providing a guide to the novel's many editions, translations, and abridgments as well as to the wealth of visual, audiovisual, and digital resources, "Materials" includes specific recommendations for further readings concerning the historical and literary context, Hugo's life, and critical studies of the novel. It also provides two additional resources: an essay on the novel's representation of the city, accompanied by a set of three maps showing some of the novel's important sites and tracing characters' itineraries in the city, and a short presentation of the characters and their networks in the novel. The maps, the data on the characters, and the graphs of the characters' networks can also be accessed on the Web site *Visualizing* Les Misérables, hosted on the *MLA Commons*.

Part 2, "Approaches," consists of essays that provide instructors with concrete, practical, and pedagogical suggestions on teaching the novel. Like the novel, this assortment of essays spins various strands of understanding that the reader can either hold apart or thread together as a productive means of coming to grips with Hugo's writing. The most urgent practical issues are the novel's length, its historical context, and its many digressions. The essays address these central problems in various ways. The responses to our survey and the essays themselves show that harnessing sections of the novel for teaching is relatively straightforward, especially in courses with a thematic focus (e.g., the courses on Paris, childhood, crime, or utopia described below). Many of the essays also indicate that adaptations can be used both to make *Les Misérables* more relevant to students and, through comparison with the novel, clarify the importance of its historical specificity. And as some of the essays illustrate, the digressions can also be used to illuminate aspects of the novel as a whole.

The contributors to the volume include Hugo specialists and scholars working broadly in the field of nineteenth-century French literature; all have experience in teaching the novel. Although many of the essays envisage teaching the novel to students of French literature and culture, the authors' suggestions can be easily adapted to comparative and interdisciplinary courses taught in English. The novel's renown in the American popular consciousness and its numerous English translations suggest that it deserves greater recognition beyond French studies.

"Approaches" is divided into three sections. The first, "Contexts," consists of contributions that explain how the historical context, the contexts of production and reception, and the afterlives of Hugo's most famous work can be used to illuminate aspects of the novel. Dean de la Motte analyzes the dissonance between the novel's spectacular popular success and its mostly hostile "literary" reception by situating them in the political, social, and cultural context of the period. Taking an approach more rooted in material history, Anne O'Neil-Henry argues that *Les Misérables* should be read in the context of mid-nineteenth-century French literary markets and the modern phenomenon of the best seller. Her essay investigates how production and distribution help shape literary forms. Bettina Lerner's essay turns to the importance of historical context by placing Hugo's famous digression about Waterloo in dialogue with other historical and literary renderings of the battle as well as with popular historical spectacles such as panoramas and phantasmagorias. The novel's conception of history is revealed as an interplay of official and unofficial accounts. Moving from the battlefield to the streets, Rachel Fuchs documents the lives of the poor, especially those of children and unwed mothers, in nineteenth-century Paris and situates Hugo's political opinions and his novel in the context of contemporary attitudes toward the destitute. Laurence Porter considers the novel's keen sociohistorical consciousness in broader terms to draw out Hugo's nonessentialist understanding of social class. Moral hierarchies in the novel depend not on wealth or social rank but on human action, enabling Hugo to highlight the potential value of individuals and groups that conservative society has dismissed. Finally, Kathryn Grossman's essay deals with the multimedia afterlives of Hugo's work and shows how this adaptive legacy constitutes a rich cultural context for thinking and talking about the novel. The novel's vast range of adaptations illustrates how works of literature can always be appropriated and reshaped to reflect changing needs.

The second section, "Specific Courses," is devoted to courses in which *Les Misérables* can be taught. Though authors present the courses at the level and to the audience to which they were originally taught, all the proposed courses can be easily modified to fit different levels and different student bodies (including non-French-speaking students). The section opens with an essay by Philippe Moisan, who describes how *Les Misérables* can be taught in a survey course on the French novel by focusing on the place of Hugo's text in the move from Romantic to realist aesthetics during the nineteenth century. Michal Ginsburg's essay treats the challenge of teaching the entire novel in an undergraduate class. It proposes ways of dealing with the novel's length and digressions, describes a "transversal" approach to the novel, and demonstrates how using film clips can illuminate broad thematic issues while keeping students close to the text. Pauline de Tholozany describes an interdisciplinary course on the representation of childhood in which the novel's treatment of children is studied alongside other texts featuring children: nineteenth-century medical reports, children's literature, and educational treatises, as well as histories of childhood. Andrea Goulet's essay presents a course on another sociocultural context—namely, crime in nineteenth-century literature. She shows how reading *Les Misérables* can be used to discuss the relation between law, ethics, and criminal justice in the nineteenth century (thus allowing reflection on these issues in contemporary culture). In the next essay, Cary Hollinshead-Strick and Anne-Marie Picard describe a course on the literature of Paris in which parts of *Les Misérables* are read. The authors link the episode of the sewers to writings by François Villon and François Rabelais, while the episode of the barricade leads to a study of Arthur Rimbaud's poetry. Brian Martin then discusses how Hugo's novel can be read as a powerful forum for social and political engagement against human suffering. He describes two courses: an introductory one on French war literature that uses a segment of *Les Misérables* and an advanced course that deals with the novel and some of its adaptations to demonstrate the enduring importance of Hugo's representation of the miseries of poverty and misogyny. Daniel Sipe's essay proposes a comparative and interdisciplinary course on nineteenth-century utopianism. He explains how *Les Misérables* can be taught as part of the tradition of utopian thought and literature and how Hugo's utopianism evolved in response to the changing cultural and political landscape of mid-nineteenth-century France. That political landscape also looms large in Julia Douthwaite Viglione's essay, which describes a course on the French Revolution that includes sections of *Les Misérables* on the syllabus. The course emphasizes the revolution's goals of creating a new man and a new nation, reconciling past and present, and identifying a moral code for the future. Bradley Stephens's essay about a course on literary adaptation details how the relation between a source and its reimaginings echoes the dialogue between past and present. He uses *Les Misérables* as a compelling example of how texts travel across time and media, analyzing versions from a range of cultures and media forms through the conceptual and methodological models articulated by adaptation studies. Finally, André Iliev's essay provides an example of how selected passages of the novel can be taught in high schools that prepare students for the international baccalaureate and other qualifications. His essay reinforces this volume's overall argument that *Les Misérables* can be productively approached by students at various levels and with varying skills.

The third section, "Critical Perspectives," centers on specific themes and formal issues by bringing a range of critical perspectives to bear on *Les Misérables*. Dorothy Kelly's essay explores teaching Hugo's novel and "la question sociale" through the lens of gender. She explains how the novel exposes the societal enforcement of normative gender roles, thereby revealing the text's relevance to a prevalent area of critical reflection. Joseph Mai's essay treats the place occupied by the moral individual in Hugo's novel as well as questions of shame and humility. Mai explores how Hugo's moral compass navigates between secular observation and spiritual fulfillment. William Paulson proposes teaching the specter of 1848 in the novel through a comparison between the novel and its musical adaptation. The presence in the musical of songs where the dead are remembered renders all the more poignant the absence of memorialization of the dead of the barricade in the novel, which reveals Hugo's own moments of doubt after 1848. The role of the digressions and how to use them in teaching the novel is the topic of Mary Anne O'Neil's essay. The philosophical and historical digressions are highlighted to clarify not only Hugo's perspectives as a thinker but also his construction of plot and character. Timothy Raser then discusses the way in which narrative motivation functions in *Les Misérables*: one cannot link it to plot causality or define it through proximity between detail and event. Instead, motivation is produced in the novel through metaphor. Another central feature of narrative is the subject of the final essay, by Isabel Roche. She addresses Hugo's conception of character and character making, arguing for the modern aspects of his conceptual, nonpsychological creations and presenting detailed analyses of the archetypal figures in *Les Misérables*. A different analysis of character can be found on the Web site *Visualizing* Les Misérables, a companion to this volume.

NOTE

[1] "Le problème capital de la littérature, depuis 1840 jusqu'en 1890, n'est-il pas: Comment faire autre chose que Hugo? Comment être visible malgré Hugo? Comment se pencher sur les cimes de Hugo?" 'Isn't literature's main problem, from 1848 up until 1890: How not to repeat Hugo? How to stand out in spite of Hugo? How to scale his heights?' (letter to Paul Souday dated October 1923 [*Lettres* 149]). That Valéry writes this in 1923 casts doubt on the idea that somehow this anxiety abated in 1890.

Part One

MATERIALS

Editions, Abridgments, and Translations

According to the Bibliothèque Nationale de France (BNF) catalog, more than three hundred French editions of *Les Misérables* have been published. The majority of our survey participants favored the edition by Yves Gohin, in the Folio classique series (reissued in 1999 in two volumes) because of the quality of its notes and its affordable price. This is the edition contributors to this volume cite. It includes, besides extensive notes, an introduction by Gohin in the first volume, and a "dossier" at the end of the second volume, consisting of a parallel chronology of Victor Hugo's life and of the events told in *Les Misérables*; a short bibliography; and, in an appendix, the text "Les Fleurs" (the first part of which became the four chapters of "Patron-Minette" [pt. 3, bk. 7]).

A good alternative to the Gohin edition is the 1998 Livre de poche edition by Nicole Savy and Guy Rosa, also in two volumes. Published research increasingly tends to reference the 1985 Laffont-Bouquins one-volume edition (part of the project of complete works led by Jacques Seebacher and Guy Rosa in the late 1980s). One of the editions mentioned by respondents is no longer in print: the Classiques Garnier two-volume edition by M.-F. Guyard. The 1993 Garnier-Flammarion three-volume edition and the Pocket one-volume edition (reissued in 2013) have no notes. All the above editions are unabridged; abridged editions (excerpts) include Classiques Larousse, edited by Alexandre Gefen (2007); Classiques Bordas, edited by Florence Naugrette (1995); and the École des Loisirs 2013 edition (designed for French schoolchildren).

The English translation of *Les Misérables* that is used in this volume is Lee Fahnestock and Norman MacAfee's 1987 revision of the original 1862 Charles E. Wilbour translation, published by Signet Classics. It is far from perfect but was judged to be more accurate (though less lively) than the Norman Denny translation (1976), published by Penguin Classics. The Signet edition has an afterword by Chris Bohjalian, and the Penguin edition has an introduction by Denny; neither one has notes. The Modern Library paperback edition, translated by Julie Rose (2008), is lengthier and more expensive than the Signet or the Penguin edition; on the other hand, it has, besides an introduction by Adam Gopnik, extensive notes by James Madden. Another option mentioned is Isabel F. Hapgood's translation, dating from 1887 and available online at *Project Gutenberg* (at the same time it is, of course, prudent to discourage students from using any online edition that has not been authenticated by scholars). Penguin Classics has more recently released a new and well-received translation by Christine Donougher (2013), with an introduction by the historian Robert Tombs. An abridged version of the novel in English is published by Barnes and Noble Classics (2003); it is edited by Laurence M. Porter, uses the Wilbour translation, and includes an introduction and notes by Porter.

Select List of Editions and Translations

Editions

Les Misérables. Edited by Alexandre Gefen, Classiques Larousse, 2007 (abridged).

Les Misérables. Edited by Yves Gohin, Folio classique, 1999. 2 vols.

Les Misérables. Edited by M.-F. Guyard, Classiques Garnier, 1963. 2 vols.

Les Misérables. Edited by René Journet, Garnier-Flammarion, 1967. 3 vols.

Les Misérables. Edited by Arnaud Laster, Pocket Classiques, 2009. 3 vols.

Les Misérables. Edited by Florence Naugrette, Classiques Bordas, 1995 (abridged).

Les Misérables. Edited by Guy Rosa and Annette Rosa, Laffont-Bouquins, 1985, 1991.

Les Misérables. Edited by Marie-Hélène Sabard, École des Loisirs, 2013.

Les Misérables. Edited by Nicole Savy and Guy Rosa, Livre de poche, 1985. 2 vols.

Translations

Les Misérables. Translated by Norman Denny. Penguin Classics, 1976.

Les Misérables. Translated by Christine Donougher. Penguin Classics, 2013.

Les Misérables. Translated by Lee Fahnestock and Norman MacAfee. Signet Classics, 1987.

Les Misérables. Translated by Isabel F. Hapgood. *Project Gutenberg*, 1887.

Les Misérables. Translated by Julie Rose. Modern Library, 2008.

Les Misérables. Translated by Charles W. Wilbour, edited by Laurence M. Porter. Barnes and Noble Classics, 2003 (abridged).

Note on Editions Cited in This Volume

In this volume, contributors cite Gohin's 1999 French edition of *Les Misérables* and Fahnestock and MacAfee's 1987 translation, unless otherwise noted.[1] Citations in the text are composed of three parts: the volume and page number(s) in Gohin's edition; the page number(s) in Fahnestock and McAfee's translation; and the corresponding part, book, and chapter number(s) in Hugo's novel.

Visual, Audiovisual, and Digital Materials

The Web site of the Paris-based Groupe Hugo (groupugo.div.jussieu.fr/) offers an unparalleled resource for readers of Hugo's work. Founded in 1969, the group brings together specialists, mainly within France. In addition to news relating to publications and conferences about Hugo, the Web site hosts a range of indispensable research tools, the highlights of which are arguably a growing archive of over 260 research presentations from the group's regular meetings since 1986 and links to nearly 100 downloadable publications, including Guy Rosa's edition of *Les Misères* (the manuscript of *Les Misérables* as it stood on the eve of the 1848 revolution), which can illustrate to students the long-term evolution of Hugo's novel.

The site provides other useful links: for example, to *Gallica*, the digital library of the BNF (gallica.bnf.fr), where original editions and illustrated versions of *Les Misérables* can be consulted alongside press reviews from the 1860s; the BNF's online exhibition for Hugo's 2002 bicentenary (victorhugo.bnf.fr/), which opens a rich interactive portal into Hugo's life and works (including his many paintings and sketches); and the Hugo museums in Paris and Guernsey (maisons victorhugo.paris.fr), which provide details on Hugo's domestic life and his personal library. The French *Wikisource* site also allows access to a wide range of Hugo's literary works, essays, and speeches in a mostly standardized format, which can become a particularly useful teaching tool when composing reading lists for students (fr.wikisource.org/wiki/Cat%C3%A9gorie:Victor_Hugo).

Broader historical information can be found at the bilingual Web site of the *Fondation Napoléon* (www.napoleon.org/en/home.asp), which covers both France's empires, and at the Web site *France in the Age of* Les Misérables, which was created by history students at Mount Holyoke College in 2001 (www.mtholyoke .edu/courses/rschwart/hist255-s01/index.html) and provides a range of social and cultural contexts for readers of Hugo's novel, from the pleasures of the bourgeoisie to the plight of the poor. Online commemorations of the Battle of Waterloo for the 2015 bicentenary offer similar context to explore, especially *The Last Stand: Napoleon's 100 Days in 100 Objects* (www.100days.eu/) and *Waterloo 200* (www .nam.ac.uk/waterloo200/), a project of the United Kingdom's National Army Museum. Both sites feature online exhibitions, time lines, and news.

The ongoing success of the stage musical ensures that a healthy interest persists in the different adaptations of *Les Misérables*. Although no portal exists as a gateway to these versions, many screen and stage recordings are regularly uploaded to video-sharing Web sites such as *YouTube*. In addition, there is a growing bank of material (including documentaries and panel discussions) at France's *Inathèque* Web site (www.inatheque.fr/index.html).

See also the section on adaptations in the works-cited list at the end of this volume.

Biographies and Reception

Hugo's life and indeed afterlife as a major cultural figure of the nineteenth century can read like something of an epic in itself and has unsurprisingly been the subject of numerous biographies and critical studies. The most recent undertaking in French is also the most substantial: Jean-Marc Hovasse embarked on a trilogy of volumes with *Victor Hugo: Avant l'exil: 1802–1851*, followed by *Pendant l'exil: 1851–1864*; a third installment is forthcoming. This biography is already greater in length (over 2,600 pages and counting) than Hubert Juin's triptych, which divides Hugo's life along slightly different political lines (1802–43, 1844–70, 1870–85), and Max Gallo's two-volume study entitled *Victor Hugo I: "Je suis une force qui va!": 1802–43* and *Victor Hugo II: "Je serai celui-là!": 1844–85*.

Single-volume biographies include works by Jean-Bertrand Barrère, Alain Decaux, and Yves Gohin. More concise and readily accessible introductions have been published by Sophie Grossiord, Maricke Stein, and Sandrine Fillipetti. These would be logical starting points for instructors and students unfamiliar with Hugo. Biographies with a more particular focus are also of interest, especially Michel de Decker's *Hugo: Victor pour ces dames* as well as Henri Pena-Ruiz and Jean-Paul Scot's *Un Poète en politique: Les combats de Victor Hugo*, both appearing during Hugo's 2002 bicentenary, and Henri Pigaillem's broad history of the Hugo family during and after the writer's life. Bernard Leuilliot's *Victor Hugo publie "Les Misérables"* recounts the novel's sensational publication in 1862, and, like Marc Bressant's relatively brief reflections on Hugo's famous state funeral in Paris in 1885, is a reminder of Hugo's impact on the popular consciousness. Although Hugo never published an autobiography, his wife Adèle Hugo's *Victor Hugo raconté par un témoin de sa vie* constitutes something of an official self-portrait that can be read alongside his journal entries from *Choses vues*.

In English, Graham Robb's 1997 biography remains the liveliest and most extensive account; it is still widely available and benefits from meticulous detail and critical impartiality. A. F. Davidson's informative 1912 study is more candid than might be expected of biographies from the early twentieth century. Elliott M. Grant offers an imaginative portrait of a forward-thinking Hugo whose resonance with the immediate postwar period makes for stimulating reading, while John Porter Houston focuses on poetry as the key thread through Hugo's life, and Joanna Richardson develops a probing, if at times moralizing, reading. A new short critical biography, by Bradley Stephens, is forthcoming.

Excellent insights into the cultural fashioning of Hugo's monumentality as a writer can be found in the fourth chapter of Michael D. Garval's *A Dream of Stone*. General overviews of Hugo's life and works are available in John Andrew Frey's *A Victor Hugo Encyclopedia* and in Marva A. Barnett's *Victor Hugo on Things That Matter*. Claude Millet and David Charles are coediting the *Dictionnaire Victor Hugo* for Classiques Garnier, which will be a major reference work for research on Hugo.

Criticism

To get a sense of the diversity of interpretations of *Les Misérables*, the reader of French can start with any of several volumes of collected essays, including those edited by Guy Rosa and Anne Ubersfeld, by Pierre Brunel, by Gabrielle Chamarat, by José-Luis Díaz, by Guy Rosa (*Victor Hugo*), and by Danielle Molinari. The chapter on *Les Misérables* in Mona Ozouf's *Les Aveux du roman* is of particular note since, through its investigation of how the French novel in the nineteenth century negotiates the old and the new, it proposes an interesting way for integrating Hugo's novel into French literary history. Myriam Roman and Marie-Christine Bellosta's Les Misérables*: Roman pensif* is another helpful tool since, besides a detailed analysis of the novel, it includes a substantial collection of texts and documents, a chronology, and a synopsis. Roman's *Victor Hugo et le roman philosophique* sets Hugo's novel within the broader context of his fiction to substantiate the link between literature and philosophy in his writing, while Georges Piroué's *Victor Hugo romancier* develops a similarly broad but equally astute overview of Hugo's narratives. In addition, Henri Meschonnic's *Pour la poétique, IV: Écrire Hugo* rigorously analyzes the shape of Hugo's "roman poème" 'novel-poem' (our trans.).

In English, five book-length studies focusing exclusively on *Les Misérables* are to be recommended. Mario Vargas Llosa's *The Temptation of the Impossible* provides an excellent analysis of the novel's narrative voice (which Vargas Llosa, half seriously, half ironically, calls "the divine stenographer" [11]) and of its utopian dimension. Kathryn M. Grossman's *Figuring Transcendence* develops a far-reaching study of how Hugo dramatizes his Romantic sublime through the novel's depiction of all life as interrelated. Grossman's Les Misérables*: Conversion, Revolution, Redemption* offers a more introductory consideration of the novel's formal and thematic concern with revolution. With Bradley Stephens, she has also edited Les Misérables *and Its Afterlives*, which analyzes the novel and its multimedia adaptations and appropriations. Similarly attentive to literary analysis and cultural history, David Bellos's *The Novel of the Century: The Amazing Adventures of "Les Misérables"* is lively and illuminating.

Works on Hugo's novelistic enterprise are also of critical value, relating Hugo's most famous novel to his other narratives. Richard B. Grant's *The Perilous Quest* gave anglophone readers access to the revisions in Hugolian scholarship, which had been under way in France since the 1950s, by stressing the visionary rather than the mimetic nature of Hugo's narrative fiction. This concept of Hugo's novels as visionary works is taken up by Victor Brombert in his influential *Victor Hugo and the Visionary Novel*, which includes a chapter on *Les Misérables*, and in *The Hidden Reader*, his comparative reading of Hugo with Stendhal, Balzac, Baudelaire, and Flaubert. J. A. Hiddleston's bilingual edited volume of essays uses the notion of the abyss as an interpretive strategy toward

Hugo's fiction, with two essays on *Les Misérables* and two essays looking at all his novels. Given the memorable nature of characters such as Jean Valjean and their importance to the novel's cultural appeal, Isabel Roche's study of character and meaning in these novels is another thought-provoking title to consult because it reads Hugo's fictive figures through his aesthetic and political ideas.

Background Materials

Hugo's novel occupies a unique and problematic place in the history of the French novel: published when realism had already been established as the dominant aesthetics, it harks back in some of its elements to Romanticism while gesturing toward what would become modernism. We therefore list suggestions for readings on all three literary movements, noting that valuable introductory essays to each are to be found in widely accessible anthologies (e.g., Hollier; Burgwinkle et al.).

Romanticism

A major reference work for French Romanticism is now available in Alain Vaillant's edited volume *Le Romantisme*. General introductions can be found in *Manuel d'histoire littéraire de la France, 1789–1848*, edited by Pierre Barbéris and Claude Duchet, and in Max Milner, *Le Romantisme, 1820–1843*, in addition to David G. Charlton's two-volume edited collection *The French Romantics*. Another useful introductory book (although primarily about English Romanticism) is Marilyn Butler's *Romantics, Rebels, and Reactionaries*. For an accessible book (which may thus also be assigned to students) that spells out the intellectual stakes of Romanticism, one can turn to Isaiah Berlin's *The Roots of Romanticism*. Discussions of Romanticism that are particularly relevant to Hugo's novel can be found in James Smith Allen's *Popular French Romanticism: Authors, Readers, and Books in the Nineteenth Century* and Claude Millet's commanding panorama *Le Romantisme*. On melodrama—an important ingredient of Romantic fiction—consult Peter Brooks's *The Melodramatic Imagination*. For a study of the French Romantic hero, one can consult Margaret Waller, *The Male Malady: Fictions of Impotence in the French Romantic Novel*, and Allan H. Pasco, *Sick Heroes*. For the relation between French Romantic literature and other arts, see David Wakefield, *French Romantics: Literature and the Visual Arts*, C. W. Thompson, *Victor Hugo and the Graphic Arts*, and the music critic Charles Rosen's *Romantic Poets, Critics, and Other Madmen*. Other discussions of French Romanticism include Jean-Pierre Richard, *Études sur le romantisme*; Pierre-Georges Castex, *Horizons romantiques*; Michel Crouzet, *Essai sur la genèse du romantisme*; Paul Bénichou, *Les Mages romantiques*; and Frank Paul Bowman,

French Romanticism. For studies of Romanticism across Europe that can help position the French tradition in continental terms, see the following edited volumes: Roy Porter and Mikulàs Teich, *Romanticism in National Context*; Michael Ferber, *A Companion to European Romanticism*; and Paul Hamilton, *The Oxford Handbook of European Romanticism*. Ferber's *Romanticism: A Very Short Introduction* provides a stellar summary of these European contexts.

Realism

Erich Auerbach's seminal *Mimesis: The Representation of Reality in Western Literature* provides a broad introduction to the question of the representation of everyday life; though it is not confined to the nineteenth-century movement of realism, it includes readings of Stendhal and Balzac. György Lukács's *Studies in European Realism* is another classic study of the movement, and Fredric Jameson's *The Antinomies of Realism* offers a contemporary perspective on the most influential theories of literary and artistic realism. Roland Barthes's essay "L'Effet du réel" is an important discussion of the role of objects in realist fiction. Vanessa Schwartz's *Spectacular Realities: Early Mass Culture in Fin-de-Siècle Paris* helps situate the French realist novel within a broader culture of realist spectacle, while Richard Lehan's *Realism and Naturalism* positions the realist text as a site of transition in Western culture. Christopher Prendergast's *The Order of Mimesis*, Margaret Cohen's *The Sentimental Education of the Novel*, Peter Brooks's *Realist Vision*, and Sandy Petrey's *In the Court of the Pear King*, as well as Lawrence Schehr's *Rendering French Realism* and *Subversions of Verisimilitude*, are all, in one way or another, critiques or questionings of the assumptions underlying realism.

Modernism

A large number of books can serve as introductions to modernism. These include *The Oxford Handbook of Modernisms*, edited by Peter Brooker et al.; *The Modernism Handbook*, compiled by Philip Tew and Alex Murray; *Modernism*, edited by Astradur Eysteinsson and Vivian Liska; Peter Nicholls, *Modernisms: A Literary Guide*; and Tim Armstrong, *Modernism: A Cultural History*. Michael Whitworth's *Modernism* discusses, among other things, modernism's relation to Romanticism, realism, and formalism. Stephen Bronner's *Modernism at the Barricades: Aesthetics, Politics, Utopia* deals with modernism in literature, visual arts, and music; *Modernism and the European Unconscious*, edited by Peter Collier and Judy Davies, emphasizes the link between modernism and psychoanalysis; Stephen Kern's *The Culture of Time and Space, 1880–1918* deals, among other topics, with modernism's relation to technology and mass culture.

History: Waterloo to the Second Empire and Beyond

For instructors looking for general history books dealing with the period covered by the novel (1815–33) or the period of Hugo's life (1802–85), suggested readings would include John Lough and Muriel Lough, *An Introduction to Nineteenth-Century France*; F. W. J. Hemmings, *Culture and Society in France, 1789–1848*; Gordon Wright, *France in Modern Times: From the Enlightenment to the Present*; the relevant parts in Eric J. Hobsbawm, *The Age of Revolution: Europe, 1789–1848*; Philip Nord, *The Republican Moment: Struggles for Democracy in Nineteenth-Century France*; Robert Tombs, *France, 1814–1914*; Francis Démier's *La France du XIXe siècle*; and Robert Gildea, *Children of the Revolution: The French, 1799–1914*.

For the history of Paris, David Harvey's *Paris: Capital of Modernity*, Johannes Willms's *Paris: Capital of Europe*, and Colin Jones's *Paris: Biography of a City* immediately come to mind. For a more literary account, one can consult Christopher Prendergast's *Paris and the Nineteenth Century*, Priscilla Parkhurst Ferguson's *Paris as Revolution*, as well as Karlheinz Stierle's *Paris, capitale des signes: Paris et son discours*. On social conditions in nineteenth-century Paris, with a special emphasis on women, see Rachel Fuchs's *Poor and Pregnant in Paris: Strategies for Survival in the Nineteenth Century*. Martyn Lyons's *Readers and Society in Nineteenth-Century France* pays particular attention to the reading habits of women, workers, and peasants during the period's expansion of the reading public. For insights into the health, education, and employment of children, see Colin Heywood's *Childhood in Nineteenth-Century France*. For a history of the police, see John Merriman, *Police Stories: Building the French State, 1815–1851*. Those interested in the episode of the barricade would benefit from *The Insurgent Barricade*, by Mark Traugott; *Barricades: The War of the Streets in Revolutionary Paris, 1830–1848*, by Jill Harsin; and Robert Sayre's *L'Insurrection des Misérables*. For the episode of the sewers, one may want to consult Donald Reid's *Paris Sewers and Sewermen: Realities and Representations*.

Characters and
Character Networks in *Les Misérables*

Les Misérables has many more characters than readers can remember or even notice while reading. Most of these forgotten, unrecognized characters remain nameless, play a marginal role in the novel's plot, appear only briefly before disappearing without leaving a trace — and therefore may not be considered "characters" at all. Conversely, one may argue that they stand precisely for *"les misérables"* of the novel's title and that our habitual reading practices demonstrate the problem Hugo sought to bring to our attention: the *misérables'* invisibility to the social world that we, the readers, represent.

The Web site *Visualizing* Les Misérables, created by Michal P. Ginsburg and hosted on *MLA Commons* (lesmiserables.mla.hcommons.org) provides, first, a sortable matrix that lists 181 characters, indicating the number of times each character appears in the novel and in what chapter or chapters as well as the number and name of the other characters with whom each one of them interacts. It also features graphs based on the data contained in the matrix, showing the characters' interrelations by grouping them into "communities" or "clusters." A graph for the entire novel is complemented by a series of five graphs, one for each of the novel's five parts, showing how the world of the novel and the relations among characters change over time. A brief essay discusses the methodological and technological issues raised by treating characters as "large data" and by graphing and visualizing their relations.

The Paris of *Les Misérables*: Maps and Commentary

Michal P. Ginsburg

The Representation of Paris in Les Misérables

The plot of *Les Misérables* moves to Paris rather late—after more than five hundred pages. But once the move occurs (pt. 2, bk. 4, ch. 1) the city is kept in the forefront of the reader's attention until the very end; there is no question of its being simply the backdrop for the plot or a bit of local color.

So what is the Paris of *Les Misérables*?[2] As in any other city novel, the parts of the city that are *not* represented are as important as the ones that are. In the case of *Les Misérables*, out of the forty-eight quartiers that constituted the city in the 1830s, nineteen quartiers on the Right Bank, Ile de la Cité, and Ile Saint-Louis are of little interest to Hugo. Only once in the novel, in the passage describing Marius's circuitous walk from the Rue Plumet to the barricade, are a few sites in this part of the city mentioned: the Champs-Elysées, Rue de Rivoli, Palais Royal, Rue Saint-Honoré. Hugo makes clear that in this novel the important parts of the city are the faubourgs—it is there that "la race parisienne apparaît" 'the Parisian race is found' (1: 754; 592–93 [pt. 3, bk. 1, ch. 12]).

In discussing the role of the city in *Les Misérables*, instructors can show how its representation is linked to some of the novel's main themes and formal aspects. When tracing the city sites mentioned in the novel, one is struck by the frequent, almost obsessive reference to the passage of time, to what has been and what is no longer. Here, instead of celebrating the passing of time as productive of positive change—progress, the removal of darkness, misery, and injustice—Hugo mourns the passage of time and the passing of all material things. Of course, what time effaces can be preserved by and in writing. This preservation, however, is not simply a matter of meticulous documentation: some of the most important sites mentioned in the novel—ostensibly preserved from the havoc of time through writing—are actually fictive constructions. Thus, the convent in which Valjean and Cosette find refuge is pure fiction. Of the quartier of Petit Picpus where it is situated Hugo writes, "Il y a trente ans, ce quartier disparaissait sous la rature des constructions nouvelles. Aujourd'hui il est biffé tout à fait" 'Thirty years ago, this neighborhood was disappearing, erased by new construction. It is now completely blotted out' (1: 585; 453 [pt. 2, bk. 5, ch. 3]). But this quartier never existed. Hugo originally placed the convent in the Rue Neuve-Sainte-Geneviève but later on changed its location. As he himself put it, "[J]'ai dû dépayser le couvent, en changer le nom et le transporter imaginairement quartier Saint-Antoine" 'I had to relocate the convent, change its name, and transport it imaginatively to the quartier Saint-Antoine' (qtd. in Chenet). Françoise Chenet rightly points out that the name of the convent is not imaginary: there was, and still is, a Picpus convent; it has a garden and a famous cemetery, with which Hugo must have been familiar. The location of the real Picpus convent, however, is not that of the imagined one but farther to the east, in the part of the city that in the map "Paris of *Les Misérables*" is covered by the legend. (It is situated in the triangular plot of land bordered by the Rue de Picpus, where the entrance to the convent is located, Avenue de Saint-Mandé and the Boulevard de Picpus, formerly the Barrière de Saint-Mandé). In writing "Le Petit Picpus, dont aucun plan actuel n'a gardé la trace, est assez clairement indiqué dans le plan de 1727, publié à Paris chez Denis Thierry" 'The Petit Picpus of which no present map retains a trace is shown clearly enough on the map of 1727, published in Paris by Denis Thierry' (1: 585; 453; [pt. 2, bk. 5, ch. 3]), Hugo goes out of his way to affirm both the reality and the facticity of the site. As critics have long ago pointed out, there is no map of Paris dated 1727 and Denis Thierry died in 1712 (Cooley 357). Playing the role of the preserver of the real city through writing, Hugo flaunts the fictionality of his account.

The second important site under the sign of fiction is the barricade. Though the streets where the barricade is erected did exist, and though it is quite likely that at some point in history there was a barricade there, critics agree that the insurrection Hugo describes in the novel took place, in reality, by the convent of Saint-Merry to the northwest of the fictive barricade. With so many real barricades available for representation, Hugo nevertheless feels the need to invent one.

Finally, the Gorbeau house, which gives its name to the first chapter of the novel taking place in Paris, is derealized by the astonishing coincidence—one of the hallmarks of fiction—on which Hugo's narrator never comments: that the same place Valjean chose for lodging when he and Cosette first arrived in Paris would become the place of lodging for both the Thénardiers and Marius. While placing Marius in close proximity with, but also in utter ignorance of, the Thénardiers is necessary for the plot, there is no reason why the ambush against Valjean should take place in his old lodging. By stretching the long arm of verisimilitude as far as it can go, Hugo highlights the fictional character of the site. Representing the reality of misery and of the *misérables*, Hugo suggests repeatedly, can be done only through fiction.

Mapping the Paris of Les Misérables

The maps presented in this volume are intended to help instructors discuss the representation of Paris in the novel. The map showing the Paris of *Les Misérables* (pp. 14–15) lists twenty-four sites (out of about 150 mentioned in the novel).[3] Fourteen of them are sites of important episodes or events (the barricade, the convent, the prison of La Force) or sites where important encounters take place (the Champ de Mars, where Éponine delivers her warning to Valjean; St. Sulpice, where Marius's father watches him unobserved; the Barrière du Maine, where Valjean and Cosette see the chain of convicts; etc.). The remaining ten are places where the novel's various characters live. We note that while we are given the address of a minor character such as la Magnon, there is no indication as to where Javert lives—suggesting clearly, though not surprisingly, that he has no home, no life outside his duties as representative of the law.

In looking into the places where characters live, we discover a curious fact: Hugo tells us that la Magnon used to live on the Quai des Célestins, at the corner of the Rue du Petit Musc, before she moved to the Rue Clocheperce (2: 267; 942 [pt. 4, bk. 6, ch. 1]). Hugo further mentions that Mabeuf used to live on the Rue des Méziers, then moved to the Boulevard Montparnasse, before settling in the Village d'Austerlitz (1: 868; 690 [pt. 3, bk. 5, ch. 4). Unlike the changes in place of residence of Marius or Valjean, which are related to major events in the plot, the former places of residence of la Magnon and Mabeuf are totally irrelevant to the plot (they precede the point in the story where these characters appear). The mention of previous sites of habitation is but one example of Hugo's habit of referring to sites in the city that are *not* part of story—as when Grantaire, attempting to convince Enjolras of his commitment to the cause of the revolution, traces the rather circuitous itinerary he could take (but doesn't) in order to recruit participants around the Barrière du Maine (2: 164; 855–56 [pt. 4, bk. 1, ch. 6]). Similarly, in a chapter describing the activities on the eve of the insurrection (pt. 4, bk. 10, ch. 4), Hugo mentions the names of streets and sites in the city over eighty times in six short pages. By repeatedly evoking sites in the city that play no role in the plot, Hugo insists that the represented city is not limited to the story he tells, that—as is evident from the various digressions—the novel exceeds the story of a certain number of characters at certain points in time and space.

The other two maps trace the walks, often described in great detail, that some of the novel's characters take through the city (pp. 16–17). A quick comparison with Balzac's *Le père Goriot* can be useful here. In Balzac's novel, the hero,

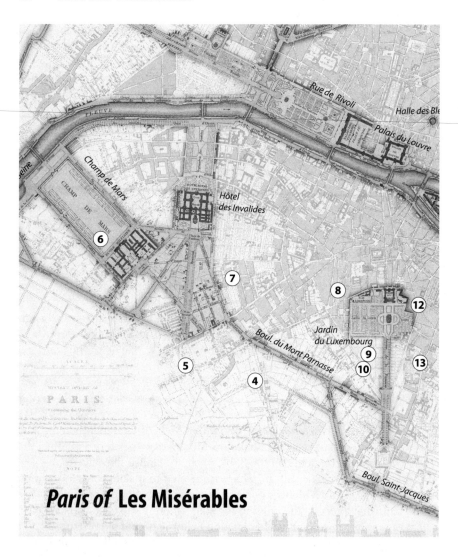

Paris of Les Misérables

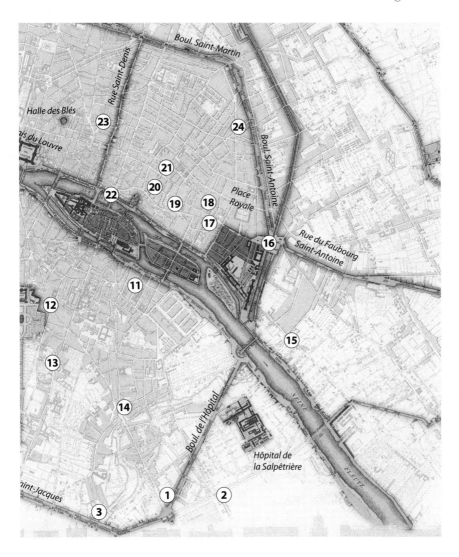

13. St. Jacques du Haut-Pas

14. St. Médard

15. Approximate location of fictive convent

16. Elephant of the Bastille

17. St. Paul-St. Louis

18. La Force prison

19. Rue Clocheperce

20. Rue de la Verrerie

21. Rue de l'Homme-Armé

22. Site of Javert's suicide

23. Barricade

24. Rue des Filles-du-Calvaire

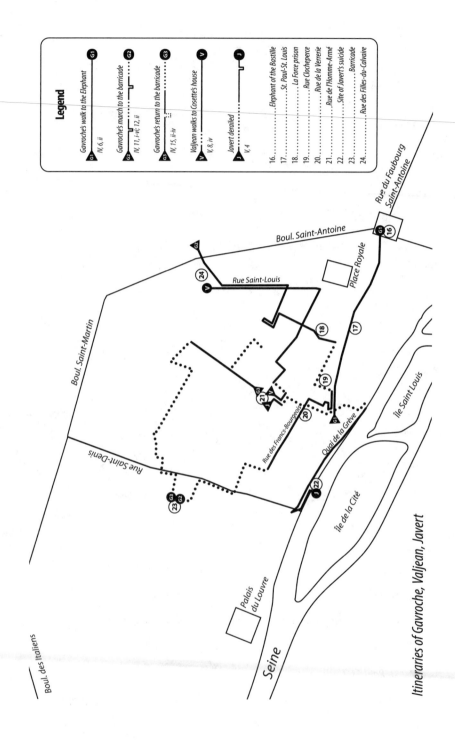

Legend

▲ **G1** Gavroche's walk to the Elephant
   IV, 6, ii

▲ **G2** Gavroche's march to the barricade
   IV, 11, i–vi; 12, ii

▲ **G3** Gavroche's return to the barricade
   IV, 15, ii–iv

▲ **V** Valjean walks to Cosette's house
   V, 8, iv

▲ **J** Javert derailed
   V, 4

16. .... Elephant of the Bastille
17. .... St. Paul-St. Louis
18. .... La Force prison
19. .... Rue Clocheperce
20. .... Rue de la Verrerie
21. .... Rue de l'Homme-Armé
22. .... Site of Javert's suicide
23. .... Barricade
24. .... Rue des Filles-du-Calvaire

Itineraries of Gavroche, Valjean, Javert

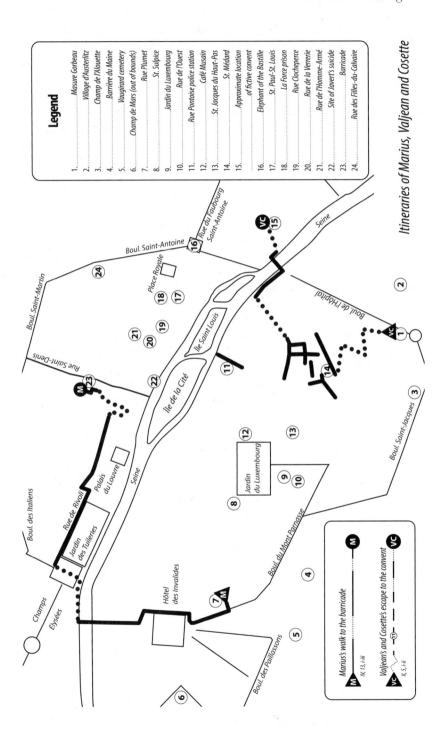

Itineraries of Marius, Valjean and Cosette

Legend

1. .... Masure Gorbeau
2. .... Village d'Austerlitz
3. .... Champ de l'Alouette
4. .... Barrière du Maine
5. .... Vaugirard cemetery
6. .... Champ de Mars (out of bounds)
7. .... Rue Plumet
8. .... St. Sulpice
9. .... Jardin du Luxembourg
10. .... Rue de l'Ouest
11. .... Rue Pontoise police station
12. .... Café Musain
13. .... St. Jacques du Haut-Pas
14. .... St. Médard
15. .... Approximate location
         of fictive convent
16. .... Elephant of the Bastille
17. .... St. Paul-St. Louis
18. .... La Force prison
19. .... Rue Clocheperce
20. .... Rue de la Verrerie
21. .... Rue de l'Homme-Armé
22. .... Site of Javert's suicide
23. .... Barricade
24. .... Rue des Filles-du-Calvaire

Marius's walk to the barricade
IV, 13, i-iii

Valjean's and Cosette's escape to the convent
II, 5, i-iii

Rastignac, walks a lot and is linked to many of the sites mentioned in the novel, sites that are in different parts of the city. But when Balzac describes his hero's movement in the city he usually tells us only his point of departure and point of arrival (the same is true for the movements of other characters in the novel). For example, we read that "Rastignac arriva rue Saint-Lazare," but there are no details about how he got there (192). Obviously, Balzac is not interested in tracing the route that leads Rastignac from one point to the other. This is because Rastignac's movement in the city physically expresses his social mobility, and what is important is that he "arrives"; the teleology of the plot of arrival is replicated in the teleology of movement in space; how one gets somewhere is not important as long as one does. Hugo's characters, on the other hand, walk rather than arrive. This is not simply because *Les Misérables* is anything but a novel of social climbing; it is also because one of the main functions of detailing the itineraries of different characters is to draw attention to the city itself, its existence beyond the characters' plot. The other function is to suggest the state of mind of the characters: Marius's long and indirect route to the barricade expresses his ambivalence and distressed state of mind; the back-and-forth movement of Valjean and Cosette during their escape to the convent shows Valjean's confusion and hesitation (as well as probably Hugo's lack of certainty, now that he moved the convent from its original site in the area near the Panthéon to an imaginary territory); Valjean's gradually shortened walks from his apartment to the house Cosette inhabits with Marius (the map represents only the full walk) give physical form to his dwindling hope and life.

It would come as no surprise that women in Hugo's novel do not walk much. Cosette walks with Valjean to the Luxembourg gardens and other unspecified places but certainly does not walk on her own. Éponine gets around—she gives warning to Valjean in the Champs de Mars, waters Mabeuf's garden in the Village d'Austerlitz, visits Marius's apartment in the Rue de la Verrerie, and finally arrives at the barricade, where she dies. We are not given an itinerary for any of her walks (as if she were invisible), and for the last part of her walk she is dressed as a man.

The detailed itineraries of characters as well as the many references to sites that play no role in the novel's plot explain the large number (over 150) of different sites and streets mentioned in the novel and the even larger number (over 1,500) of references to streets, avenues, boulevards, quais, squares, bridges, and other thoroughfares as well as to specific sites in the city. This frequency of spatial reference keeps us constantly aware of the sheer presence of the city.

NOTES

[1] The pagination of the 2013 Signet Classics edition of Fahnestock and MacAfee's translation differs slightly from that of the 1987 edition.

[2] For other studies of Paris in *Les Misérables*, see Bellosta; Combes.

[3] The 1834 map that underlies the "Paris of *Les Misérables*" map is used with the kind permission of the David Rumsey collection (www.davidrumsey.com). The three maps were produced by Michal P. Ginsburg, Matthew Taylor, and Sergei Kalugin, of Northwestern University.

Part Two

APPROACHES

CONTEXTS

The Reception of *Les Misérables* in the Context of a New Aesthetic

Dean de la Motte

The evolution of literary schools in mid-nineteenth-century France is a familiar tale to scholars, but the role it played in the complicated reception of *Les Misérables* is perhaps underestimated. It is my hope that this brief essay can assist instructors in addressing the following questions: Despite the overwhelming popular success of Hugo's book, what were the most common aesthetic reservations at the moment of its publication? What was the historical context of these critiques (many of which were privately expressed—so great was Hugo's prestige)? I limit my discussion to formal objections, though the novel was also vigorously denounced by the political and the religious right. The rejection of the novel by the partisans of modernity is most relevant here, for this rupture between the generation of Baudelaire and Flaubert and the generation of "le Père Hugo" allows us to understand why serious literary criticism would continue to disparage *Les Misérables* for nearly a century.

Such considerations are hardly the sole province of literary historians, for they allow the instructor to place the reputation of the novel in a broader context. The objections raised by some of Hugo's celebrated contemporaries can provide a pathway for discussion of aspects of the novel that twenty-first-century students might find difficult, problematic, or even distasteful: the length of the novel; its numerous long digressions; the lack, according to some, of character depth and realism overall; the "melodrama" of the work; and, finally, its overt political agenda. What follows allows the instructor to provide students with a historical framework for discussion, as well as the reassurance that they are not alone in their struggles with this celebrated, if sometimes daunting, text.

It is important, then, for the instructor to explain that, despite the immediate and enduring popular success of the novel, Charles Baudelaire and Gustave Flaubert, among others, expressed their profound disappointment: the first, who publicly praised it in the press and privately called it "immonde et inepte" 'vile and inept' (Bach 608; Grossman, Les Misérables 16). As for Flaubert, he famously found Hugo's novel a book that had been "fait pour la crapule catholico-socialiste, pour toute la vermine philosophico-évangélique" 'made for the socio-catholic riff-raff, the whole philosophico-evangelical vermin' (Bach 608; Grossman, Les Misérables 16). These comments come in a letter to Edma Roger des Genettes, dated July 1862, which deserves to be quoted at greater length, for it touches on nearly all the formal objections made upon the novel's publication and for decades to come:

> Je ne trouve dans ce livre ni vérité, ni grandeur. Quant au style, il me semble intentionnellement incorrect et bas. C'est une façon de flatter le populaire.   (*Correspondance* 3: 235–36)

> I find neither truth nor greatness in this book. As for the style, it seems to me intentionally incorrect and base. It's a way of currying favor with the common people.[1]

Not only does Hugo cater cynically to the masses; his work lacks all realism—and here it is worth reminding students that realism had, with Flaubert in fiction and Courbet in painting, gained ascendancy by the late 1850s, just before the release of *Les Misérables*—and its characters are "des mannequins, des bonshommes en sucre" 'mannequins, little men made of sugar' (*Correspondance* 3: 236). Flaubert continues:

> Décidément ce livre, malgré les beaux morceaux, et ils sont rares, est enfantin. L'observation est une qualité seconde en littérature, mais il n'est pas permis de peindre si faussement la société, quand on est le contemporain de Balzac et de Dickens.

> Despite some beautiful passages—and they are rare—this book is decidedly childish. Observation may be a secondary quality in literature, but it is impermissible to depict society so falsely when one is the contemporary of Balzac and Dickens.

Hugo has become so obsessed with the "idées banales de son époque" 'commonplace ideas of his age' that "il en oublie son œuvre, son art" 'he forgets his work, his art' (237). He has been carried away by his politics at the expense of his art; for the consummate aesthete Flaubert, such work is little better than crass propaganda.

Flaubert's candid letter provides striking insight into the conflict that lies at the heart of the sometimes violent reaction of the champions of the new aes-

thetic. I have found that to help students understand the origins of this profound disappointment it is helpful to return to French Romanticism. In the
earlier literary movement, one finds the origins of an aesthetic cleavage that not
only allows us to grasp the rupture between Hugo and his contemporaries in
1862 but also helps us understand the critical reputation of his novel well into
the twentieth century. Finally, a brief consideration of Romanticism provides
another tool for classroom discussion on those dimensions of the book that can
often challenge students, from its political message to the formal qualities noted
above.

The vehemence of Flaubert's private critique of *Les Misérables* might well be
explained as oedipal in nature, for he and Baudelaire were direct descendants of
the *École romantique* of which Hugo himself, particularly after the publication
of the "Préface" to *Cromwell* in 1827, was the acknowledged leader and spokes-
man. This manifesto underscores not only the freedom of the writer but also the
importance of *la vraisemblance*, that early form of *le réel*. For Hugo—the youth-
ful royalist who twenty years later would become a republican—it is above all a
question of throwing off the yoke of literary classicism, although political ideas
would soon enough catch up to aesthetic concerns. Indeed, there exists for the
prolific young writer no tension between political and literary engagement: we
need only note that within two years, 1829–30, he published *Le Dernier Jour
d'un condamné*, a protest against capital punishment; triumphed on the stage
with *Hernani*, a turning point in French literary history; and brought out his
Orientales, a volume of poetry whose preface may be read as a precursor of art
for art's sake:

> Si donc aujourd'hui quelqu'un lui demande à quoi bon ces *Orientales*?
> qui a pu lui inspirer de s'aller promener en Orient pendant tout un vol-
> ume? que signifie *ce livre inutile de pure poésie*, jeté au milieu des pré-
> occupations graves du public? ... où en est l'opportunité? à quoi rime
> l'Orient? ... Il répondra qu'il n'en sait rien, que c'est une idée qui lui a
> pris; et qui lui a pris d'une façon assez ridicule, l'été passé, en allant voir
> coucher le soleil.   (*Œuvres poétiques* 1: 578; emphasis mine)

> And if today the author is asked what's the point of these *Orientales*? Who
> or what could have inspired him to go traveling through the Orient for an
> entire volume? What's the meaning of *this useless book of pure poetry*,
> tossed in the midst of the public's serious concerns? ... Is this timely or
> appropriate? What does the Orient have to do with anything? ... He will
> answer that he hasn't the slightest idea, that it is an idea that simply came
> to him, and that came to him in a rather ridiculous way, last summer, as he
> was going to watch the sun set.

Despite his ability to move deftly from the political advocacy of *Le Dernier
Jour* to "pure poetry," the Romantic poet not only seeks liberation from classical models but also, in the case of *Les Orientales*, seems to flirt with the

possibility of art for art's sake, with a poetry that has little relevance to society and politics.

Indeed, we soon find under the July Monarchy (1830–48) the beginnings of a fissure between those who wish to change the world through political action and those who would limit themselves to the literary and aesthetic fields of endeavor. As early as 1835, Théophile Gautier writes memorably in his "Préface" to *Mademoiselle de Maupin*, "Il n'y a de vraiment beau que ce qui ne peut servir à rien. L'endroit le plus utile d'une maison, ce sont les latrines" 'The only true beauty is that which is useless. The most useful place in a home is the toilet' (23). The stage is already set for the political retreat of so many of the writers now associated with the Second Empire: while Hugo, after the coup d'état of Napoleon III in 1851, will go into exile and become only more engaged in the service of the republican cause, Gautier, Baudelaire, and Flaubert will retire from the political arena and maintain a largely ironic distance from society and politics. The Romantic aestheticism of Gautier, for example, will harden into the more radical and modern formalism associated with the Parnassians, and in the preface-poem of the collection *Émaux et Camées* (1852), he famously alludes to recent, violent political events: "Sans prendre garde à l'ouragan / Qui fouettait mes vitres fermées, / Moi, j'ai fait *Émaux et Camées*" 'Paying no heed to the storm lashing my closed windowpanes, I fashioned *Émaux et Camées*' (25). The satirist of 1835 has become the aesthete of 1852, his windows resolutely shuttered against political reality. He concludes his collection with the much-anthologized "L'Art," where there can be no remaining doubt concerning his views on the distinction between art and politics: "Tout passe. — L'art robuste / Seul a l'éternité. / Le buste / Survit à la cité" 'Everything passes away. — Only robust art is eternal. The bust outlives the city' (150).

If realism is also born at this historical moment, one must keep in mind that Flaubert had no political agenda in creating *Madame Bovary* (serialized 1856; published 1857). Quite to the contrary, as he notes in what is one of his best-known letters to Louise Colet, from 1852:

> Ce qui me semble beau, ce que je voudrais faire, c'est un livre sur rien, un livre sans attache extérieure, qui se tiendrait de lui-même par la force interne de son style, comme la terre sans être soutenue se tient en l'air, un livre qui n'aurait presque pas de sujet ou du moins où le sujet serait presque invisible, si cela se peut. Les œuvres les plus belles sont celles où il y a le moins de matière. . . . Je crois que l'avenir de l'Art est dans ces voies. . . . C'est pour cela qu'il n'y a ni beaux ni vilains sujets.
>
> (Flaubert, *Correspondance* 2: 31)

> What seems beautiful to me, and what I'd like to create, is a book about nothing, a book that is entirely self-contained, which would be held together purely by the internal strength of its style, just as the earth maintains itself in orbit without being held aloft, a book that would have almost

no subject or at least whose subject would be nearly invisible, if such a thing is possible. The most beautiful works are those with the least subject matter. . . . I think this is the future direction of art. . . . That's why there are no beautiful or ugly subjects.

While his insistence that there are "ni beaux ni vilains sujets" echoes Hugo's "Préface" to *Cromwell*, it is equally clear that the novel according to Flaubert has no social or political purpose. Like Gautier, Flaubert turns his back on any kind of engagement and, as if to underscore this, creates a world where the absurd apothecary Homais becomes the "partisan of progress" and where we not only hear, at the scene of the agricultural fair, the discourse of a certain M. Lieuvain but also witness, at the precise moment that Rodolphe seduces Emma, a prize loudly announced for the best "Fumiers" 'Manure' (215)!

Social progress, even if it is possible—and for Baudelaire and Flaubert this is already a doubtful proposition—has nothing to do with literature, although society itself has elevated this idea to the status of a new religion, "la véritable foi de notre âge" 'the true faith of our age,' according to Pierre Larousse, in his effusive eight-column article "Le Progrès" in the *Grand dictionnaire universel du XIXe siècle* (225). Like Larousse, Hugo has fashioned progress into a religion of sorts or, at the very least, has made it the beating heart of his sprawling tale. In this context, the twentieth chapter of part 5, "Jean Valjean," in *Les Misérables*, bears quoting at some length:

> Le progrès est le mode de l'homme. La vie générale du genre humain s'appelle le Progrès; le pas collectif du genre humain s'appelle le Progrès. Le progrès marche; il fait le grand voyage humain et terrestre vers le céleste et le divin; il a ses haltes où il rallie le troupeau attardé; il a ses stations où il médite; . . . il a ses nuits où il dort; et c'est une des poignantes anxiétés du penseur de voir l'ombre sur l'âme humaine et de tâter dans les ténèbres, sans pouvoir le réveiller, le progrès endormi.
>
> (2: 621 [pt. 5, bk. 1, ch. 20])

> Progress is the mode of man. The general life of the human race is called *progress*; the collective advance of the human race is called *progress*. Progress marches on; it makes the great human and terrestrial journey toward the celestial and divine; it has its halts where it rallies the belated flock; it has its pauses where it meditates; . . . it has its nights when it sleeps; and it is one of the bitter anxieties of the thinker to see the shadow over the human soul, and to feel progress asleep in the darkness, without being able to waken it.   (1236)

Clearly, in exile, "le Père Hugo" had developed—or perhaps, more accurately, simply retained—a sensibility utterly foreign to that of Baudelaire, Flaubert, and Gautier. Another text from this period, the letter Hugo wrote to Baudelaire from Hauteville House on 6 October 1859, underscores the "dissidence"—to use Hugo's word—between the author of *Les Misérables* and the disciples of beauty:

> Vous ne vous trompez pas en prévoyant quelque dissidence entre vous et moi. Je comprends toute votre philosophie (car, comme tout poète, tu contiens un philosophe); je fais plus que la comprendre, je l'admets; mais je garde la mienne. Je n'ai jamais dit: l'Art pour l'Art; j'ai toujours dit: l'Art pour le Progrès. Au fond, c'est la même chose, et votre esprit est trop pénétrant pour ne pas le sentir. En avant! c'est le mot du Progrès; c'est aussi le cri de l'Art.   (qtd. in Guyaux 297)

> You are not mistaken in sensing a considerable difference between our views. I understand your entire philosophy (for, like all poets, you have within you a philosopher); I more than understand it, I accept it—but I prefer to keep my own. I never said: art for art's sake; I have always said: art for the sake of progress. Ultimately it is the same thing, and your mind is far too penetrating not to sense that this is true. Onward! That is the motto of progress; it is also the battle cry of art.

Thanking his younger *confrère* for a recent dedication of two poems, Hugo credits Baudelaire with an implicit participation in progress: "Que faites-vous? Vous marchez. Vous allez en avant. . . . Vous créez un frisson nouveau" 'What are you doing? You are marching, you are moving forward. . . . You are creating the exciting shudder of the new' (qtd. in Guyaux 297). But novelty in literature does not equal social progress, and Hugo readily accepts and accentuates this crucial distinction:

> L'Art n'est pas perfectible, je l'ai dit, je crois, un des premiers, donc je le sais; . . . mais . . . il faut déplacer l'horizon de l'Art, monter plus haut, aller plus loin, marcher. Le poète ne peut aller seul, il faut que l'homme aussi se déplace. Les pas de l'Humanité sont donc les pas mêmes de l'Art.—Donc, gloire au Progrès.   (qtd. in Guyaux 297)

> Art is not perfectible; I was one of the first to say it, and so I know it all too well; . . . but . . . one must continue to push the boundaries of art, climb higher, go farther, march onward. The poet cannot go it alone; mankind must move with him. The forward path of humanity is thus the same as art.—Therefore, glory be to progress.

In conclusion, the poet dramatically links his own exile and possible martyrdom to progress itself: "C'est pour le Progrès que je souffre en ce moment et je suis prêt à mourir" 'It is for progress that I am currently suffering and for progress that I am prepared to die' (qtd. in Guyaux 297).

The date of this letter is critical, for this is the precise period during which Hugo is at last about to conclude *Les Misérables*. Baudelaire, despite his secret envy of and frequent annoyance with the great man, could warmly embrace at least that part of the letter that credits him with the creation of a *frisson nouveau*; one need only think of the final lines of the amoral and apolitical "Le Voyage," written at roughly the same time and added to the second edition of *Les Fleurs du Mal* (1861), standing as the final poem and thus the last word of the volume:

> Verse-nous ton poison pour qu'il nous réconforte!
> Nous voulons, tant ce feu nous brûle le cerveau,
> Plonger au fond du gouffre, Enfer ou Ciel, qu'importe?
> Au fond de l'Inconnu pour trouver du *nouveau*!
>
> (Baudelaire, *Œuvres complètes* 100)

> Pour us your poison and let it strengthen us! We want, such is the fire that burns our brains, to plunge into the depths of the abyss, Hell or Heaven, what does it matter? To the depths of the unknown to find something *new*.
>
> (Baudelaire, *Selected Poems* 145)

This notion of aesthetic novelty and all-consuming beauty is quite intentionally unmoored from social, moral, or religious values, and it is worth reminding students that one finds it throughout Baudelaire's work and correspondence, including—though not without occasional, even self-deprecating, irony—in the posthumous *Petits Poèmes en prose* or *Le Spleen de Paris* (1869), for example in "Le Mauvais Vitrier" 'The Bad Glazier.' In this poem, the narrator is infuriated that the humble glazier has no colored or magic windowpanes and so, after making the glazier climb six flights of stairs, shoves him back into the stairwell and, once he has descended, drops a flowerpot on him from high above, completely destroying the poor man's "fortune ambulatoire qui rendit le bruit d'un palais de cristal crevé par la foudre" 'itinerant fortune . . . which produced the brilliant sound of a crystal palace smashed by lightning,' while screaming "La vie en beau! la vie en beau!" 'Make life beautiful! Make life beautiful!' The narrator concludes with the notable phrase: "Mais qu'importe l'éternité de la damnation à qui a trouvé dans une seconde l'infini de la jouissance?" 'But what does an eternity of damnation matter to someone who has experienced for one second the infinity of delight?' (*Œuvres complètes* [Laffont] 168; *Parisian Prowler* 15).

The shattered glass of the poor glazier is an apt image for the violent rupture between the utopian Romanticism of Victor Hugo as embodied by the publication of a novel devoted in large part to social progress and the prophets of a new aesthetic whom a younger Hugo—he of the "Préface" to *Cromwell* and *Les Orientales*—had, himself, inspired. It is thus worth reminding our students, and indeed ourselves, of just how anachronistic *Les Misérables* must have seemed in 1862, published at the height of this first wave of a new aesthetic of modernity.

In the end, Flaubert and Baudelaire could not forgive Hugo for creating a text where political concerns are elevated over aesthetic imperatives as they conceived them; they could not pardon the grand old man of letters for creating a work that had a goal—indeed, a *cause*—far greater than the work itself.

Kathryn Grossman, in her helpful overview of the work, has noted that no new French editions of Hugo's novel appeared between 1914 and 1933 and that for several decades "it was fashionable to hold in contempt not only Hugo but also anyone who admitted liking or admiring his work" (Les Misérables 19). It is far from coincidental that the very generation of writers that abandoned political action in the wake of the revolution of 1848 also, in that same gesture, initiated and championed various aesthetic attitudes of an incipient *modernité*. These same writers would, in turn, not only have a profound influence on the later literary movements we might group under the larger headings of modernism and postmodernism but also provide foundational texts that would inspire many of the dominant formalistic approaches to literature of the first half of the twentieth century.

A brief review of some of the essential texts illustrating competing strands of nineteenth-century thought about the role of literature in society can thus help students not only better situate the reception of *Les Misérables* in French literary history but also understand why it took nearly a century for Hugo's novel to be enshrined in the "serious" literary canon, despite its immediate and enduring popularity with the broader reading public. Finally, and perhaps most important, the role of literature in society allows for a direct connection between the students' own frequent challenges as readers and those of some of Hugo's most illustrious contemporaries.

NOTES

An early, longer version of this essay was given as a lecture in French at the École Française of Middlebury College in July 2014. I am grateful to several members of the audience that day for their constructive criticism.

[1] All unattributed French translations are my own.

Best-Selling Hugo: *Les Misérables* and the Nineteenth-Century Literary Market

Anne O'Neil-Henry

Heralded as the "plus grand événement littéraire du siècle" 'biggest literary event of the century' even before it was available for sale (Bach, 595),[1] Victor Hugo's 1862 *Les Misérables* became an instant commercial success—in part because of an aggressive publicity campaign and the author's already well-established reputation, in part for its compelling narrative and characters. Yet while the novel's commercial success, in the nineteenth century and today, is well known, it is not often read in the context of its publication and release. *Les Misérables* embodied the burgeoning literary market of its day and prefigured our contemporary world of publishing: from elaborate contract negotiations to large-scale marketing campaigns. This essay examines the history of *Les Misérables*' publication and argues for the importance of extraliterary conditions in shaping this major literary work. I analyze Hugo's correspondence and contract negotiations with the publishers Hetzel and Lacroix and Verboeckhoven, review the publicity surrounding the novel's multicity releases, and assess the unprecedented financial achievements of the novel and its author. The conditions of the novel's production, I argue, help form readers' understanding of the structure and content of the work. Finally, by offering ways in which instructors might incorporate the novel's publication history into their teaching of *Les Misérables*, I suggest that attention to the commercial frameworks of Hugo's novel allows scholars and students of *Les Misérables* to understand the logistical origins of this canonical work and to see the consequences of those conditions in the novel. Given its continued commercial success, *Les Misérables* presents a unique opportunity to study the modern phenomenon of the best seller.

Reading *Les Misérables* in the context of its publishing history, which began long before Hugo completed this work in 1862, exposes students to all the complicated formal, commercial, and political forces that ultimately took shape in this novel, as well as to the inner workings of the nineteenth-century publishing world. Hugo, who at this point had not yet determined the nature of the novel, initially entered into a contract with the well-known publishers Eugène Renduel and Charles Gosselin, committing to them "les trois mille premiers exemplaires du premier roman en deux volumes in-8° qu'il viendrait à publier" 'the first three thousand copies of the first novel in two volumes in octavo that he would publish' for the price of twelve thousand francs (Leuilliot, *Victor Hugo* 18). As Leuilliot explains, the above contract was agreed upon on 31 March 1832 and was possibly an adjustment to the similar "traité Gosselin-Renduel de 1831" 'Gosselin-Renduel agreement of 1831' that had been drawn up in the aftermath of their successful publication of *Notre-Dame de Paris*. Gosselin reminded Hugo of his commitment in an 1847 letter, when the author was drafting the first version of the novel he had begun to outline two years earlier in 1845 under the title *Les Misères*, and offered to send him a copy of the contract (Leuilliot 18). At this point, Hugo had made adequate progress on his novel, and it seemed logical that these two volumes would come from *Les Misères*. Hugo, however, interrupted his work on the novel in February 1848; despite the lengthy pause in his writing of *Les Misérables*, this initial contract would weigh heavily on him as he sought a publisher in the early 1860s.

Both Hugo's *Les Châtiments* (1853) and *Légende des Siècles* (1859) listed *Les Misérables* among forthcoming works on their back covers, keeping readers' curiosity piqued. The 1853 cover of *Les Châtiments* described the incomplete novel as comprising three parts; the 1859 cover of *Légende,* as a two-part work. These announcements, which we might think of as teaser campaigns avant la lettre, fueled speculation about ongoing contract negotiations and even, as early as 1854, about translations of the novel—long before Hugo had neared completion of the work. Though Hugo refused the publisher and his friend Pierre-Jules Hetzel's 1856 offer to purchase his past and future production for fifteen years, he charged Hetzel with securing a contract for *Les Misérables*, who then began negotiating partnerships with other publishing houses (Leuilliot, *Victor Hugo* 24). Erroneous rumors in 1860 claimed that Hetzel, who had clandestinely published *Les Châtiments* in 1853 and is best known as Jules Verne's publisher, had purchased the novel. Hetzel wrote to a friend that "*Le Nord* avait annoncé que j'avais acheté *Les Misérables*" '*Le Nord* had announced that I had purchased *Les Misérables*' (Leuilliot 26). He had, instead, conveyed Hachette's offer to Hugo to publish *Les Misérables* for 150,000 francs, in exchange for the rights to the novel for ten years—an offer that Hugo felt was not "faite sérieusement" 'made in seriousness' (Leuilliot 28). Hetzel criticized Hugo's "pretentions financières" 'financial pretentions' and reproached him for "trop demander à ses éditeurs" 'asking too much from his publishers' (Hovasse, *Victor Hugo: Pendant l'exil* 643).[2]

Correspondence between Hetzel and Hugo from January to October 1861 shows that Hetzel had attempted to negotiate contracts with the publishers Michel Lévy and Alexandre Houssiaux. Hetzel had also drawn up a proposal for Renduel and Gosselin's successor, Laurent-Antoine Pagnerre, to release Hugo from his previous contract, and he had heard from Hugo's wife that her husband was offering to sell the novel at half the requested price to the Belgian publishers Albert Lacroix and Hippolyte Verboeckhoven, publishers to whom Hetzel had previously leaked Hugo's request of 300,000 francs. Yet despite Hetzel's active involvement, Hugo sold *Les Misérables* and its rights for twelve years to Lacroix and Verboeckhoven for 300,000 francs on 4 October 1861. After Lacroix initially wrote to Hugo about purchasing the novel, the author stated that he was impressed by Lacroix's "abord direct et son absence de circonlocutions" 'direct manner and his lack of circumlocutions' and by his ability to "paie comptant" 'pay in full' (Hovasse 668, 667). When Lacroix came to Guernsey that October, Hugo accepted his offer to pay 240,000 francs up front and to disperse 60,000 francs later. Hugo would receive 125,000 francs at the time of the submission of the first part of the manuscript, 60,000 francs two months after the publication of the first part of the novel, and 55,000 after the publication of the second part (Hovasse 669–70). The sum of 300,000 francs, equal to roughly 1.5 million dollars today, is, according to Kathryn Grossman, "an astronomical price at the time" (Les Misérables 14). It represented the largest sum paid to an author for a book contract at that point in the nineteenth century, with the exception of Adolphe Thiers's *Histoire du consulat*, for which Thiers received 500,000 francs (Charle 152). Additionally, the Belgian publishers agreed to take on the Gosselin-Renduel contract; in mid-October, Lacroix brokered a deal in which Renduel and Pagnerre forfeited their contract in exchange for "le seul droit d'exclusivité pour la diffusion du roman en France" 'the exclusive distributions rights for the novel in France' (Hovasse 670). Though Hetzel had not negotiated the final deal, Hugo included a clause stipulating that *Les Misérables* would have to be published in a format compatible with "l'édition complète in 8° que va publier M. Hetzel" 'the complete edition in-octavo that M. Hetzel will publish' (Hovasse 669). Hetzel and Lacroix would ultimately collaborate in 1865 to publish a popular edition of *Les Misérables*, selling more than 130,000 copies in that year alone. The complicated history of the contract negotiations for *Les Misérables* reveals the interconnected network of the nineteenth-century publishing world.

Hugo's choice to publish with the young Albert Lacroix was surprising. Aside from the fact that Lacroix and Hugo had briefly corresponded regarding Lacroix's own manuscript five years earlier, Lacroix did not know Hugo. Unlike more established publishers like Gosselin-Renduel and Heztel, with whom Hugo had worked previously, Lacroix was not well known in Belgium "hors des cercles des lettrés, . . . en France, il commence seulement à l'être" 'outside erudite circles . . . in France, he was only becoming known' (Sartorius 17). Lacroix had recently joined forces with Hippolyte Verboeckhoven and established the publishing house A. Lacroix, Verboeckhoven et Cie. Their catalog boasted the names of Alphonse de Lamartine and Edgar Quinet, among other already established figures, but Lacroix felt this list was weighted too heavily toward history and philosophy, and he hoped that purchasing *Les Misérables* would compensate for this imbalance (Hovasse 667). Here was an opportunity to redefine their nascent publishing house as well. While this was a financial boon for Lacroix and Verboeckhoven, Lacroix had to borrow much of the 300,000 francs promised to Hugo: Francis Sartorius reports that some critics viewed Lacroix's actions as an "abus de confidence" 'abuse of confidence' and Lacroix as an example of "un flibustier de l'édition" 'a publishing bandit' (18). Hugo himself was unconcerned by Lacroix's financial tactics (18). Lacroix's serious risk ultimately paid off, and with the wildly successful *Les Misérables*, the publishers had recouped their advance by the end of 1862 (Martin 198).

The format in which the novel would appear was debated until its publication, revealing that formal aspects of literary works can be determined by commercial and political factors. Hugo's friend Paul Meurice, also an author, warned him not to allow editors to publish the book first in a newspaper, because the government "peut interdire du jour au lendemain la publication même" 'can ban the publication overnight' (Leuilliot, *Victor Hugo* 27) and because of the financial risks of limiting the exclusive rights to the novel to one newspaper (Hovasse 671). The choice not to publish the novel first as *feuilleton* ("serial novel") influenced not only the form, then, but also the potential readership of the novel, since newspaper subscription prices could have made the novel more accessible to readers. Additionally, Lacroix and Verboeckhoven suggested, among other options, publishing the novel "d'un seul coup" 'in one go' (Hovasse 696) in order to prevent counterfeit publications, a pressing issue for nineteenth-century publishers. To complicate matters, Hugo himself did not offer a clear picture of the organization of the novel until close to the initial publication date of "Fantine"; he had stayed "flou sur la dimension totale de son œuvre" 'flexible on the total dimension of his work' (Hovasse 695), before deciding in February 1862 that the novel would be published in five parts, of two volumes each. Lacroix also had concerns that a longer novel would reduce readership, claiming that "le nombre d'acheteurs diminue en proportion de l'étendue de l'ouvrage et de l'importance de la somme nécessaire pour acquérir le livre" 'the number of purchasers diminishes in proportion to the length of the work and of the importance of the sum necessary to purchase the book' (Hovasse 669). In order to sustain the public's interest, therefore, Lacroix chose to release the first part, "Fantine," and, subsequently, the second and third parts together and the fourth and fifth parts together. The format and strategy behind the release of the novel were based on a variety of political and commercial tactics, which played a decisive role in the final publication success of *Les Misérables*.

The marketing push for the novel was massive and coordinated, anticipating modern practices of global release and multiplatform distribution. "Fantine" was released in Belgium on 30 March 1862, and four days later in Paris, London, Milan, Naples, Saint Petersburg, and other major cities. In the lead-up to the launch, Hugo meticulously chose passages from the volumes of *Les Misérables* to be published in the press, having directed his publishers to "[c]ommuniquer des extraits à tous les journaux à la fois le même jour, *la veille de la publication* ou le *jour même* . . . *Ne rien donner à l'avance à aucun journal*" 'communicate the excerpts to all the newspapers the same day, *the day before the publication or even the day of the publication . . . Do not give anything in advance to any newspaper*' (Hovasse 699). *Le Constitutionnel, La Presse, Le Journal des débats, Le Siècle,* and other papers printed short articles and sample chapters on 2 April 1862 before "Fantine" was made available; on 14 May when "Cosette" and "Marius" were released; and on 30 June for the release of "L'Idylle rue Plumet et l'Épopée rue Saint-Denis" and "Jean Valjean." Large advertisements for the novel appeared in many of these same newspapers on the day of each release, indicating the cost of the volume and where customers could find copies. In addition, rumors and anecdotes about the novelist and his work circulated in the local press. While the reception of the novel is discussed in another essay in this volume, it is important to note here that critiques of the novel—both positive and negative—proliferated in the press following the release of each new part: regardless of their content, these provided even more publicity for *Les Misérables*.

The campaign worked, and the book was a sensational success. In his biography of Hugo, Jean-Marc Hovasse notes that the first print run of "Fantine"—six thousand copies—sold out instantly, so extra copies from Belgium were imported to satisfy customers until the next print run several days later (700–22). At the launch of the second and third parts, printers were better prepared, having doubled the number of copies (48,000 volumes in total, since each part comprised two volumes). Nothing could have prepared them, however, for the "véritable émeute" 'veritable riot' outside Pagnerre's bookstore: "La boutique . . . ouvrit ses portes le jeudi 15 mai à 6h40 du matin. Depuis une heure, une foule de libraires et de commissionnaires encombrait la rue et tentait d'entrer par force" 'The boutique . . . opened its doors on Thursday, 15 May, at 6:40 a.m. For an hour, a crowd of booksellers and agents crowded the street and tried to enter by force' (Hovasse 710). Once again, the book sold out instantly. As they prepared the final launch, Lacroix and Verboeckhoven released some impressive figures: "Cinq éditions de *Fantine* épuisées rien qu'en France, vingt-cinq mille exemplaires originaux du triple tirage parisien, belge et allemand enlevés; neuf traductions vendues simultanément dans les deux mondes; et le tout en un mois" 'Five editions of *Fantine* sold out in France alone, twenty-five thousand copies from the triple Parisian, Belgian, and German print run snapped up; nine translations sold simultaneously in the two worlds; all of this in one month' (Hovasse 720). Once the last two parts were released and the final calculations made, an estimated 100,000 copies had been sold throughout the world, and continued orders required further print runs (720). Impressive figures were not unheard of, but compared with other best-selling works of fiction—Alexandre Dumas's bound editions of *Le Comte de Monte Cristo* sold, in high estimates, 44,000 copies between 1846 and 1850 (Lyons, "Les best-sellers" 377)—Hugo's sales dwarfed those of most previous best sellers.

The sales tactics continued even after initial publication. After the release of the entire novel, Lacroix and Verboeckhoven planned an elaborate banquet to celebrate the unprecedented success of Hugo's work. The event was scheduled in Brussels for 16 September and included the author's guests and members of the press, Belgian and foreign (Trousson 11). Most sources estimate about eighty-five guests in attendance, among them "essentiellement des grands noms de la politique, de la littérature et de l'art, ainsi que les deux fils de Hugo" 'essentially the biggest names in politics, literature, and art, as well as both of Hugo's sons' (Despy-Meyer 33). The event, for Despy-Meyer, was proof of Lacroix and Verboeckhoven's "avant-gardisme de bon aloi" 'avant-gardisme in good taste' (33). While the banquet certainly celebrated Hugo's and the publishers' success, it also functioned as a major publicity event, garnering enormous attention in newspapers both opposed to and supportive of Hugo's politics. The press not only noted the details of the event—the location, the decor, even the menu—but also analyzed the speeches and toasts. Whether the articles were favorable or negative, found on the front page or hidden among the *faits divers,* the Belgian banquet contributed to the media storm surrounding the novel (33). Because "ces polémiques assuraient une publicité nouvelle aux *Misérables*" 'these polemics assured renewed publicity for *Les Misérables*' (Aron 46), the banquet demonstrated the publishers' sustained and modern sensibility about fame, publicity, and the literary market.

By considering *Les Misérables*'s status as a commodity of the nineteenth-century literary marketplace, students can arrive at a better understanding of the historical, social, and economic forces shaping Hugo's best seller. In my upper-division course Nineteenth-Century French Bestsellers and Mass Media Culture, students read many of the most widely sold (but not necessarily the best received) works of the nineteenth century; learn about how they were published, marketed, and received by critics and readers; and locate their place in today's literary canon. We frame our analyses of these literary works with essays on developments in print technology, literacy, and publishing in the nineteenth century. In the context of this ongoing study of literary value and mass culture, students can use the case of *Les Misérables* as a best seller to delve more deeply into a broad study of nineteenth-century print culture. For example, in addition to studying the publication history of the novel, students might examine extraliterary materials related to the publication of the novel—such as Hugo's correspondence with his editors, as well as the advertisements for and reviews of the novel—to understand the publicity campaigns behind *Les Misérables* and to begin appreciating the dynamism of Second Empire media culture.

Instructors can locate these documents on the Bibliothèque Nationale de France's digital database *Gallica* and might ask students to apply close-reading techniques to such publicity articles to study the language used to promote Hugo's work. In the 14 May issue of *La Presse,* a popular *quotidien* founded in 1836, the author J. Mahias appealed to the sensibilities of the newspaper's readers by underscoring the unprecedented popularity of the novel:

> Demain, ainsi que nous l'avons annoncé, paraîtront quatre nouveaux volumes des *Misérables*, de Victor Hugo. Le succès de la première partie a été sans précédents: plus de trente mille volumes ont été vendus en France, la cinquième édition s'épuise avec la rapidité des premières. Un pareil succès pour un pareil livre est plus qu'un événement littéraire.

> Tomorrow, as we announced it, four new volumes of Victor Hugo's *Les Misérables* will be published. The success of the first part was unprecedented: more than thirty thousand volumes were sold in France, the fifth edition has sold out with the same speed as the first. Such success for a such book is more than just a literary event.

The word "succès" is used twice in the first three sentences of the article, in addition to the expression "sans précédents" 'unprecedented'; the large number of volumes and the quickness with which they were sold are also suggested. The author's repeated references to the phenomenal achievements of "Fantine" emphasize his attempt to use the popularity of the work to sell even more volumes. Despite the mixed reception of *Les Misérables* among critics, Mahias notes that even the most hostile reviewers are impressed by the "grandeur" of the novel, and "ont signalé les incomparables beautés que renferment les deux premiers volumes. Il est des œuvres que l'admiration publique impose au respect de tous; les *Misérables* sont une de ces œuvres-là" 'signaled the incomparable beauty contained within the first two volumes. There are works that command the respect and admiration of the public; *Les Misérables* is one of these works.' The novel is announced as a best-selling, universally appreciated literary phenomenon.

Similar marketing tactics can be found in the large ads splashed across the back page of *La Presse*, *Le Journal des débats*, and others, on 15 May, date of the release of "Cosette" and "Marius." These advertisements offered the address of Pagnerre's bookshop and a description of the physical object with emphasis on the quality and aesthetic attributes of the work: "two beautiful volumes in-octavo *cavalier* vellum" (*La Presse*). The advertisement also explains the pricing of the volumes—12 francs per part—prompting questions about the affordability of the novel and the class of the novel's readers. Finally, the ad evokes the fact that, a mere five weeks after it went on sale, "Fantine" was now in its fifth edition, an approach that leverages the established popularity of the novel to entice more readers to participate in the phenomenon.

As if to underscore the "grandeur" of the novel implied in the 14 May 1862 article (Mahias), *La Presse* excerpted the chapter "Le Plateau de Mont-Saint-Jean," from "Waterloo," the first book of "Cosette," a chapter that announces the battle as "monstrueuse" 'monstrous' (1: 438; 331 [pt. 2, bk. 1, ch. 10]) and climaxes with Wellington's one-word proclamation "sublime" 'splendid' (1: 440; 332). Students might discuss the particular merit of the choice of this chapter to advertise the novel and examine the chapter's place within the larger arguments of the novel. Instructors could consider asking students to read the articles publicizing *Les Misérables* or the excerpted chapters in the context of the relevant issue of *La Presse* (or any other *quotidien*) to determine how reading "Le Plateau de Mont-Saint-Jean" next to that issue's court or stock or foreign correspondence reports affect our understanding of the novel. Short, analytic engagements with extraliterary elements of the novel can improve students' comprehension of the context in which the novel was initially received and better their understanding, more generally, of nineteenth-century mass culture.

Hugo's novel opens historical and contemporary questions about how material conditions of production and distribution help shape literary form. Studying Hugo's negotiations with his Belgian publishers, his decision to publish the novel in volumes and not serially, his need to coordinate compatible formats across publishing houses—all this enables students to see how these extraliterary aspects of *Les Misérables* affected the final form of this sprawling novel. Analyses of the publicity strategies chosen to promote the novel and of the Belgian banquet after the release indicate how the "biggest literary event of the century" came into being and encourage scholars and students to consider the important context of *Les Misérables* as a best seller in their studies of this canonical work.

NOTES

[1] Translations are mine unless otherwise indicated.

[2] All citations to Hovasse are to *Victor Hugo: Pendant l'exil*.

Hugo's Waterloo:
History, Politics, Commemoration

Bettina R. Lerner

In a letter to Edma Roger des Genettes dated July 1862, Gustave Flaubert berates Victor Hugo for the endless parentheses, detours, and asides that make *Les Misérables* such a difficult read: "Et les digressions," Flaubert complained, "Y en a-t-il! Y en a-t-il!" 'And the digressions! So many of them! So many of them!' (*Correspondance* 235).[1] Most of these maligned digressions date from relatively late in the development of *Les Misérables*. In 1845 Hugo had begun work on an early version of the novel that bore the title *Les Misères*, but this project was interrupted by the revolution of 1848 and his exile in 1851. When he returned to it in 1860, the lengthy manuscript already laid out the major outlines of the plot. By the time the final two parts were delivered to the public in the same month as Flaubert's letter to des Genettes, Hugo had added a fifth and final part and increased the original 101 chapters to a monumental 365, most of which, according to Flaubert, were extraneous and useless, containing "Des explications énormes données sur des choses en dehors du sujet, et rien sur celles qui sont indispensables au sujet" 'enormous explanations on matters beside the point, and none on matters essential to the subject at hand' (235–36).

It is precisely these apparent digressions that make *Les Misérables* such a challenging novel to teach to twenty-first-century American undergraduates, whose French language skills, knowledge of European history, and overall attention spans may not always equip them to handle a novel of Hugolian proportions. My students would more than likely agree with Flaubert's rather harsh indictment, and frankly I have never attempted to teach the novel in its entirety. Instead, I have found that the best way to broach *Les Misérables* when teaching it in a typical undergraduate French literature seminar is to leave out Valjean, Javert, Cosette, Marius, and the barricades altogether and to focus, paradoxically, on one of the selfsame digressions that Flaubert so despised: the chapters describing the Battle of Waterloo (in pt. 2, bk. 1). Because these chapters are structurally and thematically self-contained, they do not require any previous knowledge of the novel's characters or of the central plot. However, pace Flaubert, the pages on Waterloo are hardly irrelevant. In fact, building in part on Victor Brombert's argument in *Victor Hugo and the Visionary Novel*, I present these chapters as the key to understanding that *Les Misérables* wrestles with some of the major questions that shape modernity.

Brigitte Mahuzier reminds us that the Battle of Waterloo holds a privileged place in French collective memory as "another name for the experience of modernity, the failure of the witness on the battlefield and by extension the failure of the fiduciary" (5). I draw on these points when teaching Hugo's chapters on Waterloo in a course for advanced undergraduates entitled France in the

World: The Modern Age. Taught in French, the course covers novels, poetry, and theater from the nineteenth and twentieth centuries. It generally attracts French majors as well as students from francophone backgrounds who are majoring in other disciplines that include history, international relations, and political science. I teach Waterloo in two class sessions approximately three weeks into the semester, typically following Balzac's novella *Le Colonel Chabert* and before Flaubert's *Un cœur simple*. During our sessions on Hugo, discussion builds from close readings of specific passages to broader questions on witnessing and the instability of realist assumptions about reference.

I begin my reading of Hugo's text by situating Waterloo as a historical event and cultural touchstone. I then turn to the chapters on Waterloo in *Les Misérables*, looking at key passages in close detail, in order to model close reading while underlining some of the major themes that characterize French literary modernity: historiography, realism, narrative instability, and the experience of revolution. Toward the end of our discussion, I engage with alternative literary accounts of Waterloo and its aftermath, including Stendhal's *La Chartreuse de Parme* and Jules Vallès's lacerating indictment of the war tourism that, by the end of the nineteenth century, had begun to draw visitors to the battlefield, to encourage broader reflections on the culture of commemoration in which Waterloo is inscribed.

Waterloo between History and Fiction

On the morning of 18 June 1815, Napoleon's armies clashed with an Anglo-Prussian coalition led by the Duke of Wellington and the Prussian general Gebhard von Blücher near the Belgian town of Waterloo, not far from Brussels. Fought over more than twelve exceedingly bloody hours, the battle brought to a close more than twenty years of near-constant military conflict throughout Europe, albeit at a heavy cost. By some estimates, the battle left at least 54,000 soldiers dead or wounded on the battlefield.[2] Four days after his defeat, Napoleon abdicated for the second time; by the fall of 1815, the Bourbon monarchy was sitting once again on the throne, Napoleon was exiled to Saint Helena, and the West's "first total war," to use David A. Bell's phrase, had come to an end (304–06).

To this day Waterloo has a contested set of meanings, thanks in large part to the dozens of poets, novelists, and historians, including Hugo, who have written about Napoleon's final defeat.[3] Still, what most of my students know of Waterloo usually comes from the Swedish pop group ABBA, whose eponymous hit single from 1974 only serves to underscore the extent to which the last great Napoleonic battle has transcended the annals of military history to become firmly embedded in Western popular culture. As students readily note from the song's repeated chorus "Waterloo / Couldn't escape if I wanted to," ABBA's idea

of Waterloo is synonymous with unavoidable surrender and inescapable destiny—albeit in love, not war. By the mid-nineteenth century, however, Hugo had
already famously associated Waterloo with fatality and destiny in his lengthy
"L'Expiation" (1853). The thirteenth (and central) poem of *Les Châtiments* describes the army's retreat from Russia in 1812 and then moves on to Napoleon's
final defeat. The poem's second part sounds a mournful knell, "Waterloo! Waterloo! Waterloo! morne plaine!" 'Waterloo! Waterloo! Waterloo! Dismal plain'
(136) and evokes the Belgian battlefield as a mythical locus where "chance"
plays out in a "moment fatal," as well as a physical site of remembrance that the
poet visits almost half a century after the battle: "Quarante ans sont passés, et ce
coin de la terre, / Waterloo, ce plateau funèbre et solitaire, / Ce champ sinistre
où Dieu mêla tant de néants, / Tremble encor d'avoir vu la fuite des géants!"
'Forty years have passed, and this corner of the earth / Waterloo, this funereal
and somber plateau / This sinister field where God stirred in so much nothing-
ness / Still trembles from the sight of fleeing giants' (136). Reading these stanzas
early in our discussion prepares students to look for a similar mythologizing of
this event and site in *Les Misérables*.

Napoleon's famous defeat at the hands of Wellington is told over the length
of nineteen chapters that make up the first book, in part 2 of *Les Misérables*,
"Cosette." The narrator, identified as "celui qui raconte cette histoire" 'the author of this story' (1: 403; 301 [bk. 1, ch. 1]), delves into an excruciatingly detailed
account of the battle that telescopes the reader back and forth between the
battlefield as it looks in the narrative present of 1861 and its appearance forty-
six years earlier.[4] Under the narrator's gaze, crumbling walls, stones, and trees
recall wounded, fallen bodies. The text swerves from realist precision to fantastic
projection to the downright macabre, such as the skeletons crowding the bottom
of the well in the courtyard of the Hougomont farm (1: 409; 306 [pt. 2, bk. 1,
ch. 2]).[5] The detailed accounts of the landscape and ruins within it not only fix
the battlefield as a physical place but also serve as witnesses to a past that the
narrator seeks to bring into the narrative present. The chapters take readers
from the initial late-morning skirmishes at Hougomont to the afternoon lull near
Haie-Sainte before the unexpected arrival of Blücher's troops in the evening
leads to the defeat on Mont-Saint-Jean, where the Imperial Guard makes its last
stand. The description of the battle proper lasts through chapter 15 and is followed by three chapters of an extended meditation on the battle's significance
and impact on Napoleon's legacy. The account closes with a final, apocryphal
scene in the hours after the battle, while the craven Thénardier scavenges valu-
ables from the battlefield's dead and wounded, among them Marius's father.

This last chapter brings readers back to the central plot after a long detour
that makes little, if any, narrative sense. The cliffhanger at the end of part 1
("Fantine") leaves readers wanting to know whether Jean Valjean will manage
to escape Inspector Javert and save Cosette. These questions, however, remain
unanswered in part 2 ("Cosette"), which dislocates readers in space, time, and
even genre: Montreuil-sur-Mer in 1823 suddenly becomes Waterloo in 1815,

and fiction seems to yield to the demands of detailed military history, a point to
which I will return below. Instead of carrying the narrative forward, the chapters on Waterloo bring the reader back in time, specifically to the first line of
the novel, which opens in 1815, as well as back to Cosette's birth, which, we
are told, occurs in the same year. Moreover, the narrator asserts that "une des
scènes génératrices du drame que nous racontons se rattache à cette bataille"
'One of the key scenes of the drama we are telling hangs on that battle' (1: 414;
311 [pt. 2, bk. 1, ch. 3]). In the same paragraph, the narrator denies giving a
historical account of the Battle of Waterloo, yet that is precisely what these chapters do, albeit not without raising a number of complex questions about the writing of war.

   This instability can be felt in the structure of the narration itself, which recounts the battle as a series of false starts. The description begins at Hougomont, "le commencement de l'obstacle, la première résistance que rencontra à
Waterloo . . . Napoléon" 'the first obstacle encountered at Waterloo by . . . Napoleon' (1: 405; 303 [pt. 2, bk. 1, ch. 2]). This origin is, however, soon displaced
by a second beginning in the orchard where the English and the French armies
have their bloodiest clash: "Waterloo commença ainsi" 'Thus began Waterloo'
(1: 411; 308 [pt. 2, bk. 1, ch. 2]). These two origins are in turn displaced by
other beginnings, including the fall of the cavalry—"Ceci commença la perte
de la bataille" 'Here began the loss of the battle' (1: 436; 329 [pt. 2, bk. 1,
ch. 9])—and the arrival of the Prussian troops led by Blücher, when "le su-
prême carnage commença" 'the final carnage began' (1: 446; 337 [pt. 2, bk. 1,
ch. 12]). The battle begins at once everywhere and nowhere. Similarly, with
each new stage in the fighting, the reader seems to arrive at an explanation
for Napoleon's loss, only to find it displaced a few paragraphs later by another,
equally definitive cause. Thus, the weather is first blamed for the outcome of
the battle: "S'il n'avait pas plu dans la nuit du 17 au 18 juin 1815 l'avenir de
l'Europe était changé" 'If it had not rained on the night of June 17, 1815, the
future of Europe would have been different" (1: 412; 309 [pt. 2, bk. 1, ch. 3]).
Soon thereafter, however, the blame shifts to a local peasant guide who provides
misleading information about the terrain: "On pourrait presque dire que de ce
signe de tête d'un paysan est sortie la catastrophe de Napoléon" 'It may almost
be said that from this shake of a peasant's head came Napoleon's downfall' (1: 436;
329 [pt. 2, bk. 1, ch. 9]). Ultimately, the blame shifts to Napoleon himself: "Si
Napoléon en ce moment-là même eût songé à son infanterie, il eût gagné la bataille" 'Had Napoleon at that very moment remembered his infantry, he would
have won the battle" (1: 439; 331 [pt. 2, bk. 1, ch. 10]).

   The chapters thus hover between the impulse to script the moments of battle
down to the most gruesome details and the avowal of the impossibility of this
selfsame task: "Ajoutons qu'il y a toujours un certain instant où la bataille dégé-
nère en combat, se particularise et s'éparpille en d'innombrables faits de détails"
'We should add that there is always a certain moment when the battle degenerates into combat, particularizes itself, scatters into innumerable details' (1: 420;

315 [pt. 2, bk. 1, ch. 5]). The narrator's archaeology of violence strains under the pressure of his own claim to bear witness to an event at which he was not present. Detailed descriptions claim to order space and time into a seamless and credible account of the past. But in passages like the one above, the text points to its own constructedness and to the ultimate unattainability of narrative order. The accumulation of constantly shifting beginnings and endings disrupts the linear and chronological order that characterizes the narration of historical events, but unless attention is drawn to this, students tend to accept the narrator's voice as historical authority—to take what Hugo writes for what "really" happened. Even as they complain (like Flaubert) about the lengthy descriptions, they must at times be nudged into noticing how some passages undermine realist assumptions.

Roland Barthes's classic essay "L'effet de réel" can provide a helpful framework for understanding the text's simultaneous deployment and subversion of realist strategies of description. I focus on the equivalence that Barthes establishes between nineteenth-century realism and history:

> L'histoire (le discours historique: *historia rerum gestarum*) est en fait le modèle de ces récits qui admettent de remplir les interstices de leurs fonctions par des notations structuralement superflues, et il est logique que le réalisme littéraire ait été, à quelques décennies près, contemporain du règne de l'histoire "objective." (*Bruissement* 185)

> History (historical discourse: *historia rerum gestarum*) is in fact the model of those narratives which consent to fill in the interstices of their functions by structurally superfluous notations, and it is logical that literary realism would have been—give or take a few decades—contemporary with the regnum of "objective" history. (*Rustle* 146)

What Barthes calls the "regnum of 'objective' history" includes Romantic historians like Jules Michelet as well as Edgar Quinet and Adolphe Thiers, whose accounts Hugo draws from in his description of the battle. For Barthes, both historical and realist discourses invest in superfluous descriptive details in order to denote an apparently unmediated, exterior reality. Yet if Hugo willingly uses realist strategies to bring the battlefield to life, he also repeatedly interrupts their referential illusion by calling attention to the limits of language: "il n'est donné à aucun narrateur, si consciencieux qu'il soit, de fixer absolument la forme de ce nuage horrible qu'on appelle une bataille" 'it is given to no narrator, however conscientious he may be, to fix absolutely the form of the horrible cloud that is called a battle' (1: 420; 316 [pt. 2, bk. 1, ch. 5]). For all the ways in which the narrator tries to circumscribe the event, Waterloo defies stable description and definition. As the title of chapter 5 reminds us, the battle is "quid obscurum," partly incomprehensible and unrepresentable. Ultimately, Hugo's battlefield stages a different use of language.

From Napoleon to Cambronne: Language and Revolution

Napoleon's presence and legacy loom large in the chapters on Waterloo and throughout *Les Misérables.* Initially described as content and even jovial, and later "hagard, pensif, sinistre" 'haggard, pensive, gloomy' (1: 449; 340 [pt. 2, bk. 1, ch. 13]), Napoleon in these pages gradually takes on a distinctly mythical dimension. He is less a military genius than an abstract figure whose downfall is the result of divine intervention. In Hugo's progressivist teleology Napoleon "gênait Dieu" 'annoyed God' (1: 437; 330 [pt. 2, bk. 1, ch. 9]) and his defeat was an inevitable step toward what still remained in 1861 the elusive promise of a democratic ideal.

Napoleon is ultimately overshadowed at the end of Hugo's account by a somewhat unlikely hero, identified as "Ce Cambronne, ce passant de la dernière heure, ce soldat ignoré, cet infiniment petit de la guerre" 'This Cambronne, coming at the final hour, this unknown soldier, this infinitesimal particle of war' (1: 452; 342 [pt. 2, bk. 1, ch. 15]). Hugo neglects to mention that this member of the Imperial Guard was a general, yet he appears in these pages as a figure of the people. The phrase "infinitesimal particle" affirms Cambronne's place among the overlooked and downtrodden figures on whom the novel claims to shed light. His heroism consists in voicing an infamously irreverent word, "le mot de Cambronne," during the Imperial Guard's last stand. Faced with the English artillery's call for him to surrender, Hugo writes that Cambronne yells out "Merde!" (1: 451; 341 [pt. 2, bk. 1, ch. 14]), a phrase that Alphonse de Lamartine euphemistically circumvents in his own account of the event, calling it "une de ces trivialités sublimes de sens, cyniques d'expressions, que le soldat comprend" 'one of those trivialities sublime in meaning, cynical in expression, that soldiers understand' (256).

Although the veracity of this version of events is contested, Hugo chooses to underline Cambronne's carnivalesque flouting of norms and linguistic registers. Even the most abject of terms can inspire poetry. He compares Cambronne's *mot* to the "Marseillaise": "Cambronne trouve le mot de Waterloo comme Rouget de l'Isle trouve la Marseillaise, par visitation d'un souffle d'en haut" 'Cambronne finds the word for Waterloo, as Rouget de l'Isle finds the "Marseillaise," through an inspiration from above' (1: 453; 343 [pt. 2, bk. 1, ch. 15]). In the face of defeat and even death, Cambronne offers a linguistic insurrection that prefigures another famous digression in the novel: the seven chapters on *argot* ("slang") in part 4. Here, Hugo stages a history and defense of street slang as the language of misery shared by the poor, marginal, and otherwise silenced members of society whose plight Hugo claims to give voice to. Cambronne's outburst can be read as an example of the "idiome abject qui ruisselle dans la fange" 'this abject idiom streaming with filth' (2: 314; 980 [pt. 4, bk. 7, ch. 1]). Seen in this light, Cambronne fits right into the gallery of otherwise anonymous *misérables* who stake their claim in society.

As abject as it may be, *argot* is also the source of creative resistance to social pressures and norms. We read later on that "Le même éclair formidable va de la torche de Prométhée au brûle-gueule de Cambronne" 'the same powerful lightning darts from the torch of Prometheus and Cambronne's clay pipe' (1: 753; 592 [pt. 3, bk. 1, ch. 11]). Cambronne marks the people's coming into language and onto the stage of history as an actor. It is hardly surprising then to note that the description of Cambronne as a "passant" explicitly aligns him with Jean Valjean, who is described by the same term when he first makes his appearance in the novel (pt. 1, bk. 2, ch. 1), as well as with the narrator, who gives himself the same epithet in the opening sentence of these chapters. Cambronne, like Hugo himself, unlocks language's revolutionary potential and wages war through words.

From Hugo to Vallès

Hugo's chapters on Waterloo should be understood in the context of numerous other fictional and historical accounts of the famous battle. Most famous among these, perhaps, is the third chapter of Stendhal's *La Chartreuse de Parme* (1839), in which Fabrice blunders his way through the battlefield in less-than-heroic fashion. Nonetheless, it is Hugo's account that resonates most strongly in the culture of commemoration that emerged in the second half of the nineteenth century specifically in relation to the Napoleonic Wars. It certainly stood out as such in 1879 to the radical-left-wing journalist and novelist Jules Vallès, whose short essay "Le Champ de bataille de Waterloo" (available on *Gallica*) takes aim at Hugo's text and at the dangers of memorializing in general. Published posthumously in *La Revue universelle* of 22 June 1901, it is a moving and deeply ironic essay that can help steer discussion toward the broader politics of commemoration.

In 1879, while still exiled from France for his participation in the Commune, Vallès was commissioned to write the entry on Waterloo for the *Grand dictionnaire universel du XIXe siècle*, but his finished piece was rejected.[6] Recovered several decades later, it appeared in *La Revue universelle* to commemorate the eighty-sixth anniversary of the battle. The photographs and map accompanying the article allow undergraduates to better visualize the battlefield, the ruins of Hougomont, and the Lion's Mound built by the Dutch monarchy in 1820 on the spot where William of Orange was wounded. The photographs alone convey the eeriness of the landscape Hugo describes. In particular, the photograph of the farm and the well on page 580 of the *Revue* documents the sense of ruin and decay that Hugo's text underlines.

For advanced undergraduates and graduate students, reading Vallès's critique of Hugo can be revealing, not just as an illustration of the different positions the two writers occupied in the nineteenth-century literary field but also as a way of exploring the politics of memorialization in the modern West.[7] Hugo's own description of his visit to the battlefield hints at the exploitation of France's wartime past when he notes that a peasant tried to charge him three francs to explain "la chose de Waterloo!" 'the battle of Waterloo' (1: 247; 309 [pt. 2, bk. 1, ch. 2]; the English translation omits the word "chose" 'thing'). Nearly two decades later, Vallès found that the battlefield had been further commodified and reified within a growing tourism industry. Unearthed bullets from the battle can be purchased and taken home as souvenir "bibelots" 'trinkets' (582), history is for sale, and Hugo's legend has become part and parcel of this commercialization. The personnel at the hotel and the guides Vallès pays to take him on a tour of the battlefield all invoke Hugo's name in the same breath as the battle itself. In Vallès's view, such mythologizing of the past goes hand in hand with its commodification, and both stand in the way of a viable future. Indeed, Vallès's essay is a manifesto in favor of pacifism and the still-unrealized rights of labor: "Je hais la guerre! . . . Non. Je ne salue pas les héros morts, mais les travailleurs vivants" 'I abhor war! . . . No. I won't salute dead heroes, but rather living workers' (582). Vallès critiques *Les Misérables* and the sentimental democracy it embraces for its apparent glorification of a violent, imperial past and its failure to enact social and political change. Vallès's searing attack thus brings Hugo's dangerous mythologizing of violence into sharp relief. Read together, Hugo's and Vallès's texts offer students a chance to explore the politics of commemoration and the privileged yet problematic roles literature can play in confronting the past.

NOTES

[1] All translations are mine unless otherwise indicated.

[2] For a detailed military history of Waterloo, see Adkin; Hofschröer; and Lefebvre.

[3] As Heinzen shows, debates over the meaning of Waterloo continue to resonate and have earned new valences in the contemporary geopolitical context of the European Union.

[4] On Hugo's visits to Waterloo and personal investment in the event and the battlefield, see Descotes 32–43 and Desné 321–28.

[5] Claude Mettra discusses the symbolic significance of the water well at Hougomont both as an improvised tomb for the victims within and as a more general but particularly potent, Romantic commonplace referring to a source of inspiration and life (76–77).

[6] See the note accompanying the entry on Vallès in the second supplement to the *Grand dictionnaire universel du XIXe siècle* (1890), vol. 17, 1726–28. For a detailed reading of Vallès's article in the *Revue*, see Corinne Saminadayar-Perrin.

[7] Waterloo's privileged place in the so-called European Heritage Industry is explored by Neil Silberman in his article on the archaeology of the battlefield.

Beyond Fiction:
Misère in Historical Context

Rachel G. Fuchs

What does it say about a society when a young unwed mother such as Fantine feels compelled to leave her baby to a family she happens to encounter? Does she really need to disencumber herself of a child and remove evidence of her sexual activity in order to find work? What are her alternatives? And what does it say about a society when she is then fired from her job and subsequently sells her hair, her teeth, and her body—all for her child? And what does the life of the young child, Cosette, tell us about an economy and culture where such a tiny girl could suffer as a servant? Is Gavroche, the *gamin* ("street urchin"), really illustrative of "les enfants errants [qui] abondaient dans Paris" 'truant children [who] abounded in Paris,' always hungry and shivering in winter (1: 740; 581 [pt. 3, bk. 1, ch. 6])?

Gavroche's siblings fare hardly better than he, as the girls try to survive in the dilapidated Gorbeau lodging house located in a liminal part of the city near the large public hospitals mainly for the aged, criminals, and the insane, La Salpêtrière and La Pitié. Éponine and Azelma go about in flimsy rags (2: 19; 736 [pt. 3, bk. 3, ch. 4]), and the boys are abandoned twice, first by their parents and then by la Magnon, who used them for extortion. They are "monstres impurs et innocents produits par la misère" 'impure innocent monsters produced by misery' (2: 22; 738 [pt. 3, bk. 8, ch. 4]). And there are others in poverty: the aging Mabeuf sells his precious books for a pittance, becoming destitute.[1] The harshness of poverty is everywhere—from the "blanchisseuses" 'laundresses' (1: 365; 272–73 [pt. 1, bk. 7, ch. 10]) to the "chiffonnières" 'ragpickers' (2: 426–27; 1072 [pt. 4, bk. 11, ch. 2]) to the Thénardiers.

Fiction, obviously, is not history, but *Les Misérables* lends itself to teaching history. Although novels do not typically claim historical accuracy or supply the verifiable facts that historians insist on, they provide the emotions and sensibilities of the time. This essay first places Victor Hugo in the context of contemporary theories on poverty and then provides the historical context for Hugo's characters. With oftentimes mundane descriptions mixed with elegant philosophy and exquisite poetry, Hugo's romantic fiction creates compelling characters living in the world of poverty (*misère*) that historians immediately recognize. The pawnshops (*monts-de-piété*) where Marius would "manger ses habits et sa montre" 'eat his coat and his watch' (1: 854; 678 [pt. 3, bk. 5, ch. 1]) were necessary for survival not only for starving students but also for men in construction and women in the needle trade, especially when they faced unemployment during the dead season. Poverty also existed in rural areas. Petit Gervais, a Savoyard, was typical of young peasant boys who trekked seasonally from their poor rural villages in the Alps of Savoy (annexed to France in 1860) to work mainly as chimney sweeps.

Poverty was as widespread in Paris as it is in the novel. The historian Jeanne Gaillard estimated that from 1831 to 1869 between five and ten percent of the people in eastern Paris were impoverished, with indigence increasing in Paris during the Second Empire (1851–70), particularly in the eastern part of the city (154–56, 162, 488). Urban industrialization and increased rural-urban migration, especially during the depression of 1830 and during the "hungry forties," often resulted in family dislocation and disruption.

Victor Hugo was a politician as well as a poet and novelist. He participated in the parliamentary debates of the Second Republic (1849–51), and on 9 July 1849 delivered an emotional and combative address, "Détruire la misère" ("To Destroy Misery"), to the Legislative Assembly. Legislators and reformers of his time wanted to reduce *misère* as a means to reducing crime, but Hugo wanted to do more: he sought to eradicate *misère*. In his impassioned speech, employing some of the images and techniques designed to arouse emotion that he had incorporated into *Les Misérables*, Hugo painted pathetic portrayals of poverty to evoke a reaction that would inspire legislative action:[2]

> Il y a dans Paris . . . des rues, des maisons, des cloaques, où des familles, des familles entières, vivent pêle-mêle, hommes, femmes, jeunes filles, enfants, n'ayant pour lits, n'ayant pour couvertures, j'ai presque dit pour vêtement, que des monceaux infects de chiffons en fermentation, ramassés dans la fange du coin des bornes, espèce de fumier des villes, où des créatures s'enfouissent toutes vivantes pour échapper au froid de l'hiver.
> (qtd. in Kahn 614)[3]

> In Paris, there are streets, houses, sewers where families, entire families, live pell mell, men, women, girls, children, having no beds, having no blankets, I almost said clothing, except for stinking heaps of fermenting rags gathered from the muck of the street corners, a sort of urban manure, where all living creatures burrow to escape the cold of winter.[4]

To celebrate the victory of the Second Republic after the Revolution of June 1848 and to combat the socialism of the 1840s, Hugo also proposed to the Legislative Assembly a controversial solution that was decades ahead of his time:

> Il faut . . . créer sur une vaste échelle la prévoyance sociale, pour substituer à l'aumône qui dégrade l'assistance qui fortifie, pour fonder de toutes parts, et sous toutes les formes, des établissements de toute nature qui rassurent les malheureux et qui encouragent le travailleur.   (qtd. in Kahn 613)

> We must . . . create social welfare on a large scale, to replace the charity that degrades, supporting aid, by establishing all sorts of institutions, everywhere and in all forms, that would comfort the unfortunates and encourage the worker.

Despite his view of charity as degrading, Hugo recognized the tradition of giving alms to the poor who begged outside churches, as Jean Valjean does at Saint-Médard and as do Marius and Cosette, who bestow coins to the poor on their wedding day. Hugo also recognized the importance of well-ordered charity, such as the Sisters of Charity and the Société de Saint-Vincent-de-Paul (1: 292–93; 213 [pt. 1, bk. 7, ch. 1]), two prominent religious charitable organizations throughout the century, primarily before 1870. Jean-François Kahn argues that Hugo's appeal for remedies to *la misère* rested on "une politique chrétienne de soulagement de la misère" 'a Christian policy to alleviate poverty' to combat the socialism of the 1848 revolution (609). Although Hugo deviated from Christian policy in declaring that alms degraded the recipient, he did agree that religious charity was an important form of relief for the poor. His views resembled those of some later nineteenth-century republican politicians who argued that religious charity was necessary when social welfare was absent or insufficient.

Hugo was a man of his time and had faith in religious redemption, but he was also ahead of his time with his call for a republican government to cure the social ill of poverty. Only in the 1880s did republican politicians disassociate religion and morality from *misère* and promote public assistance, a needs-based secular social welfare, to alleviate poverty. Hugo's ideas about poor relief related to his views of the early-nineteenth-century French economy. He recognized the positive impact of industrialization and urbanization concomitant with an increase in manufacturing, business, national prosperity, and progress, but he also recognized the negative impact of industrialization in spawning crowded cities and factories, unhealthy workplaces, long hours for factory workers, minimal pay, and deplorably harsh working conditions. In an ideal world, factory owners would be responsible. In the figure of M. Madeleine (Valjean), Hugo depicted an idealistic factory owner and the mayor of a new company town who wanted to increase industry, factories, and families while enabling people to become prosperous because then "la misère disparaît, et avec la misère disparaissent la débauche, la prostitution, le vol, le meurtre, tous les vices, tous les crimes!" 'poverty disappears, and with poverty disappear debauchery, prostitution, theft, murder, all vices, all crimes!' (1: 314–15; 231 [pt. 1, bk. 7, ch. 3]).

Debates in the legislature of the Second Republic and Hugo's language in the novel resemble those of social reformers of the 1830s and 1840s who had investigated conditions of poverty. The social question in Hugo's time was, What are the causes and remedies of *la misère*? Social reformers replied that urban industrial development, with its mixing of men and women in the workplace, led to immorality. In addition, these commentators generally believed that the workers were ignorant and lazy and that these presumed character traits led to their *misère*, which in turn led to crime; eliminating crime was the reformers' primary concern, and they linked crime and immorality to urban poverty, especially in Paris, which experienced an in-migration of rural men and women in search of work.

Hugo's descriptions of *misère* demonstrate the influence of two social economists who published monumental and widely read works in the 1840s, Louis-René

Villermé and H.-A. Frégier. They investigated workers' lives, much as Hugo did, but their conclusions differed on some levels. Like Hugo, Louis-René Villermé eschewed alms and proposed paternalism in which individual manufacturers would create situations that separated men and women in the workplace, as in the manufactory of the fictional M. Madeleine. And like Hugo he did not view children such as Gavroche as immoral or criminal. Rather, he viewed them as the unfortunate victims of their parents' "debauchery" and lack of financial and family planning. In spite of their similarities, their conclusions differ: Villermé maintained that the moral disorder that produced inadequate income was at the root of the misfortunes of the working classes. Unlike Hugo, he reserved much of his moral indignation for women who, like Fantine, succumbed to sexual pleasure and bore a child. The argument of the oft-cited H.-A. Frégier resembled that of Villermé and many others: immorality led to *misère*, which led to crime. Frégier intoned: "the poor and vicious classes have always been and always will be the most fertile crucible for all categories of wrongdoers" (1: 9). To Frégier, *misère*, more than criminal inclinations, led a starving child disowned by his parents, such as Gavroche, to steal. Villermé and Frégier exemplified the urban propertied population who feared Thénardier and his gang of four. In the social imaginary, the laboring classes had become the dangerous classes, but Hugo does not seem to have shared their ideas of the general immorality of the laboring classes.

Joseph Marie de Gérando, a moral economist of the 1820s and 1840s, may have influenced Hugo. Gérando pitied unwed mothers who succumbed to men's false promises of love. He acknowledged that these seduced and abandoned women would have difficulty keeping their babies and their jobs and proposed institutions where they could work. His Asile-Ouvroir, established in Paris two decades after 1817–18, when Fantine would have given birth, might have welcomed Fantine because it was her "first fault"—if she demonstrated that she was otherwise moral and hardworking. Women entering the Asile were forced to abandon their infants to the Hospice des Enfants Trouvés. Gérando along with other moral economists and social Catholics allowed for the redemption of unwed mothers, as did Hugo.

Social Catholics, such as Armand de Melun, the author of the 1849 legislation that Hugo supported, also related poverty to immorality. They were critical of the industrial capitalism of the 1830s and 1840s, which they thought fostered immorality by mixing the sexes in the workplace, by separating families, by creating conditions where entire families shared one room and often one bed, by employing single women who lived without family, and by other means leading to a loss of religious morality. Thus they tried to ameliorate social ills through Catholic charity grounded in personal relationships between donors and recipients. Hugo represented some of these ideas in his depiction of the relationship between the Bishop of Digne and Jean Valjean. Church spokesmen during the July Monarchy of the 1830s and 1840s were conservative and paternalistic, moved by a sense of moral obligation. Religious leaders such as Frédéric Ozanam founded the Société de Saint-Vincent-de-Paul, which became the best-known Catholic relief organization, and in which the Sisters of Charity, represented in the novel by Sister Simplice, played a prominent part. Socialists, such as Eugène Buret, differed; they clearly placed the blame for poverty on the economic system and not on the workers' immorality. Hugo embodied some of Buret's ideas along with those of the economists and social Catholics, but without a dominant morality component.

In the novel, Hugo humanized the face of poverty and provided vivid descriptions, sometimes using language reminiscent of his 1849 speech as well as that used by reformers when visiting dwellings where several workers unrelated to each other shared living quarters. Like many reformers of the 1830s and 1840s, Hugo visited textile workers and reported on their lives. His heartrending description of Cosette as a servant for the Thénardiers provided an emotional example of what he and others may have seen (1: 224–25; 156–57 [pt. 1, bk. 4, ch. 3]). Along with the young Cosette, the Thénardiers, Fantine, and Gavroche emerge as Hugo's central characters in the world of poverty. Aside from some romantic imagery, their lives do not stray far from the historical context.

Fantine, Hugo's naive and pure victim, born in Montreuil-sur-Mer (in the northern department of Pas-de-Calais), leaves home at age ten for domestic service with nearby farmers, a typical trajectory for poor girls (1: 183; 122 [pt. 1, bk. 3, ch. 2]). At fifteen she comes to Paris to work in the needle trades, becomes a *grisette*, and, like other young women in her situation, falls in love and has a sexual liaison. Poor, pregnant, and abandoned by Tholomyès, her options are few. Hugo does not mention the birth of Cosette. Fantine could have entered the free public hospital, La Maternité, where almost all women admitted before the 1830s were unwed. Almost a third worked in the needle trades and almost five percent were born in the Pas-de-Calais (Fuchs, *Poor* 23, 26, 28). The much-preferred home delivery with a midwife was another possibility, but that necessitated having money to pay the midwife. Religious charities eschewed helping unwed mothers because they thought such aid would encourage immorality. Because the Napoleonic civil code forbade paternity searches, Fantine could not pursue Tholomyès for support (Fuchs, *Contested Paternity*).

Most women at La Maternité abandoned their newborns to the Hospice des Enfants Trouvés within two days of the birth. It was legal for a parent to abandon a child and, as Hugo accurately mentioned, Jean-Jacques Rousseau did so (2: 268; 943 [pt. 4, bk. 6, ch. 1]). About half of all illegitimate babies born in the 1820s in Paris were abandoned; a third of the mothers abandoning their babies resembled Fantine in giving their occupation as seamstress or worker (Fuchs, *Abandoned Children* 64–67). The hospice sent the abandoned infants to unregulated wet nurses in the countryside. The odds of an abandoned child dying were over fifty percent (206–32). Only about two percent of all abandoned children were reclaimed by a parent, and most of those were among the older children, such as the Thénardier boys, brought to the hospice by the police if the police found them. In 1874 the Roussel law regulated the wet-nursing industry, and, given associated advances in medicine, infant mortality declined.

Fantine chose to keep and nurse her baby, but few avenues for help existed. The Bureaux de Bienfaisance in Paris, established in July 1816, was one of the earliest forms of relief for the poor, but it helped only married women. Fantine was on her way to the village of her birth, where she hoped someone would take her in, possibly along with Cosette. Some unwed mothers had close ties with their families, who would forgive a pregnancy outside marriage (Fuchs, *Poor* 14–16). But Fantine had no known family. Since most people considered an unmarried mother immoral, Fantine is probably correct when she says, "Voyez-vous, je ne peux pas emmener ma fille au pays. L'ouvrage ne le permet pas. Avec un enfant, on ne trouve pas à se placer" 'You see I can't take my child into the country. The work will prevent it. With a child I could not find a job there' (1: 218; 152 [pt. 1, bk. 4, ch. 3]).

The earliest welfare began in 1837, when the Minister of Interior advocated assistance to women who gave birth in public hospitals so they could stay there for several days, breast-feed their infants, and take them with them when they left. But insufficient funds made this program available only to very few, and it existed for only a short time. In 1876 the Assistance Publique of Paris instituted a program of aid to unwed mothers to prevent abandonment. Hugo lived to see this program expand in 1885 and change its name to Secours d'Allaitement ("Aid for Maternal Infant Feeding"). Fantine also had no available infant day care. Private *crèches* ("day-care centers"), established in 1844, accepted only children of married mothers. Municipal *crèches* that accepted children of unmarried mothers began in 1874. After Hugo's death in 1885, *consultations des nourrissons* ("well-baby clinics") and homes for unwed and parturient mothers increased in number—all with the goal of preventing child abandonment and infant mortality. With a new concern with depopulation caused by the Franco-Prussian War of 1870, political discourse shifted from criticizing the poor for the immorality of having children they could not support to encouraging childbirth, and the government started to provide relief for the poor in order to prevent infant mortality.

Without family or social services, in her economic and emotional misery emanating from her love for Cosette, Fantine succumbs to prostitution. To Hugo's contemporaries, prostitutes exemplified women's immorality and were a source of pollution and crime. The social hygienist Alexandre Parent-Duchâtelet examined prostitution as an aspect of criminality, publishing his results in 1836. Hugo, however, differed: he blamed poverty for prostitution. In his sympathetic portrayal of Fantine as a virtuous victim of desperation, Hugo considered prostitution slavery:

> C'est la société achetant une esclave. À qui? À la misère. À la faim, au froid, à l'isolement, à l'abandon, au dénuement. Marché douloureux. Une

âme pour un morceau de pain. La misère offre, la société accepte. La sainte loi de Jésus-Christ gouverne notre civilisation, mais elle ne la pénètre pas encore. On dit que l'esclavage a disparu de la civilisation européenne. C'est une erreur. Il existe toujours, mais il ne pèse plus que sur la femme, et il s'appelle prostitution.   (1: 261 [pt. 1, bk. 5, ch. 11])

It is about society buying a slave. From whom? From misery. From hunger, from cold, from loneliness, from desertion, from privation. Melancholy barter. A soul for a bit of bread. Misery makes the offer; society accepts. The holy law of Jesus Christ governs our civilization, but it does not yet permeate it. They say that slavery has disappeared from European civilization. That is incorrect. It still exists: but now it weighs only on woman, and it is called prostitution.   (187)

Along with the prostitutes, the *gamins* who roamed Paris as runaways or abandoned children existed in historical imagery as part of the social tragedy of poverty. The *gamin* was a child "bien affublé d'un pantalon d'homme, mais il ne le tenait pas de son père, et d'une camisole de femme, mais il ne la tenait pas de sa mère. Des gens quelconques l'avaient habillé de chiffons par charité. Pourtant il avait un père et une mère. Mais son père ne songeait pas à lui et sa mère ne l'aimait point" 'well decked out in a man's pair of pants, though he did not get them from his father, and in a woman's jacket, which was not from his mother. Strangers had clothed him in these rags out of charity. Yet he did have a father and a mother. But his father never thought of him, and his mother did not love him' (1: 755; 594 [pt. 3, bk. 1, ch. 13]).

Propertied Parisians and the police thought of *gamins* as gangs of criminals—begging, robbing, or stealing. Although Gavroche steals, it is for survival. Demonstrating a generous soul, Gavroche robs Montparnasse (a member of his father's gang of thieves) of his purse and, although hungry himself, throws it to Mabeuf upon overhearing the latter's tale of destitution (2: 237–38, 245; 916–917, 923 [pt. 3, bk. 4, ch. 2]). Gavroche also provides food and shelter for his abandoned younger brothers, without knowing their identity. Those two children had become homeless, dressed in tatters, and wandering at night into the Luxembourg gardens after the gates had closed: "Ces êtres appartenaient désormais à la statistique des 'Enfants Abandonnés' que la police constate, ramasse, égare et retrouve sur le pavé de Paris" 'These beings belonged from then on to the statistics of 'abandoned children,' whom the police report, collect, mislay, and find again on the streets of Paris' (2: 599–600; 1218–19 [pt. 5, bk. 1, ch. 16]). Policemen, or *gardiens de la paix*, were scarce in Paris in the 1830s, and none had found these children. Hugo estimated that on average the police rounds annually resulted in 260 homeless children, whom they would find "dans les terrains non clos, dans les maisons en construction et sous les arches des ponts" 'in open lots, in houses under construction, and under the arches of bridges' (1: 740–41; 581–82 [pt. 3, bk. 6, ch. 6]). Admission registers of the Hospice des Enfants Trouvés reveal that the police would occasionally bring in groups of vagrants under age twelve. Hugo voiced the sentiments of some of his contemporaries and foresaw the opinions of conservatives later in the century who maintained that vagrancy in Paris was a "blight" of modern civilization and led to all types of crime (1: 741; 582 [pt. 3, bk. 1, ch. 6]). Authorities treated vagabond children over age twelve as delinquents and sent them to an *ouvroir*, or a *colonie agricole*, a reformatory, or a prison for young delinquents (Fuchs, *Abandoned Children* 239). Child-protection agencies appeared after midcentury to protect children who were abandoned or guilty of some crime, such as Gavroche's petty theft.

Hugo did not live to see the law of 1889 on the *déchéance de la puissance paternelle* ("denial of paternal authority") designed to protect *moralement aban-donnés* ("morally endangered") children.[5] The law allowed the state to disempower parents with egregiously bad behavior, who were not ensuring the moral order, and to remove their children. Such parental behavior included improperly clothing and feeding the children; living in extreme filth; habitual drunkenness; sexually or physically abusing the children; beating the children beyond what was considered normal correction; being arrested for begging, theft, or other crime; leaving the children alone; or engaging in prostitution. Under this law, Éponine, Azelma, and Gavroche and his two brothers would have been taken away from the Thénardiers to become wards of the state and doled out to relatives, if any existed, or shipped off to foster parents in the countryside, or sent to a workhouse where they might learn a trade, or taken to a *colonie agricole* or other institution (Fuchs, *Contested Paternity* 207–17; Schafer 130, 167–69, 176, 191).

The Thénardiers and Marius rented rooms in the Gorbeau hovel, consisting of "planches vermoulues grossièrement reliées par des traverses pareilles à des bûches mal équarries . . . On ne sait quels chiffons couleur de poussière pendaient comme des draperies au vasistas triangulaire" 'worm-eaten boards crudely held together by cross ties that looked like rough-cut logs of firewood . . . dust-colored rags that served as curtains around the triangular ventilator' (1: 558; 429 [pt. 2, bk. 4, ch. 1]). The most wretched of the residents were the Thénardiers and their two girls, a family of four sharing a single garret room (1: 756; 594 [pt. 3, bk. 1, ch. 13]). The Gorbeau building did not differ significantly from the dilapidated nineteenth-century lodging houses that were occupied by the least stable Parisian population of urban poor, who moved to ever-cheaper rooms when they could not pay the rent. Hugo's descriptions also resemble many of the reports on workers prepared during the July Monarchy. An 1831 police report on the area near Gorbeau mentioned the despair of the residents who were told to leave: "I saw unfortunate fathers of families, with their four or five children around them, without bread and with no notion how they were going to be able to support them the next day. To make matters worse, the soup kitchen in the rue Mouffetard is closing down on Friday by order of the Mayor" (Chevalier 266–67).

Marius's poverty was temporary and self-imposed, unlike the *misère* of the others, but his life in the Gorbeau rooming house illustrates that of Paris's "floating population" ("population flottante") of indigents. The population of Paris doubled from 1801 to 1851, but housing did not increase proportionally, especially in the areas inhabited by immigrants and workers, resulting in overcrowding, disease, filth, and congestion (Chevalier 188–99). In the marginal area of the Boulevard de l'Hôpital where Marius and the Thénardiers lived, the population was not as dense nor rents as high as in the more central areas until the Second Empire, when density and rents there increased substantially. According to Hugo, Marius lived on roughly seven hundred francs a year, which was possible, and a larger income than that of a woman worker. In 1830 he would have paid between fifty and two hundred francs a year for an unheated rented room in a lodging house. By midcentury, rent in such a room ranged from two hundred to five hundred francs a year. Just the most minimal food and shelter, such as rooms in Gorbeau, would have taken his entire income (Gaillard 136–46, 151, 174; Fuchs, *Poor* 34; Berlanstein 11–14, 26).

Historians provide evidence about conditions of poverty and the survival strategies of the poor, and they place the novel in a historical context. In so doing, they analyze the nineteenth-century shift from an understanding of poverty as caused by immorality and laziness to an understanding of poverty resulting from the upheavals brought about by industrialization and urbanization. The shift in understanding led to new ideas and remedies. Social reformers redefined the moralistic casting of the social question of the 1840s to a positivist one in the 1880s; this resulted in governments taking measures to alleviate poverty in the name of national solidarity. *Les Misérables*, however, affords personal insights into nineteenth-century poverty. The novel provides an understanding of poverty on another level than that of historians. The imagery is vivid, transcends historical data, and creates a reality for its time.

NOTES

I thank Katie Jarvis, who read and commented on this essay with an eye on teaching *Les Misérables* to history students.

[1] See, e.g., 2: 237–39, 917 (pt. 4, bk. 4, ch. 11) and 2: 390–93, 1043–46 (pt. 4, bk. 9, ch. 3).

[2] See, e.g., 1: 756–57; 595 (pt. 3, bk. 1, ch. 13) and 2: 19–20, 27–41; 728–55 (pt. 3, bk. 8, ch. 5).

[3] See also "Discours à l'Assemblée Législative."

[4] Unless otherwise indicated, all translations from the French are mine.

[5] On the question of paternal, or parental, authority, see Fuchs, *Contested Paternity* 207–17.

Teaching Social Class and the Dynamics of History in Hugo's *Les Misérables*

Laurence M. Porter

The keen social and historical consciousness of Victor Hugo's *Les Misérables* helps students discover the relevance of imaginative literature to their own experience and to their society. Admittedly, *Les Misérables* is redoubtably long. Even some first-language speakers of French in graduate school grumble at having to read it in a month. The instructor must carefully select limited readings and artfully sequence topics to enable students to become active participants in discussion. Fortunately, Hugo's pointedly contrasting depictions of various social groups illuminate his intentions and messages.

Students need historical background to understand Hugo's novel (see Wright's chapter "The Varieties of History," covering 1789–1835, in *France in Modern Times*). During the revolution, the three doctrinal pillars that had legitimated the ancien régime collapsed: the divine right of kings (who rule because God ordains it), the privileges (such as freedom from taxation) conferred by birth to a noble family, and the state-supported Catholic Church. Nobles and clergy who refused to support the new republic were persecuted, forced into exile, or executed. European monarchies united to invade France and restore the monarchy, but failed. The prominent English conservative Edmund Burke warned that universal suffrage invited barbarism: if all were considered equal, he warned, "the swinish multitude" would be justified in appropriating and redistributing the wealth of the rich (68). Meanwhile, and up until the present day, some conservatives have adopted an even more hostile stance, believing that any gathering of workers or others united in collective protests—however organized and peaceable—became a "multitude" and therefore forfeited their rights. In contrast, the liberal view, such as that of Thomas Carlyle in *The French Revolution* (1837), tried to individualize and humanize the masses. The major political project of *Les Misérables* (reflected in nearly all Hugo's novels) runs along the lines of Carlyle's advocacy of humanistic inclusivity.

About six percent of the fifteen hundred pages of *Les Misérables* can provide an overview of Hugo's views on class structure, guide students toward understanding Hugo's social thought, and integrate his views with a broader view of the novel. To prepare students for a general discussion a few days ahead of the first class meeting on *Les Misérables*, one could ask them to consider their home country by briefly answering the following questions in writing: How would you define a social class? How are classes arranged in a hierarchy in your home country? What arguments are used to justify this hierarchy? Which persons are denied the full rights of citizenship, including participation in public affairs? When students have finished their reading assignments, the instructor can ask them to reflect on how political conditions in Hugo's novel differ from those they have experienced in person.

From the beginning of his career, Hugo gave important roles to groups without suffrage: slaves (*Bug-Jargal*); street people and criminals (*Notre-Dame de Paris*, *Les Misérables*, *L'Homme qui rit*); working-class people (*Les Misérables*, *Les Travailleurs de la mer*, *Quatrevingt-treize*). Thus he implies that society should value them and ensure their welfare. There are many socially conscious passages in *Les Misérables* from which one could choose. Twelve passages, with suggestions for a discussion topic, appear below. (They are labeled according to the class hierarchy in nineteenth-century France and arranged from highest to lowest degree of status.)

The Emperor and His Army

"Quot libras in duce?" 'How Much Does the Leader Weigh?'
(1: 453–59; 343–48 [pt. 2, bk. 1, ch. 16])

"Faut-il trouver bon Waterloo?" 'Should We Approve of Waterloo?'
(1: 459–61; 348–50 [pt. 2, bk. 1, ch. 17]).

Hugo's preoccupation with Waterloo is in part linked to his family history. His parents separated when he was very young, and he lived with his mother, a royalist. She influenced his views during his youth until, like his young hero Marius in *Les Misérables*, he came to admire the military career of his father, who had been promoted to general and whose name appears on the Arc de Triomphe. But later, also like Marius, he came to wonder whether the slaughter and tyranny—costs of an expansive empire always at war and ruled by one person alone—were preferable to the peace and constitutional rights of the people in a republic. Students could be asked to take sides in a debate over which form of government seemed preferable to Hugo and why.

The Church: The Male Clergy

"Solitude de Msgr. Bienvenu" 'Monseigneur Bienvenu's Solitude'
(1: 94–97; 49–52 [pt. 1, bk. 1, ch. 12])

The bishop's actual name is "Myriel," a near anagram for *lumière*, which for Hugo represents both the social reform movement of the Enlightenment ("les Lumières") and the light of redeeming grace. Students could examine and report on how the bishop preaches by outreach and personal example and how he politely recommends best practices of community organization by telling one impoverished mountain village about the achievements of another that is poorer or equally poor. But he has few connections to the rich and powerful.

Why? What kind of "solitude" does the bishop experience, and why? Which comments by Hugo suggest a dereliction of duty by the ambitious young prelates and moral failures on the part of the church? How does the passage on the nobility (below) ironically anticipate Hugo's critique of the church? The two highest classes have abdicated their social responsibilities in favor of personal gain. In contrast, a scrutiny of "Bienvenu's" (Myriel's) finances shows that he reverse-tithes, giving ninety percent of his revenues to the poor.

The Church: Nuns

"Parenthèse" 'A Parenthesis'   (1: 653–66; 509–23 [pt. 2, bk. 7, chs. 1–5])

The instructor could point out that Hugo does not question the rigid gender-based distinction between male leadership and female self-abnegation in the French Catholic Church of the nineteenth century. Here, students might reflect on what Hugo considers morally admirable in the nuns he depicts, and which practices of their rule (for the conduct of a life of prayer and service, as prescribed by each religious order) he considers excessively harsh and unproductive in modern times. Because the revolution had seized much of the church lands and property, religious orders often had to partially support themselves. In consequence, the fictitious order described by Hugo has had to admit some wealthy single women—former aristocrats—as boarders, and also runs a boarding school for little girls. Moreover, the charitable vocation of the nuns has led them to admit refugee sisters from convents that had been destroyed or rendered too small to be viable during the revolution. (Napoleon did cynically decide to tolerate nuns in France, when he realized that they would provide a valuable source of free labor in primary schools and in hospitals.) These refugees were generously allowed to worship each in their own way, instead of following the rule of their host order. But, as a result, the hosts' strict observance of labor-intensive prayer and perpetual adoration in the convent could no longer be maintained, because of a shortage of participants. Here the instructor could point out that religious vocations actually increased overall in France once persecution of Christians ceased. Vocations continued to increase throughout the nineteenth century until one French person in a hundred was in lay or holy orders.

The Nobility (a Count)

"Philosophie après boire" 'After Dinner Philosophy'
                                (1: 67–71; 28–31 [pt. 1, bk. 1, ch. 8])

The cynical attitude of the first speaker, a *sénateur* and a count, is that religion serves well as an opiate for the masses, dulling their rage at the gross inequities of the distribution of wealth in their world, but that in a world without God, a self-serving, materialistic attitude is the only sensible guide to a good life, and that anyone who does not take care of himself first is a fool. Students could be asked to seek and comment on examples of Bishop Myriel's sarcasm in his rejoinder as he rejects his dinner partner's crude selfishness. This count is far from assuming the responsibilities that, from medieval times, would have given him legitimacy: to protect his lands, farmers, and workers from attack (knighthood) and to ensure their health and welfare (a duty implied by the term "noblesse oblige"). On the other hand, even veterans with aristocratic titles who were wounded while serving under the republic or the First Empire were often neglected and impoverished by reductions of their pensions, as Marius's father had been (see next paragraph, and compare with Balzac's *Le Colonel Chabert*). The frequent changes of regime in nineteenth-century France disadvantaged good and faithful servants of a former regime.

The Haute Bourgeoisie

"Le grand bourgeois" 'The Grand Bourgeois'
(1: 758–63; 597–607 [pt. 3, bk. 2, chs. 1–4])

"Le grand-père et le petit fils" 'The Grandfather and the Grandson'
(1: 797–804; 630–36 [pt. 3, bk. 3, ch. 6])

Referring students to the first set of these chapters, one could ask them to characterize the well-to-do grandfather: lusty, energetic, superficial, self-satisfied, and with a powerful, unreflective sense of entitlement that allows him to overlook, berate, and abuse people of lesser rank without scruples. He often forces servants, as if they were slaves, to take new names that he has chosen. His frivolous attitude toward love and toward women and his general facetiousness create a barrier between him and his moody, idealistic grandson, who needs and cannot find a suitable role model. The second passage (pt. 3, bk. 3, ch. 6) traces the political awakening of young Marius: he is raised to accept unquestioningly the divine-right monarchy and to recoil with horror from the bloodthirsty revolution and the tyrannical empire for which his father had bravely, loyally fought. Students might consider the inherent self-contradiction in Marius's newfound dual admirations: "la république dans la souveraineté du droit civique restitué aux masses, l'empire dans la souveraineté de l'idée française imposée à l'Europe" 'The Republic in the sovereignty of civil rights restored to the masses, the empire in the sovereignty of the Idea of France imposed on Europe' (1: 798; 631). One could pair this passage with the telling rejoinder of Marius's revolutionary friend Combeferre, when both meet later at a gathering of Les Amis de l'ABC (a pun on "l'abaissé," referring to the downtrodden peasants and workers). When Marius finishes extolling the grandeur of Napoleon's Empire and asks what could be more sublime, his friend retorts simply "Être libre" (1: 847–49; 671–75 [pt. 3, bk. 4, ch. 5]). Later, Marius's participation in the insurrectionists' resistance behind a barricade is of questionable ideological purity. One could ask students to discuss what may have motivated it, using quotations from the text as evidence.

(As I read *Les Misérables* I found that Marius seems motivated partly by a despairing lover's desire for suicide and partly by a perverse, rationalized emulation of his father as a war hero—although that father innocently reinforced tyranny rather than opposing it, as Marius did). Marius is the sole survivor among the rebels who remained behind the barricade, but so far as one can tell at the end of *Les Misérables*, his commitment to righting social wrongs seems to have been ephemeral. His devotion to and marriage with Cosette illustrate a romantic view of life, but one that contains no interactive social function. By the end of *Les Misérables*, we know nothing of his plans for a career. He will perhaps become "a useful public man" like young Ladislaw at the conclusion of George Eliot's *Middlemarch*.

The Middle Bourgeoisie: Provincials of Moderate Means, Educated in Paris

"Double quatuor" 'Double Quartet'
(1: 180–85; 120–23 [pt. 1, bk. 3, ch. 2])

"Le désœuvrement de M. Bamatabois" 'The Idleness of M. Bamatabois' and "Solution de quelques questions de police municipal" 'Solutions for Some Municipal Police Issues'
(1: 262–76; 188–99 [pt. 1, bk. 5, chs. 12–13])

Two other, less favored bourgeois youths are depicted in diptychs. The first panel contains a scene from their idle youth, exploiting poor, defenseless working women, and the second—a flash-forward—points to their unmerited success later, in provincial society. In "Double quatuor," Tholomyès and his three friends, perpetual students, date and support working girls who enter this subservient relationship by mutual consent, in order to escape their dull lives of drudgery and to be courted, supported, and entertained. Three of the girls are as cynical as their partners and readily move on to other relationships when they are suddenly abandoned. But one, Fantine, truly loves Tholomyès and believes his promises. She becomes pregnant, has a child, and then is left without any possibility of finding work again unless she conceals her child, Cosette, from a self-righteous, moralistic society. She works herself to death, sickens, and dies. "Le désœuvrement de M. Bamatabois" and "Solution de quelques questions de police municipal," her last scene before her final illness, shows her as a prostitute. Bamatabois sneaks up behind her, stuffs snow down the back of her low-cut dress, and brings on a fatal crisis of tuberculosis or pneumonia. Because of her lower-class standing, she is blamed for the resulting scuffle, arrested (while the perpetrator scurries off), and sentenced to six months in jail until Jean Valjean, as mayor, rescues her. Bamatabois, a social parasite, eventually plays a minor role as a juror in the Champmathieu trial. He has no commitment or sensitivity to the less fortunate. Students can be asked to consult the *ARTFL* database of keywords in context and decide what kinds of men Tholomyès and Bamatabois become in their maturity.

The Police

> Les paysans asturiens sont convaincus que dans toute portée de louve il y a un chien, lequel est tué par la mère, sans quoi en grandissant il dévorerait les autres petits. Donnez une face humaine à ce chien fils d'une louve et ce sera Javert.   (1: 240 [pt. 1, bk. 5, ch. 5])

> The peasants of the Asturias believe that in every litter of wolves there is a dog who is killed by the mother for fear that on growing up he would devour the other little ones. Give a human face to this dog and you will have Javert.   (170)

Like other public servants and like merchants, policemen occupy the lowest rung of the bourgeoisie, or the highest rung of the underclass. They do not own the means of production, but suspects must obey them. Their class prejudices are explained in Javert's background portrait quoted above. Unlike the savage wolf, Javert seeks respectability through absolute conformity to social rules, but he overcompensates by being insensitive and cruel to those who break them, unless they hold a higher social rank than his own. Javert later undergoes a wrenching moral conversion when Jean Valjean saves his life at the apparent cost of his own freedom. Just before he commits suicide, Javert leaves for his chief a limited but thoughtful list of practical ways to improve the efficacy and moral decency of operations through the more humane and respectful treatment of prisoners, but his chief simply thinks he has gone mad and throws the list away (2: 718–32; 1319–30 [pt. 5, bk. 4, ch. 1]). From bitter experience in the "Chambre des pairs" 'Chamber of Peers' (Porter 66–70, 81–85), Hugo realizes that proposed reforms often fail to interest politicians.

Skilled Craftsmen

Although craftsmen's medieval guilds inspired Hugo with nostalgia for their democratic, self-regulating structures (see *Notre-Dame de Paris*), they have no role in *Les Misérables*. Although in *Les Travailleurs de la Mer* sailors and farmers form other guild-like groups and the hero, Gilliatt, is an expert sailor, farmer, carpenter, and mechanic, in *Les Misérables* Hugo's main interest is in social outcasts. By means of calling attention to them, he advocates for social reforms, although his viewpoint remains paternalistic.

Unskilled Workers

In *Les Misérables*, these are the janitor-concierges (who may sleep in a cubbyhole under the stairs) and, below them, those among the working urban poor who are scavengers with no permanent home, who are tolerated by the police but occupy the lowest rung among legitimate members of society. They perform humble chores such as rag collecting and selling trash from their wheeled carts, in or under which they may take shelter. Hugo quickly sketches four of them and their hierarchy in the middle of "Gavroche en marche": "La chiffonnière était humble. Dans ce monde en plein vent, la chiffonnière salue, la portière protège. . . . Cette chiffonnière avait la hotte reconnaissante" 'The ragpicker was humble. In this outdoor society, the ragpicker bows, the concierge patronizes. . . . The ragpicker was a grateful recipient' (2: 426; 1072–73 [pt. 4, bk. 11, ch. 2])—she saved for the concierge choice bits from what she swept up in the street. Times are getting hard, but at least, she says, "moi j'ai un état" 'I have an occupation'—and social standing (2: 427; 1073). They all blindly accept economic injustice; Gavroche, however, more lucid, satirizes the lazy, pampered bourgeoisie (2: 99, 102; 1072, 1074 [pt. 3, bk. 3, ch. 20]). Lower in status, as a nonproductive member of society he possesses a higher social awareness.

Street Urchins (Gamins)

"Paris étudié dans son atome" 'Paris atomized'
(1: 733–57; 575–96 [pt. 3, bk. 1, chs. 1–13])

Gamin, meaning "street urchin," is a term Hugo boasts of having invented, although it is actually attested by *Le Petit Robert* in 1804, when Hugo was two. For Hugo, concern for the welfare of children is the touchstone of morality. He implies that the tens of thousands of neglected, orphaned, or abandoned children wandering the streets of Paris are the symptom of a pervasive social problem caused by society's lack of constructive solutions. The *gamins'* basic innocence is masked by impudence. But treating them as a nuisance binds the problem of their existence down to the lowest possible level and encourages defiant transgressions as a game. The *gamins* and the members of the next two categories do not belong to the accepted social order; they are outcasts considered by the powers that be to have no possible redemption or constructive social role.

Criminals

"Patron-Minette"   (1: 902–07; 718–22 [pt. 3, bk. 7, chs. 1–2])

In the first chapter of this section, "Les mines et les mineurs" 'Mines and Miners,' Hugo likens reformers to gangsters. Both live (literally or figuratively) in a *"troisième dessous"* 'third substage,' more accurately, 'second subbasement' (1: 904; 720), and they undermine society from beneath, evading repression. An evil and destructive subsociety such as a criminal gang, Hugo emphasizes, can be just as cohesive and well-organized as a socially sanctioned group formed to arrange political protests—and the latter can be even more destructive than a gang of bandits if it is outlawed and forced underground, as we see from the bloody battle at the insurgents' barricade. The Patron-Minette gang totally fails, but (as Hugo showed us earlier in the novel) so did Napoleon and his armies. Although Thénardier is smaller and weaker than other members of his criminal gang, he is more clever. He inspires them to find a more lucrative form of crime than muggings and burglaries: a scheme to kidnap, torture, and blackmail Valjean or Cosette. Although the supremely evil Thénardier callously sacrifices every member of his family without a qualm, the escaped convict Jean Valjean lovingly creates a replacement family for the orphan Cosette. Students could be invited to develop this contrast, which demonstrates that a former convict can be redeemed.

Republicans Fomenting Uprising with a Worker-Student Alliance

> "Un groupe qui a failli devenir historique" 'A Group That Almost Became Historic'   (1: 816–31; 646–59 [pt. 3, bk. 4, ch. 1])

Royalists see this group as the lowest: they see republicans as traitors to the king and to France, causing disorder and many deaths, in comparison to the criminals, who cause only a few. From the republican viewpoint, revolutionaries are heroes uprooting entrenched privilege in order to promote liberty and justice for all. Hugo, not blindly partisan, presents a balanced view. The group he depicts is intelligent and idealistic, but they fail to organize effectively: few workers come to join them, and they rely as much on rumor as on advance planning for recruitment. Moreover, as Hugo implies, although they are ready to fight and die together, the personal motives of most of the participants behind the barricade are divergent, conflicted, or unclear. They include a police spy, a criminal double-agent agitator, and several—M. Mabeuf, Éponine, and Marius—seeking to die because of their despair, as well as one, Grantaire, who sacrifices himself to demonstrate his chaste love for his leader. Students could be invited to identify the insurrectionists' diverse motives and then to comment on how their urgent situation behind the barricade, and the inspiring example of their leaders' idealism, produces temporary unanimity. Students will probably be interested in Hugo's careful distinctions between a riot, insurrections, and a revolution. He explains: "Dans les états démocratiques, les seuls fondés en justice, il arrive quelquefois que la fraction usurpe; alors le tout se lève, et la nécessaire revendication de son droit peut aller jusqu'à la prise d'armes" 'In democratic states, the only governments founded on justice, it sometimes happens that a faction usurps power; then the whole rises up, and the necessary vindication of its right may go so far as armed conflict' (2: 399; 1050 [pt. 4, bk. 10, ch. 2]). Any repression of the majority, Hugo defines as an *émeute* ("a riot"); a revolt against a tyrannical minority is an *insurrection*, morally justified ("Le fond de la question" 'The essential question' (2: 399–406; 1050–56 [pt. 4, bk. 10, ch. 2]). Later, however, he presents both sides of the argument in "Les morts ont raison et les vivants n'ont pas tort" 'The dead are right and the living are not wrong' (2: 618–28; 1234–42 [pt. 5, bk. 1, ch. 20]). The people must decide whether to support a revolution; many are premature. "Pour nous, qui préférons le martyre au succès, John Brown est plus grand que Washington" 'For ourselves, who prefer martyrdom to success, John Brown is greater than Washington' (2: 623; 1237–38) — and Hugo declares that somebody has to speak for the vanquished. In exile, he was one of the latter and pleaded their cause while affirming his faith in inevitable, eventual progress. He prefers peaceful solutions. Students could be asked to analyze the two extreme viewpoints as well as Hugo's compromise between them.

Hugo repeatedly points out that even the most respected institutions and persons are often corrupt. For example, Jean Valjean goes on trial when he is mayor, and the outcome is favorably influenced by his well-known, regular religious observance. And even the rigidly moralistic Javert is blindly prejudiced against the lower classes. He automatically assumes that a bourgeois must always be in the right in a quarrel with a member of "the people." Reacting against the complacency of the privileged, Hugo grants recognition and calls attention to those who in his time were usually shunned or exploited, neglected or forgotten: he pauses his narrative to present brief essays on the needs of unwed mothers, orphans, prostitutes, convicts, and the sick or elderly poor. These are not the movers of history; his discussions of them are digressions from the central epic or dramatic tale. Moreover, Hugo knows that even benevolent leading actors, such as Bishop Myriel, Jean Valjean as factory owner, or the Benedictine nuns, to say nothing of the historical author as a member of the governing legislative body of the Second Republic, often fail to achieve lasting reforms.

Nevertheless, for Hugo class membership is not an essence but an attribute. He shows that individuals can move from one class to another. Myriel transforms himself from a frivolous, pleasure-seeking, aristocratic womanizer into an idealistic prelate. Jean Valjean starts out as a hardworking rural tree pruner, the sole support of his sister and her seven children; becomes a convict, spending nineteen years at hard labor; transforms himself into a respectable industrialist and a revered mayor; and voluntarily returns to prison so that an innocent man will not be condemned in his place. He escapes, becomes a convent gardener, and finally retires as a bourgeois *rentier*, living on his savings. Students may enjoy seeking and finding other examples of social mobility in *Les Misérables*, such as Javert, and especially Cosette, the symbolic vehicle of the hopes of the next generation.

Morally, poverty is an empty signifier, correlated neither with vice nor virtue. Hugo calls it "la misère," which has the double meaning of extreme deprivation and of moral turpitude: individuals must be judged by their actions, not their wallets. But Providence intervenes as well, to test a few select persons with stark moral choices. Conscience, says Hugo, is the voice of God in us, reinforced in *Les Misérables* by "The Communion of Saints" (see *The New Catholic Encyclopedia*): a person who has benefitted from a generous act by another is inspired to "pay it forward" by selflessly helping someone else. Students could be asked to trace the chain of such influences from Bishop Muriel to Jean Valjean (1: 167–73; 106–13 [pt. 5, bk. 1, ch. 20]) to Fauchelevent (1: 671–73; 525–27 [pt. 2, bk. 8, ch. 1]). Through such individual conversions, Hugo believes that providence haltingly, unpredictably, and slowly guides humanity toward the consecration of a classless, egalitarian, democratic republic.

Les Misérables in/as
American Pop Culture

Kathryn M. Grossman

In popular culture, *Les Misérables* has taken on a life of its own—and not just since the 1985 musical version became a worldwide sensation. From the start, the novel had a profound impact on the American consciousness, yielding numerous representations in other media, in extrapolations and allusions in the press and in other writers' literary works, and in commodified spinoffs. The pervasiveness of *Les Misérables* in the American cultural landscape continues to this day, not just through stage, film, radio, and television adaptations but also through the digital, interactive new media in which our students are continuously immersed. For most of the students in my semester-long freshman seminar on *Les Misérables*, Hugo's masterwork is already a familiar cultural landmark. Some have read excerpts from the text in high school English classes. Others have seen Bille August's 1998 film adaptation with Liam Neeson, Uma Thurman, and Geoffrey Rush on *Netflix*; the Broadway production either in New York or on tour; or Tom Hooper's 2012 movie version of the musical starring Hugh Jackman, Anne Hathaway, and Russell Crowe—or even all three. Still others have participated in staging the musical either at school or in a community theater. Without realizing it, they have already been engaged for a number of years in the evolving adaptive process for the work.

The adaptive legacy of *Les Misérables* constitutes a rich cultural context for considering not just the text but also its multimedia afterlives. Hugo's novel can be approached as the subject and object of pop culture, while providing a critical frame for understanding the different film, musical, and parodic material that we subsequently view—as well as the broader issue of importing works into new contexts and media.[1] In this essay, I look first at some of the ways in which *Les Misérables* was adapted early on in the American popular press and on stage, then at its twentieth- and twenty-first-century cinematic versions, and finally at its many afterlives in digital media, all of which can be used in the classroom to frame discussions of the novel itself.

Appropriations of Characters

To supply students with a context for many of the extratextual activities in the course, I begin by using class discussions on the text to weave in pertinent cultural and historical information regarding the reception and early adaptations of the novel. Since first-time readers tend to focus on the portrayal and interaction of the major characters, students enjoy knowing that the explosive entry of Hugo's work onto the United States literary stage was largely fostered by the *adoption* of its characters by the American public, who *adapted* them to their own cultural mythology. Thanks to modern print journalism, abetted by the arrival of the transcontinental telegraph in 1861, Fantine, Jean Valjean, and Gavroche came alive again through the triumphs and woes of real people in a clear illustration of what Michel Espagne terms "les transferts culturels" 'cultural transfers' (13). The plight of poor and fallen women was, for example, a recurring motif in the American press. Thus, a country girl in Missouri sold her waist-length hair to a pawnbroker for a pittance, "like Fantine, stepped from . . . 'Les Miserables'" ("Forced").[2] Another journalist exposed the plight of a woman who had been enslaved, like Fantine, in order to reimburse a Thénardier-like figure for her child's care (*"Les Miserables* in Real Life"). And a paper in North Dakota reflected the growing women's rights movement by recalling the seduced and abandoned Fantine and proposing a law that would make "every child born out of wedlock legitimate" ("Mrs. Bough's Paper Feature"). Gavroche surfaced in a series of photographs titled "The American Gamin," taken in New York City's Lower East Side and in the poor districts of other cities in the United States, that vividly evoked the pathos of Hugo's creation while focusing on very real American versions of "outcast childhood" (Hine). Likewise, a founder of the "Berkshire Industrial Farm" evoked Hugo's portrait of Gavroche before describing the institution where "boys with criminal tendencies" can "try for a respectable life" (Burnham)—a positive and hopeful approach to street boys living on their own or with unfit parents. The American myth of the self-made man, like the constructed identities of homeless and reeducated urchins, found an echo in Hugo's indomitable Paris *gamin.*

More than any other character, though, it was Jean Valjean who was most often appropriated by the press to embody ideas about American know-how, society, and justice. Student identification with the protagonist tends to run very strong, especially at the beginning of the novel, given the paucity of other candidates (surely not Bishop Myriel or the heartless senator). Even when their attention turns elsewhere—say, to Cosette or Marius, who are closer to their own age—the fate of the outlaw hero retains their fervent interest. In the late-nineteenth-century American press, many of the references to Valjean invoke his escape wizardry as a way of framing local events.[3] Spectacular jailbreaks— whether of Confederate soldiers held in a Union penitentiary ("Morgan's Escape") or of other prison escapees ("Unsuccessful but Novel Attempt"; "Depravity")—evoked Jean Valjean's prowess, both mental and physical, in outwitting the criminal justice system. The ingenuity and derring-do required to conquer the ever-expanding new country were modeled in the popular consciousness after Hugo's ex-convict. At the same time, *Les Misérables* remained a top reading choice of inmates in the United States well into the twentieth century, perhaps not so much as a template for reforming one's life as a handbook for escapist artistry. The press also multiplied reports of reformed criminals relentlessly pursued by the law (see, e.g., "Western Jean Valjean"), thus adapting the backstory of Valjean's upward mobility to local human interest stories.

As the "most eloquent plea for the under dog ever penned,"according to *The Fort Worth Telegram* ("Art"), *Les Misérables* appealed not only to American inmates looking for escape schemes but also to a nation of migrating, enterprising settlers who often lived off their sweat and wits. To root for Jean Valjean was, in a way, to root for oneself—or for someone else struggling to overcome adversity. The character's example of repentance and redemption, through repeated self-sacrifice, might even prepare readers to cheer for real-life fugitives who had succeeded in reforming their lives. One could both admire the skill required to outsmart the criminal justice system and lament the overzealous application of the law to anyone then recaptured. In case after case, escaped convicts or vanished parolees in the United States who had assumed new identities and lived upright lives, like Jean Valjean as Madeleine, were largely supported by their communities when their criminal backgrounds were exposed and they were faced with returning to prison. The social reformers who in 1895 had begun speaking out against the American penal system by citing Valjean's example clearly had an impact on the public. Hugo's belief in the ability to change, to become truly *other*, as does Jean Valjean after his encounter with the bishop, provided a legitimating frame for expressing American optimism about human nature.

In this way, allusions to *Les Misérables* were used early on as hooks to draw readers to human interest stories in the media—a practice that continues today. If we consider Linda Hutcheon's discussion of how adaptations work, we can in fact view all these *faits divers* not just as points of reception or of *transferts culturels* but as mini-adaptations of Hugo's tale in an American context. Functioning as "repetition without replication, bringing together the comfort of ritual and recognition with the delight of surprise and novelty" (Hutcheon 173), such adaptations allowed for ample variations on, and even inversions of, Hugo's plot line in order to capture their own audiences. Reactivating in other contexts the strong emotions attached to Jean Valjean and Hugo's other characters, these stories did more than just illuminate current cases; they proclaimed a collective vision of what it meant to inhabit a new continent with vast horizons and opportunities for self-reinvention.[4]

Early Plays and Movies

The novel also permeated the American cultural consciousness through its theatrical presence. Dramatic renditions dated back to January 1863, when an English-language version of a play by Hugo's son Charles was booked in Alexandria, Virginia ("Charles Hugo"), and a musical drama by Albert Cassedy entitled *Fantine, or the Fate of a Grisette* was performed in Washington, DC ("Grover's Theatre"). A few months later the British-born American actress Laura Keene was heralding "a splendid dramatic version of Victor Hugo's 'Les Miserables'" at her own theatre in New York City ("Amusements"). Every few years, another stage version cropped up—local attempts to profit from the book's popularity might even have been adapted (if not plagiarized) from English plays, like Henry Neville's 1868 take on Jean Valjean in *The Yellow Passport*, rather than from Hugo's text.

Once moving pictures were invented, the staging moved to the silver screen—engendering huge box-office hits nationwide. Indeed, in the first decade of the twentieth century, theatrical interpretations of *Les Misérables* gave way to increasingly long film versions of the novel. Montaville Flowers's 1901 one-man show of *Les Misérables* resembled the way readers today enact all the characters in Charles Dickens's *A Christmas Carol* or the kinds of elaborate performances by individuals on *YouTube*. By the time William Lackeye's 1906 adaptation *The Law and the Man* toured the eastern United States that year and the next, Albert Capellani's five-minute silent French film, *Le Chemineau* (1905), depicting Jean Valjean's encounter with Myriel, was making the rounds in the States as *The Strong Arm of the Law*. And the accomplished American actor James Hackett's nine-year theater circuit, beginning in 1909, of the British one-act play *The Bishop's Candlesticks* (1901) coincided with the release not only of the first two feature-length movies in the United States (1909), both based on *Les Misérables*,[5] but also of Capellani's 1912 two-and-a-half-hour French megahit in 1913, whose epic run in the States lasted until 1918. That Hugo himself was complicit in the adaptation of his fiction for the stage—a pattern established as far back as *Notre-Dame de Paris* (see Stephens's essay in this volume)—suggests that the writer, who explicitly prioritized the public domain over his own copyright, would have applauded the arrival of new media to introduce his work to an even broader public.[6] Hugo's unerring dramatic flair, visual dynamics, and general sense of what would appeal to an audience made *Les Misérables* a familiar, even household, name to generations of readers and spectators, all the way to the present day.

Students are amazed to learn about the long history of theatrical and cinematic adaptations of *Les Misérables*, which many initially imagine to have sprung up for the first time with the British West End musical in 1985 (Nunn and Caird)—which itself was adapted from Alain Boublil and Claude-Michel Schönberg's original 1980 French version—and then to have been reincarnated in the 2012 Tom Hooper movie. They are also surprised that student drama clubs put on *The Bishop's Candlesticks* during the early years of the twentieth century, much as universities and high schools today produce their own adaptations of the stage musical. The availability of this play on *Amazon* makes it possible to do a dramatic reading in class, something I find effective as a break between parts 1 and 2 of the novel. As for the widely reviewed *The Law and the Man*, it is useful to inform students that in 1906 one critic's description of the scenes depicted ("Stage"), right up to the death of Jean Valjean, sounds in many respects like a prototype for the 1985 musical. The opinion of another journalist in 1907 that "[t]he effective use of incidental music in connection with this play suggests that a good opera might be built upon 'Les Miserables'" ("Drama") likewise suggests the possible germ of our own modern stage version of the text. At the least, students apprehend the very long tradition of adapting Hugo's novel, of borrowing from other versions, and of experimenting with new media.

Film Clips

To expand students' awareness of the cultural legacy of *Les Misérables* while driving home its historical currency in the United States, I accompany discussions of the novel with clips from various movie versions—not just the ones from 1998 (Bille August's) and 2012 (Tom Hooper's) but also Richard Boleslawski's 1935 adaptation with Fredric March and Charles Laughton, Jean-Paul Le Chanois's 1958 French film starring Jean Gabin, and the 2000 French television miniseries with Gérard Depardieu and John Malkovich. By so doing, I illustrate how key characters, episodes, and scenes have been interpreted and invite discussions on the book's "cultural work." Besides comparing the text with its cinematic interpretations, we compare the films with one another, the better to determine what aspects of the original are modified, which are not, and what social and artistic purposes those decisions serve.

Several scenes in particular have lent themselves to extended exchanges in my class: Jean Valjean's encounter with Myriel, Champmathieu's trial, Valjean's rescue of Cosette from the Thénardiers, the police chase that leads Valjean and Cosette to take refuge in the convent, the barricade and sewer scenes, and Javert's death. In the novel these episodes constitute much of the main action in parts 1, 2, 4, and 5. Part 3, on the other hand, is largely devoted to Gavroche and to Marius and his revolutionary friends, as well as to the "conjunction" between Marius and Cosette and the confrontation in the Gorbeau ambush between Valjean, Thénardier, and Javert—much of which is elided in all but the longest movie version (Dayan). Hugo's lyrical and philosophical interludes lend themselves less well to film than do his action scenes, and while part 3 ends with a bang, it is difficult to set up the ambush without a lot of time-consuming preliminaries. It is much more efficient to have boy meet girl on the eve of insurrection and to proceed quickly to the barricades. But such cuts to Hugo's plot, let alone to his many digressions, fuel debates about what parts of the text are absolutely essential to both his story line and to his core argument.

A comparison of cinematic depictions of Javert's crisis of conscience and subsequent suicide is particularly instructive. In "Javert off the Track" (pt. 5, bk. 4), Hugo probes the policeman's ethical dilemma about how to deal with the sublime ex-convict from multiple angles in a lengthy interior monologue—the counterpart to Jean Valjean's famous "Tempest within a Brain," regarding whether to save his prospering factory workers or the wretched Champmathieu (pt. 1, bk. 7, ch. 3). As a literary historian, I find that the two scenes are equal to the best psychological narratives found in a French work and thus stand as precious resources for understanding the complex moral construction of the two characters. One dilemma leading to resolution in public confession and self-sacrifice saves Valjean's soul from perdition; the other completely undermines Javert's sense of self after he comes to grasp his opponent's moral superiority. How could one leave them out of any adaptation of the novel? And, yet, how could one possibly present the full drama of a man pitted against himself on the stage or silver screen? This becomes a very teachable moment regarding media specificity as a generator of meaning. Generally speaking, novels can *tell* some things, like one's inmost thoughts, that plays or movies cannot always *show*.[7]

In Boleslawski's movie, Javert's internal struggle is translated through Laughton's trembling lips and upturned, blinking eyes as the Inspector waits for Jean Valjean to finish saying farewell to Cosette before the agreed-on surrender. How convenient that the outlaw hero lives within sight of the Seine, because in the final scene, Valjean finds Javert's dropped manacles by his doorstep and a small crowd assembled at the agitated water's edge. The chorus offstage signals with lofty music that Valjean is now finally free to live the happy life that he deserves. What is left out, then, is not only the substance of the Inspector's agonized reflections but also the events in the last 132 pages (in the Signet edition) of the novel, which include Marius and Cosette's wedding; Valjean's confession to Marius and subsequent withdrawal from their lives; Thénardier's unwitting revelations to Marius about Javert's suicide, Valjean's alter ego as M. Madeleine, and his rescue of the unconscious young man at the barricade; and Jean Valjean's reunion with the couple on his deathbed. Some students like the fact that this adaptation puts the conflict between Javert and Valjean at the center of the action, while others are put off by the abrupt happy ending that avoids dealing with Hugo's more tragic conclusion. When we then view the *dénouement* of August's interpretation, where Rush's Javert commits suicide right in front of Neeson's Jean Valjean—who walks away swiftly, breaking a smile just before the credits roll—students understand that the scene does not reimagine Hugo's work so much as it does Boleslawski's. They also tend to argue that, even according to the logic of August's movie, it is completely out of character for Valjean to abandon a person in need, including his drowning lifelong nemesis.

Contrasting both films with Hooper's, for example, itself an adaptation of the stage musical adaptation of the novel, opens up yet another line of discussion. In Hooper's film, Javert leaps from a bridge over the Seine into the swirling waters below, well out of Valjean's sight. The movie then goes on to depict much of Hugo's ending, followed by the famous revolutionary coda on an immense imaginary barricade. Is the prolonged conclusion, I ask, dictated mainly by the extra twenty-four minutes of running time? No, most students decide, that's just backward thinking. Is it dictated by an attempt to adhere more closely to Hugo's text? Wrapping up the loose ends regarding Cosette and Marius (marriage), the Thénardiers (unmasking), and Valjean (confession to Marius and a beatific death, where he is reconciled with the younger generation) is certainly more "faithful" to the novel, even though many details, such as the Thénardiers' presence at the wedding reception and Valjean's return to the convent to die, are inexplicably modified. Therefore, students do not consider fidelity to the text to be the operative principle, especially since the grand finale turns the quiet presence of Fantine and Myriel at Valjean's death into the spectacular assembly of all the deceased characters, not in heaven, but on a massive, limitless barricade that presages future revolution in the here and now. Concluding on a romanticized vision of popular revolt—the resurrected dead seek to galvanize the living, including the audience, to espouse a higher cause—resonates deeply in an era of multiple financial crises, large antigovernment protests, and the seemingly unstoppable rise of the one percent.

In what ways, then, might the conclusion be tied to the musical's internal logic? Once students perceive that it picks up many of the motifs established earlier in the film, they understand that the movie, like the musical, is an original work of art in and of itself. That the Thénardiers are at the wedding feast in order to reprise their comic role stands in contrast to Valjean's continued nobility and his tragic end. The convent setting for Valjean's death brings him full circle, from the bishop's abode into other caring hands, and underscores the religious imagery in the musical, which far surpasses Hugo's. The closing barricade scene provides a rousing choral epilogue that restates not only the forceful "Do You Hear the People Sing?" near the end of act 1—a modern version of our own "Battle Hymn of the Republic"—but also elements of the revolutionaries' utopian vision of "One Day More" in that act's finale. In so doing, the scene translates much of the spirit of Hugo's classic even as it violates strict fidelity to the text. Using film clips to analyze the complex relationships among Les Misérables and various renditions of key scenes prepares students to begin exploring the wide world of adaptations on their own. It also shows how successful reinterpretations of famous texts address contemporary concerns while rehearsing new patterns of thought, feeling, and action.

New Media

As digital natives, students can assume an even more active role in such exchanges by researching and demonstrating how the novel has been reimagined, remixed, and adapted for new cultural purposes. Once they have completed part 3, I assign students to find five online references to Les Misérables in pop culture that appeared in the last ten years and to post the URLs, along with a brief explanation about what was evocative or striking about each reference. They share their posts the night before class, then present their selections in class first in small groups and then at the podium, prompting the entire class to discuss them in turn. If time is limited, some present and comment on their favorites, while other students participate in the general discussion.

The universe of possibilities ends up being so large that there are surprisingly few redundancies, and this variety is one point of the exercise. (It also provides me with materials that can be incorporated into future iterations of the course.)

Students are astonished at the proliferation of allusions to Hugo's work on the Web. Their findings range from a South Korean parody on *YouTube* and a Jean Valjean action figure on *Tumblr* to comic book versions and a *"Les Misérables* Board Game" to blogs and Halloween costumes inspired by the musical. As a result, students are much more aware of the scope of appropriations and commodification of the novel—and of adaptations of other media versions—and engage readily in considerations of the textual features that have spawned these digital afterlives.

Is "One Term More!" (Colcord)—the political parody of "One Day More" published on *YouTube* in summer 2012 in support of the Obama presidential campaign—an original adaptation of Hugo's work, an extrapolation, or something else? How does the video of the South Korean military conscripts lamenting the endless task of snow removal from their airbase runways to the tune of the convicts' "Work Song" reflect the transposition of the novel into a completely different time and culture (Kim and Chung)? Students are eager to pose and to try to answer their own questions over one or two class periods, as time allows. They are inspired by their contemporaries' productions in the new media, aware that any "borrowings" from either the book or the show are part of a very long tradition of remixing and recycling material from other sources. What students really learn is that universal works of literature are always being reshaped to meet and respond to current cultural needs, sometimes to striking effect and with stunning artistic originality.

NOTES

[1] For an excellent overview of this subject, see Griffiths et al.

[2] Since the book's title often appeared without the accent mark, possibly because of typesetting constraints, I have reproduced the original spellings throughout this essay.

[3] These sources are accessible online through such databases as *ProQuest, Newsbank,* and the *Library of Congress.*

[4] For a more thorough overview of the reception and early adaptations of *Les Misérables* in the United States, see my essay "The Making of a Classic: *Les Misérables* Takes the States, 1860–1922."

[5] One was produced by the Edison Manufacturing Company (Porter) and the other by the Vitagraph Company of America (Blackton).

[6] See Hugo's declaration to the International Literary Congress on 21 June 1878 (Hugo, *Œuvres complètes: Politique* 1000). Indeed, "[e]ach version of the story that has appeared marks an example of an audience taking ownership of the work that Hugo has bequeathed to the public . . ." (Stephens and Grossman 9).

[7] The exception, of course, is musicals, where characters are able to express their feelings and reflections, albeit in abbreviated form, through the medium of song (Hutcheon 60).

Les Misérables and the Nineteenth-Century French Novel

Philippe Moisan

Teaching *Les Misérables* to undergraduate students in the context of a course introducing the nineteenth-century French novel entails two major difficulties. The first and most evident obstacle pertains to the length of the work, which renders reading the whole text in one semester virtually impossible, even with advanced students. The other, a more theoretical difficulty, concerns how Victor Hugo's novel, completed in the early 1860s, fits within the greater context of nineteenth-century French literary history. *Les Misérables* does not at first seem to conform to *"l'air du temps"* 'the mood of the times' of the 1860s and could seem anachronistic when we consider that *Madame Bovary*, published five years earlier, was meant to have signaled the death of Romanticism and announce the rise of realism and modernity. With its narrative twists and epic story line, as well as the way in which important characters always meet up at crucial moments and places, *Les Misérables* resembles a historical novel written in the first half of the nineteenth century in the style of Alexandre Dumas. How, then, can we situate *Les Misérables* within literary history in a way that is accessible to students discovering nineteenth-century French literature for the first time?

Students must first of all read and analyze *Les Misérables* in relation to other works representing the major literary and cultural currents of the period. In a fourteen-week course, the list of works studied could include Chateaubriand's *René*, Balzac's *Eugénie Grandet*, Flaubert's *Éducation sentimentale* or *Madame Bovary*, Zola's *Thérèse Raquin*, and Colette's *La Vagabonde*. With the exception of Flaubert's novels, these texts are all relatively short, making the reading load manageable for students; more important, they represent the major literary and cultural currents in France between 1789 and 1914. In the context of this course, *Les Misérables* would be read between *Eugénie Grandet* and *L'Éducation sentimentale*, and would thus serve the critical role of helping students understand the transition from Romanticism to realism.

Because of the length of *Les Misérables*, students should read not the entire text but rather passages selected for their relevance to our analysis of the novel as a pivotal text; sections to be covered could include all the chapters in the books listed below:

> Part 1: "La chute" 'The Fall'; "En l'année 1817" 'The Year 1817'
>
> Part 3: "Le grand-père et le petit-fils" 'The Grandfather and the Grandson'; "Les Amis de l'ABC" 'The Friends of the ABC'; "Le mauvais pauvre" 'The Noxious Poor'
>
> Part 4: "Les enchantements et les désolations" 'Enchantments and Desolations'
>
> Part 5: "La guerre entre quatre murs" 'War Between Four Walls'; "La boue, mais l'âme" 'Muck, but Soul'; "Le petit-fils et le grand-père" 'Grandson and Grandfather'

The objective is to provide a selection that is representative of the entire work and to have a realistic reading program of about five hundred pages (more or less the same length as *Madame Bovary*), spread out over three to four weeks in the middle of the semester. Since students do not read the entire text, it would be useful to let them read a short summary of the novel so that they know the major story lines and are able to situate the studied chapters within the course context. And finally, since the goal is to show how *Les Misérables* represents a literary turning point for the nineteenth-century novel, the selected passages can be read *not* in chronological order but thematically.

The first phase of reading *Les Misérables* guides students to view the novel as fundamentally a Romantic text and to make connections to Romantic themes, images, and characters they will have encountered in texts already studied in the course (*René*, *Eugénie Grandet*). The book entitled "Le grand-père et le petit-fils," for example, shows narrative dynamics and tensions similar to those we find in *Eugénie Grandet*. Just like Eugénie, Marius is under the influence of his grandfather, Gillenormand, and has an outlook on the world that is filtered through his immediate entourage, and thus he unoriginally reflects the thoughts and attitudes of his social milieu: "Cette jeune âme qui s'ouvrait passa d'une prude à un cuistre. Marius eut ses années de collège, puis il entra à l'école de droit. Il était royaliste, fanatique et austère" 'This young awakening soul passed from a prude to a pedant. Marius went through secondary education, then entered the law school. He was royalist, fanatical, and austere' (1: 790; 624 [pt. 3, bk. 3, ch. 3]). Later, when he uncovers his father's story and learns of the Napoleonic Wars, Marius frees himself from the weight of his family ideology and becomes a truly Romantic hero—a young man who says no, and who comes to reject and insult everything he previously loved: "À bas les Bourbons, et ce gros cochon de Louis XVIII!" 'Down with the Bourbons, and that great hog Louis XVIII!' (1: 814; 644 [pt. 3, bk. 3, ch. 8]). Alongside this revolt against the father (or in this case, the grandfather), Marius suddenly starts to explore a forbidden political space. He reads the *Bulletins de la Grande Armée* every night, and the images generated by the Napoleonic myth become linked to his adopting his father's ideology and to the nocturnal pleasure of discovering something that is monstrous and fabulous. Napoleon, who was "une sorte de monstre presque fabuleux" 'a sort of almost fabulous monster' during his childhood (1: 800; 632 [pt. 3, bk. 3, ch. 6]), becomes for Marius the source of physical and metaphysical turmoil, described in the most Romantic of terms: "Il avait le cœur serré. Il était transporté, tremblant, haletant; tout à coup, sans savoir lui-même ce qui était en lui et à quoi il obéissait, il se dressa, étendit ses deux bras hors de la fenêtre, regarda fixement l'ombre, le silence, l'infini ténébreux, l'immensité éternelle, et cria: Vive l'empereur!" 'His heart was full. He was transported, trembling, breathless; suddenly, without knowing what moved him, or what he was obeying, he rose, stretched his arms out the window, stared into the darkness, the silence, the infinite, the eternal immensity and cried out: Vive l'empereur!' (1: 801; 633 [pt. 3, bk. 3, ch. 6]). It would not be difficult for students who had previously read *René* to make the connection between René's stormy desires and the troubling and mysterious symptoms of Marius's Bonapartist fever. Marius explores his political self in the same modes and terms as René explores his emotional self. The similarities between Marius and René trace a direct line between Hugo's character and the *jeunes hommes romantiques* that we find, for example, in Balzac and Musset; he is part of a postrevolutionary or postempire generation whose members are crushed by shadows of their father's generation and prey to unspeakable emotions. Like other young men of this generation, Marius suffers from the "mal du siècle" 'malaise of the century.'

Marius continues to act like a Romantic character, as his political self and sentimental self both develop in parallel symbolic spaces. Indeed, the same lexical and semiotic fields are used to describe his meetings with Cosette in the garden of the Rue Plumet as well as his feelings about Napoleon:

> La nuit, quand ils étaient là, ce jardin semblait un lieu vivant et sacré. Toutes les fleurs s'ouvraient autour d'eux et leur envoyaient de l'encens; eux, ils ouvraient leurs âmes et les répandaient dans les fleurs. La végétation lascive et vigoureuse tressaillait pleine de sève et d'ivresse autour de ces deux innocents, et ils disaient des paroles d'amour dont les arbres frissonnaient.
>
> (4: 343 [pt. 4, bk. 8, ch. 1])

> At night, when they were there, this garden seemed a living, sacred place. All the flowers opened around them and offered them their incense; they too opened their souls and poured them out of the flowers: The lusty, vigorous

vegetation trembled full of sap and intoxication around these two innocent creatures, and they spoke words of love at which the trees thrilled. (1005)

Just like his relationship to Napoleon, his love for Cosette builds in a nocturnal, clandestine space. His love for her is at once an intimate physical experience and a spiritual communion with the surrounding nature, the night, the sky, the flowers, and the trees. In the passages from the novel dealing with Marius, for example, "Les Amis de l'ABC" 'The Friends of the ABC,' "Les enchantements et les désolations" 'Enchantments and Desolations,' and "La guerre entre quatre murs" 'War between Four Walls,' Hugo shows the permeability between the Romantic realm and the political realm: events that precipitate the episode of political revolt are intertwined with the trysts of the Rue Plumet, as if both were part and parcel of the same process. And indeed Marius ends up on the barricades more because of despair in love than because of politics. For Marius, love and politics represent quests for an ideal, for self-fulfillment. Exploring this connection between an intimate or personal Romanticism and a collective Romanticism gives students in this course a more complete and complex understanding of how this literary movement functions on several levels.

This first phase of reading *Les Misérables* could conclude with an analysis of Tom Hooper's 2012 film musical, which emphasizes the Romanticism of the text. In addition to working with this film, students could also examine Eugène Delacroix's famous painting *La Liberté guidant le peuple*, which is often associated with Hugo's novel and clearly highlights revolutionary Romanticism. By the end of the first phase, it is important that students retain the idea that Romantic aspirations in *Les Misérables* begin with an identity crisis that is at once familial, political, and sentimental—a crisis that morphs into either despair and apathy or fervor and revolutionary engagement.

The second phase of reading the novel should then examine how *Les Misérables* is also a realist novel, written after the revolution of 1848 and during the Second Empire. In the general framework of the course, the students, having read *Eugénie Grandet*, should be able to identify and articulate the major characteristics of realism. It would nevertheless be useful to show them how the failure of the 1848 revolution, the coup d'état of December 1851, and, in Hugo's case, the painful experience of exile all contribute to altering the Romantic vision of history, as embodied in Delacroix. After 1848, history shows the failure of revolutions and reveals the reality of political and social inertia.

The major theme contributing to the novel's realism is, of course, that of misery. Selections like "La chute" 'The Fall,' "L'année 1817" 'The Year 1817,' or "Le mauvais pauvre" 'The Noxious Poor' provide a detailed account of social injustice and the living conditions of the poor in nineteenth-century France. For example, in "La chute" Jean Valjean's family's tragic poverty is not described in abstract terms but in the hold that hunger exerts on the body. Hunger in fact serves as a major driving narrative force. For one, Jean Valjean's descent toward imprisonment is due to fatal food shortage that dictates the Valjean family's every action in Faverolles. Young Valjean's days are completely governed by work and the evening meal:

> Le soir il rentrait fatigué et mangeait sa soupe, sans dire un mot. Sa sœur, mère Jeanne, pendant qu'il mangeait, lui prenait souvent dans son écuelle le meilleur de son repas, le morceau de viande, la tranche de lard, le cœur de chou pour le donner à quelqu'un de ses enfants; lui, mangeant toujours, penché sur la table, presque la tête dans sa soupe, ses cheveux longs tombant autour de son écuelle et cachant ses yeux, avait l'air de ne rien voir et laissait faire.   (1: 135 [pt. 1, bk. 2, ch. 6])

> At night he came in weary and ate his soup without a word. While he was eating, his sister, Mother Jeanne, frequently took out of his bowl the best of his meal — a bit of meat, a slice of bacon, the heart of the cabbage — to give to one of her children. Eating steadily, his head down nearly in the soup, his long hair falling over his dish, hiding his eyes, he did not seem to notice and let it happen.   (83)

This passage comprises two important elements. First, we see the detailed portrait of Valjean at twenty-five: he is hungry, silent, withdrawn; "his head down nearly in the soup, his long hair falling over his dish"; the soup and the bowl become extensions of his body and part of his identity. Second, the sister takes the best bits from his plate, as if, in effect, she were removing all his personal potential, as if his miserable condition were a perpetual mutilation. In this passage Valjean is described, furthermore, only in negative or restrictive terms. He is deprived of language, of potential speech: "without a word." He is deprived of an outlook: "he did not seem to notice." And he is shown to be passive in the face of events and injustice, letting his sister do as she will. The linkage between identity and material reality can be found in descriptions of the children: "habituellement affamés" 'always famished' — they too only exist through their hunger (1: 135; 83 [pt. 1, bk. 2, ch. 6]). They drink a pint of stolen milk "si hâtivement que les petites filles s'en répandaient sur leur tablier et dans leur goulotte" 'so greedily . . . that the little girls would spill it on their aprons and their throats' (1: 136; 83 [pt. 1, bk. 2, ch. 6]) — another image showing a metonymic shift from food to clothes to corporeality. In both passages hunger reduces the poor to mere body parts, preventing the children from realizing their humanity. In this reading, *Les Misérables* signals the grip that the real has on the development of the characters and the plot. Poverty in its most material and physical form constructs the text, pushes Valjean toward crime and prison, and creates the conditions for the rest of the novel.

The materiality of the world as a dominating force can be found again in "Le mauvais pauvre" 'The Noxious Poor.' In the description of the Thénardier family members and their living space, it is not hunger that signals poverty but rather the silent presence of objects and bodies. For example, Thénardier is described in entirely physical terms: "Cet homme avait une longue barbe grise. Il était vêtu d'une chemise de femme qui laissait voir sa poitrine velue et ses bras nus hérissés de poils gris" 'This man had a long gray beard. He was dressed in a woman's blouse, which showed his shaggy chest and his naked arms bristling with grey hair' (1: 32; 747 [pt. 3, bk. 8, ch. 6]). He is no more than an enumeration of body parts (long beard, hairy chest, gray hair) that give him a certain primitive animality. By contrast, Marius and Cosette, or the Friends of the ABC, are often described in terms connecting them to emotions or political concepts. Enjolras, for example, is described as a "soldat de la démocratie; au-dessus du mouvement contemporain, prêtre de l'idéal" 'a soldier of democracy; above the movement of the time, a priest of the ideal' (1: 818; 648 [pt. 3, bk. 4, ch.1]). Meanwhile, the Thénardier family remains enclosed in their corporeal reality and environment. This is indeed the fate of all the *misérables* of the story—the Valjean family; Fantine; and Cosette, when she lives with the Thénardiers, are all imprisoned by material realities; subject to their physical needs, such as hunger; and suffering from situational constraints such as cold.

During this second phase of reading, students should be encouraged to identify the precise aspects that make *Les Misérables* a realist text. Indeed, the novel stages the disappearance of Romanticism in much the same way as does Flaubert's *Madame Bovary* or *L'Éducation sentimentale*. Hugo's novel signals the destruction of a world. The episode of the sewers in "La boue, mais l'âme" 'Muck, but Soul' perfectly shows how corporeal realities consume characters and expunge the ideals of revolutionary utopias. The opening to the sewer is like a gaping black hole in the middle of the rubble, and Valjean's long underground trajectory represents a departure from the revolutionary universe and a plunge into material reality. This reality almost literally consumes and swallows Valjean, as can be seen in the passage where he almost drowns in the mire.

> L'eau lui venait aux aisselles; il se sentait sombrer; c'est à peine s'il pouvait se mouvoir dans la profondeur de bourbe où il était. . . . Il avançait; mais il enfonçait. Il n'avait plus que la tête hors de l'eau.
>
> (2: 692–93 [pt. 5, bk. 3, ch. 6])

> The water came up to his armpits; he felt that he was foundering; he could scarcely move in the deep mire. . . . he kept moving; but he was sinking deeper. Now, he had only his head out of the water.   (1297)

Thus the sewer represents the space, or rather the matter, that absorbs world and people, light and sound, and, in a more global fashion, almost everything previously articulated, including Romantic elements. Indeed, toward the end of the novel almost nothing remains of the previous world. This idea can be seen in "Le petit-fils et le grand-père" 'Grandson and Grandfather' when Marius, convalescing at his grandfather's house, tries to recall his adventures on the barricade but encounters a black hole in his memory that resembles the black hole of the sewer opening: "Il y avait dans sa mémoire un trou, un endroit noir, un abîme creusé par quatre mois d'agonie" 'In his memory, there was a hole, a black place, an abyss scooped out by four months of agony' (2: 763; 1358 [pt. 5, bk. 5, ch. 7]). The fragments that he is able to pull from oblivion appear to him only in the instability and immateriality of a dreamed memory: "[T]ous ses amis se dressaient devant lui, puis se dissipaient. Tous ces êtres chers, douloureux, vaillants, charmants ou tragiques, étaient-ce des songes? Avaient-ils en effet existé?" '[A]ll his friends would rise up in front of him, then dissipate. All these beings, dear, sorrowful, valiant, charming, or tragic—were they dreams? Had they really existed?' (2: 734; 1358 [pt. 5, bk. 5, ch. 1]). And later: "Une chute dans les ténèbres avait tout emporté excepté lui. Tout cela lui semblait avoir disparu comme derrière une toile de théâtre" 'A fall into darkness had carried off everything, except himself. It all seemed to him to have disappeared as if behind a curtain at a theater' (2: 764; 1358 [pt. 5, bk. 5, ch. 7]). What disappears at this point in the text is of course all the Romantic elements that were generating the plot, all the drama of the revolution, all the political and social questions debated by the Friends of the ABC; in short, everything that made the novel a quest for the ideal. All that remains is the bourgeois melodrama of Cosette and Marius's wedding; even their love has stopped existing in the realm of the Romantic ideal, since they no longer exhibit the passionate emotions they did in the garden of the Rue Plumet. For Marius, for example, the image of Cosette exists henceforth in disturbing contiguity with the image of Valjean the convict: "Qu'était-ce que ce sombre jeu de la providence qui avait mis cet enfant en contact avec cet homme?" 'What was this gloomy game of providence that had placed the child in contact with this man?' (2: 824; 1409 [pt. 5, bk. 7, ch. 2]). Furthermore, the dowry—the six hundred thousand francs displayed in a bundle of banknotes in the middle of Gillenormand's salon—is now at the center of their relationship. The novel is here clearly and fully in the realist realm.

To conclude this study of *Les Misérables*, the class could spend some time analyzing Gustave Courbet's *Enterrement à Ornans* as a transition from Hugo to Flaubert and then to Zola. This painting, which Courbet executed just after the 1848 revolution and exhibited for the first time in the 1851 salon, inaugurated a new art-historical period and a new way of representing the world. It signals a tipping point when revolutionary Romanticism was losing its hold on history, and the world was forced to see the real. Like *Les Misérables*, *Enterrement à Ornans* represents a passage, a transition from one symbolic system to another; it shows the end of an ideal and the period of mourning associated with that end, and it introduces a new system of representation, which contains a new way of situating humanity in the world. After the mourning period, the characters in the painting attain a new status, that of survivors exiled in a new symbolic space, a space that has no ideal, no transcendence, be it political or religious. All that remains is a silent, anonymous, mysterious reality that does not seem to speak to the spectator, a new reality no longer founded on the exaltation of energy, optimism, and heroism. What is more, the space is shown to have no exit, since the only opening, between two rocky barriers, appears to be inaccessible and too far away. The crowd comes together around a new center, a hole around which the painting is organized, the open tomb. This emptiness, which is the only possible escape, also recalls the sewer opening in which Valjean and Marius are swallowed, and both the tomb and the sewer opening represent the reality of the world in which the characters are going to disappear.

The discussion of Courbet would be important at this moment in the course, for it not only serves as a counterweight to *La Liberté guidant le peuple*, a work often associated with *Les Misérables* in the popular imagination, but also helps connect Hugo's work to realism, to the idea and the representation of modernity that was emerging at the time.

This approach to teaching *Les Misérables* thus seeks to use the novel to understand the historical shifts in thought and symbolic representation that characterize nineteenth-century French literary history. This text enables students to perceive what we might call the agony of Romanticism while also sketching an emerging realism. And the intersection of those two worlds, of two periods of the nineteenth century, is precisely the originality and the power of *Les Misérables*—a narrative space that blends the two literary modalities of Romanticism and of realism.

Teaching an Undergraduate Course on *Les Misérables*: Ways of Doing It

Michal P. Ginsburg

The challenges Hugo's *Les Misérables* presents to instructors and students seem especially formidable when one is teaching an undergraduate course devoted to the novel and thus, in principle, engaging with it in its entirety. Whether the novel is taught in French to senior majors or in English to a more general student population, in a ten-week quarter or over a semester, its sheer length as well as its particular narrative structure and literary style introduce enormous difficulties. In this essay I suggest ways in which instructors can make reading and appreciating the novel more manageable for students.

Solving the problem of the length, unless you use an abridged version (always an option), means making some cuts (which, in my opinion, is preferable to telling students to skim). The easiest way to cut is, obviously, to eliminate the digressions, but this means doing away with one of the elements that make Hugo's novel unique, thus distorting its nature (on teaching the digressions, see O'Neil's essay in this volume). One solution is to ask students to choose and read *one* of the novel's digressions. This way students can acquire a sense of the nature of the digressions and their role in the novel. In my course, students did their oral presentations on the digression they had chosen, discussing its main themes and using *PowerPoint* to display important quotes (put online for their classmates to consult). The digressions pose a particular challenge to students: they can, for example, read the whole "Waterloo" digression and miss the importance and meaning of "Cambronne's word."[1] It is therefore necessary to point out, ahead of their presentation, the issues you consider important in each digression and to be ready to supplement the presentations with your own commentary, tying each digression to other parts of the text.

Asking students to read only one of the digressions may not solve the length problem entirely, and further cuts might be necessary, especially if you teach the course in a quarter (and in French). You may want to consider asking students to read the first part, "Fantine," in its entirety, so that, as with the digressions, they get a sense of what the uncut novel looks like. What you cut would ultimately depend on your particular focus in the course so the list of cuts proposed below is just one possible way of achieving that goal (the digressions are indicated by a dagger):

> Part 1: Fantine. Bk. 1, chs. 5, 6, 9, 11–14; bk. 3, chs. 1, 4–7, 8 (except last two paragraphs); bk. 7, ch. 2
>
> Part 2: Cosette. Bk. 1†; bk. 2, ch. 2; bk. 3, chs. 2, 6; bk. 4, ch. 1; bk. 5, chs. 4, 6, 7, 10; bk. 6†; bk. 7†; bk. 8, chs. 2, 3

Part 3: Marius. Bk. 1†; bk. 2, chs. 2–5, 7; bk. 3; chs. 1 (except last two paragraphs), 3 (except last three paragraphs); bk. 4, ch. 4; bk. 5, ch. 6; bk. 6, chs. 3–6; bk. 7†

Part 4: St. Denis. Bk. 1†; bk. 2, ch. 2; bk. 3, chs. 3, 6; bk. 4, ch. 1; bk. 5, chs. 1–3; bk. 6, ch. 1; bk. 7†; bk. 8, ch. 1 (except first paragraph); bk. 10, chs. 1, 4; bk. 12, chs. 5–6; bk. 13, ch. 2; bk. 15, ch. 4

Part 5: Jean Valjean. Bk. 1, chs. 1 (except first two pages), 10, 12–13, 20; bk. 2†; bk. 3, ch. 5 (except first sentence); bk. 5; ch. 1

Together these cuts would reduce the length of the book by about a third, leaving a more manageable 1,200 pages (in French); they leave the plot intact and intelligible (which is important) but reduce the novel to its plot and thus, again, distort it. You can counter this distortion as you discuss the novel's main themes throughout the course (as I show below). One general issue you can raise at the very beginning of the course is that of Hugo's style, a key for understanding *Les Misérables*. As soon as students have started reading the novel, you can ask them to choose one or two short passages they consider good examples of Hugo's style and present them in class. This is a difficult exercise, and you may want first to discuss with them what "style" means (the author's "signature," by which one can recognize his or her writing, what can be imitated and parodied) and how you identify it. Even so, there is a good chance that many of the chosen passages would be examples not of Hugo's particular style but of nineteenth-century literary style or even simply of French writing. In the discussion that follows you can sort out these differences while proposing your own examples of Hugo's style. One such example can be the chapter "L'Année 1817" (pt. 1, bk. 3, ch. 1). This chapter may have been omitted from their reading schedule (it is a very difficult one for students to comprehend since it consists of more or less obscure allusions to people and events), but it is a good example of one of Hugo's signature figures—the catalog—which, narratively speaking, is a cumulative and open form. (Another example is the list of barricades in pt. 5, bk. 1, ch. 1.) "L'Année 1817" also shows Hugo's understanding of history and thus tells us something about the nature of the novel as story: it aspires to be a "total" novel (hence, cumulative and without closure), it is not limited to the major events in the lives of the main characters, and it gives equal importance to material that may be considered marginal.

The style exercise can also be used to complicate, from the very beginning of the course, the view that Hugo's novel is predicated on a simplistic moral reading of the universe, where good and evil are in clear opposition. It is true that Hugo sometimes speaks the simplified language of melodramatic morality, as when he writes: "Le livre que le lecteur a sous les yeux en ce moment, c'est, d'un bout à l'autre . . . la marche du mal au bien, de l'injuste au juste" 'The book the reader has now before his eyes—from one end to the other . . . is the march from evil to good, from injustice to justice' (2: 628; 1242 [pt. 5, bk. 1, ch. 20]). However, the plot of the novel contradicts such simplification, and Hugo's style repeatedly undermines Manichean thinking by complicating binary oppositions: instead of opposing Valjean and Javert as good versus evil, the narrator says that Javert's face reveals "tout le mauvais du bon" 'all the evil of good' (1: 389; 291 [pt. 1, bk. 8, ch. 3])—a distinctive Hugolian formulation. Another example of undermining categorical oppositions is the bishop's response to his housekeeper's remark that growing flowers is useless: "Madame Magloire . . . vous vous trompez. Le beau est aussi utile que l'utile.—Il ajouta après un silence: Plus peut-être" '"Madame Magloire . . . you are mistaken. The beautiful is as useful as the useful." He added after a moment's pause, "Perhaps more so"' (1 : 62; 23 [pt. 1, bk. 1, ch. 6]). The opposition between the beautiful and the useful seems self-evident: art, for example, is supposed to be beautiful rather than useful, whereas industry produces a lot of ugliness but is considered useful. The bishop first denies the opposition, claiming usefulness for beauty—which also makes sense. But when he says that what is beautiful may be more useful than the useful, we have to completely change our understanding of what useful might mean—including the "usefulness" of the novel itself, to which Hugo refers in the short preface to the novel: "tant qu'il y aura sur la terre ignorance et misère, des livres de la nature de celui-ci pourront ne pas être inutiles" 'so long as ignorance and misery remain on earth, novels such as this one may not be useless.' We have to rethink our categories—both aesthetic and moral; this is what Hugo challenges us to do throughout the novel. (Another example is when Hugo recasts the opposition between civilized and barbarian as the difference between "les barbares de la civilisation et les civilisés de la barbarie" 'the barbarians of civilization and the civil advocates of barbarism' [2: 162; 854 (pt. 4, bk. 1, ch. 5)].)

Another problem in teaching such a long and difficult novel over a short period of time is that limiting discussion to what the students have already read (as we normally do) is not very efficient; more can be accomplished by analyzing themes, characters, and problems of representation as they manifest themselves in the novel as a whole. Since this is difficult to do if students are not familiar with the entire novel, you can ask them to watch a filmic adaptation at the very beginning of the course. For this purpose you would want an adaptation that is relatively faithful to the text, and the French ones would be your best bet. I usually suggest Jean-Paul Le Chanois's 1958 adaptation since it is shorter than the other French ones (the longer 1934 adaptation, by Raymond Bernard, is another possibility).

Asking students to interpret and reflect critically on issues that pertain to the entire novel—reading it "transversally"—is challenging. I found that showing short film clips from the novel's many adaptations can help. When viewing several versions of the same episode, several ways of representing the same character, students are immediately aware of differences; they can then start reflecting on the choices made by the different filmmakers and how these choices produce different meanings. As I show in what follows, this can help them see the choices made by Hugo and thus gain a ground from which to start reflecting on the novel's ideas and meaning.

In my course I used clips to discuss the novel's beginning and end; the characters of Javert, Marius, and Cosette; the episode of "Le guet-apens" (the main episode of pt. 3, bk. 8, "Le mauvais pauvre"—the novel's dead center) and that of the barricades; and a seemingly minor detail: what is produced in M. Madeleine's manufactory. I used the adaptations by Bille August, Raymond Bernard, Marcel Bluwal, Richard Boleslawski, Josée Dayan, Robert Hossein, Jean-Paul Le Chanois, and Lewis Milestone.[2] I also used Tom Hooper's filmic version of the musical and Orson Welles's 1937 radio drama. With the exception of Bluwal's, these adaptations are widely available.

Playing clips can help illuminate a particular episode and can also provide a framework for discussing more general issues. To discuss how the novel begins, I used adaptations that markedly differ in their beginnings, each choice highlighting a somewhat different theme: Welles, for example, starts with Valjean's entry into Digne and his being refused food and lodging, thus signaling the issue of social exclusion, of the feared other, the pariah. But August's film begins just as Valjean is about to knock on the bishop's door and so brackets the issue that concerned Welles in order to highlight Valjean's conversion. Since all the adaptations I have shown differ from the way Hugo starts the novel, students become aware of the strangeness of a novel beginning with what, in the light of the various adaptations, must be seen as a digression; this in turn impresses on them the need to interpret the way Hugo's novel begins.

But the same clips can be used also for introducing broader issues. For example, Boleslawski's film starts with Valjean's trial for the theft of bread and therefore with the right to work and the failure of the legal system to act justly. As students watch Boleslawski's handsome Valjean pleading his cause with eloquence and passion they may remember (with or without your help) that Hugo does not represent Valjean's trial (just states that it took place). The trial, however, is not entirely absent from the text; it is represented indirectly when M. Madeleine watches the trial of Champmathieu, his double, and relives through him his own trial. By noting the differences between the speeches of Boleslawski's Valjean and Hugo's Champmathieu, by reflecting on the indirect way in which Hugo represents Valjean's trial, students can start understanding what Hugo means by "misérables" (people who are not merely poor, lack work, or are reduced to stealing) and the challenges that representing them pose to Hugo.[3]

Boleslawski's trial scene is a clear parody, or caricature, of the legal system (a symmetrical reversal of the assumption of innocence); this can help bring up the question of how *Hugo* represents the legal system. Boleslawski's caricature treats the problem as a simple abuse of a practice caused by an existing social structure rather than as a failure of the legal system to mete justice. By contrast, Hugo never parodies Javert, the man who represents absolute adherence to the letter of the law. Instead of pointing out an abuse of the legal system, Hugo suggests, through Javert, the limits of a legalistic understanding of social relations, just as through Myriel, the purest manifestation of Christian love, he shows the limits of Christian charity. The critique of Myriel's position is as rigorous as that of Javert's but more difficult to see since Valjean, who models himself on Myriel, is blind to the way acts of charity fail to solve the problem of misery, and because the shortcomings of charity are spelled out most clearly by the "mauvais pauvre," Thénardier (2: 89–93; 794–97 [pt. 3, bk. 8, ch. 20]).

Discussing the novel through its characters and using film clips for this purpose is particularly rewarding. By looking at several versions of Javert, for example, students see how different Hugo's character is from that of most of the adaptations, and these differences can be used to help them better understand the nature and role of this character in the novel. For example: whereas both Charles Laughton in Boleslawski's version and John Malkovich in Dayan's, with all their differences, psychologize Javert,[4] the novel shows him as totally impersonal in his obedience to the law and to authority (see, e.g., his description when he comes to M. Madeleine to ask for his own dismissal [1: 282; 204 (pt. 3, bk. 8, ch. 20)]). Milestone's adaptation as well as August's present Javert as a villain and a brute. In the novel, however, the role of the villain is played by Thénardier, while Javert is the antagonist, the hero's adversarial double (as we can see from the almost anagrammatic relation between their names, Javert/Valjean). The novel insists on traits they share: frugality, chastity, probity (Javert is "l'homme qui n'a jamais menti" 'a man who has never lied' [2; 472; 1112 (pt. 3, bk. 8, ch. 20)]).[5] Several adaptations (those by August, Boleslwaski, Milestone, among others) see the novel as mainly a conflict between Javert, the hunter, and Valjean, the hunted, and therefore place the end of the novel right after the death of Javert—once Javert is dead, Valjean can live happily ever after. But in fact it is ultimately *Valjean* who affects Javert. The effect on Javert of Valjean's acts at the barricade is parallel to the effect Myriel's acts had on Valjean; in both cases a character's entire world falls apart as he encounters a radically different system of values. Insisting on the conflict between Javert and Valjean also misses the point that the character who mostly affects Valjean's life and brings it to its end is neither Javert nor Thénardier but Marius, the rival who robs Valjean of the one being he could love and who stands for bourgeois society, whose view of the *forçat* Valjean has internalized (cf. his speech to Marius in pt. 5, bk. 7, ch. 1). The idealization of Marius (whose meanness to Valjean after he reveals his real identity is often left out in the film adaptations) obfuscates this point.

In teaching the episode of the insurrection, I start with its anomalous status: on the one hand, the true revolutionaries, the Friends of the ABC, are marginal to the novel's plot; on the other hand, with the notable exception of Gavroche, the characters who do play an important part in the novel's plot are not at the barricade to fight with and for the insurrection. This suggests a disconnect between the cause of the revolution, to which these pages are dedicated, and the main plot of the novel. In other words, the episode of the barricade is important in the novel for reasons other than its main plot. As stated before, the novel resists being contained within a linear plot that deals with a group of named individuals.

That Mabeuf, Valjean, Marius, Javert, and Éponine are at the barricade for reasons that have little to do with the goals of the insurrection does not mean that the insurrection is simply the background for a personal drama (as is the case in Milestone's adaptation, for example). Political events and private concerns intersect and impact one another (as Bluwal's adaptation shows most successfully). This means that political events are not "purely" political. Film adaptations, however, often idealize the insurrection by presenting all its agents as committed revolutionaries—from Mabeuf, presented as a hero of 1789 (in Le Chanois), to Marius, who is often transformed into a dedicated revolutionary (e.g., August, Hopper). The novel, though, shows the mixed nature of political events while also representing the urge to idealize them. When Enjolras exclaims apropos of Mabeuf, "Quels hommes que ces régicides!" 'What men these regicides are!,' Courfeyrac tells him, "Ceci n'est que pour toi, et je ne veux pas diminuer l'enthousiasme. Mais ce n'était rien moins qu'un régicide" 'This is only for you, and I don't wish to diminish the enthusiasm. But he was anything but a regicide' (2: 498–99; 1134 [pt. 4, bk. 14, ch. 2]).

As I mentioned above, I also use film clips to analyze a relatively minor detail—the nature of M. Madeleine's manufactory. Here I have two goals: first, to show how choices of even relatively unimportant details produce meaning; and second, to further clarify the social issue at the heart of the novel.

In the part of the novel that deals with M. Madeleine, Hugo's interest is not Valjean's social and economic success but rather the impossibility of his escaping his past. Therefore, he tells us very little about the way Valjean metamorphosed from an ignorant peasant who learned how to read and write in prison to an inventor and successful businessman. But Hugo needs to say something about how Valjean became rich and respectable and so he tells us that he revolutionized the manufacture of jet beads. The choice of a light industry makes historical sense: in spite of early investment in the railways, industrialization (organization of production into large units, greater use of machine labor, reliance on steam power) did not come to France until the end of the nineteenth century.

It is therefore interesting to note that Dayan changed Valjean's jet bead manufactory into a spinning mill, tightly linked with the evils of industrialization, and that August changed it into a brick factory, emphasizing hard, physical labor and stern discipline.[6] Milestone seems at first closer to the novel in choosing a ceramics manufactory—that is, artisanal work. Milestone, however, recruits Hugo's novel to celebrate the myth of the self-made man who starts with nothing but, thanks to his brain, becomes rich and successful (and can forget his past). At the same time, Milestone's film shows that the self-made man's success is due to new methods of industrial production (in his version Valjean's revolutionary idea is the rationalization of labor that turns the artisan into a cog in the machine and whose main advantage is an increased efficiency and productivity—that is, a gain to the manufacturer at the expense of the worker). Hossein does not change the product but presents the manufactory as dark, oppressive, and permeated by violence. This can be read as a critique of paternalist capitalism (especially in the scene where we hear a guide leading schoolchildren through a tour of the factory, telling them—and us—about M. Madeleine's good deeds). But such a critique obscures the fact that since Valjean brings great improvement to the town, his manufactory is not a site for class conflict between capitalist and proletariat.

We see, then, that in one way or another these film adaptations attempt to link the story of Valjean to industrialization and the rise of the working class. This, however, is not the story Hugo tells, and this is important for two very different reasons. On the one hand, in spite (or because) of the specter of June 1848, Hugo skirts the issue of class conflict: he declares that the bourgeoisie is not a class (2: 132; 829 [pt. 4, bk. 1, ch. 2]); Enjolras's utopian vision is of a world where all men are brothers, regardless of nation, let alone class. The only character in the novel who sees the insurrection in terms of class interest is the child, Gavroche (who tells the ragpicker: "Tu as tort d'insulter les révolutionnaires, mère Coin-de-la-Borne. Ce pistolet-là, c'est dans ton intérêt. C'est pour que tu aies dans ta hotte plus de choses bonnes à manger" 'You're wrong to insult the revolutionaries, Mother Heap-o'-dust. This pistol is in your interest. It's so that you'll have more good things to eat in your basket' (2, 428; 1074 [pt. 4, bk. 11, ch. 2]). On the other hand, what Hugo is concerned with in the novel is not the working class but *les misérables* — those who are excluded from society and belong to no class, the pariahs, whose extreme destitution as well as their brutalization by the legal system deprive them of most of the attributes of humanity, those who remain invisible to society except when they come into contact with the law or with charity and who can become part of society only in the fairy tale of Cosette-Cinderella.

Showing clips takes relatively little class time (10–15 minutes for 4–5 clips), and the discussion the clips provoke can extend to many of the novel's central concerns while directing students toward particular passages in the text. It is especially useful in a course such as the one I describe here, where we need to approach the novel thematically rather than by following the plot step by step. This can be a powerful heuristic tool as long as we make clear that the point in analyzing adaptations is not to fault them for their lack of faithfulness to the text but to show, through comparison, how novel and adaptations both involve choices that produce meaning.

NOTES

[1] For the "Waterloo" digression and Cambronne's word, see Brombert, *Victor Hugo,* esp. 106–18.

[2] For useful commentary on these films, see Gamel and Serceau's edited volume.

[3] On both these points, see Rosa, "Histoire" and "Jean Valjean."

[4] On the "destruction" of novelistic psychology in *Les Misérables,* see Vernier, "*Les Misérables*: Ce livre est dangereux" and "*Les Misérables* ou: De la modernité," esp. pp. 57–62.

[5] For an analysis of Javert, see Dubois, "L'affreux Javert."

[6] Although the English translation uses "factory," a more accurate rendering of Hugo's "fabrique" would be "manufactory" or "works."

Les Misérables and Childhood in Nineteenth-Century France

Pauline de Tholozany

This essay presents pedagogical strategies and assignments that I have used to teach *Les Misérables* in a multidisciplinary course on childhood in nineteenth-century France. Although I teach this class in French and all readings are in French (with the exception of one chapter in Bruno Bettelheim's *The Uses of Enchantments*), most of the texts I use are available in translation and it would be possible to teach this class in English. The goal of the course is to familiarize students with the main debates of the period regarding the literature and history of childhood, which we approach through close analysis of various primary materials. Because the novel borrows certain aspects of its treatment of childhood from the pedagogical and ontological debates of the time as well as from contemporaneous children's literature, reading *Les Misérables* leads us to a fuller exploration of the overarching themes of the course. Students work on this novel in the second half of the semester, once they are able to recognize its polyphony and can interweave various approaches to analyzing the notion of childhood.

In what follows, I first present the goals of the course and its general progression; this sheds light on the place that Hugo's novel occupies in the semester's sequence of readings. I then examine two particular pedagogical challenges to reading *Les Misérables* in the context of a class on childhood: the unstable representation of child characters as individuals and the novel's intertextuality. Meeting these challenges requires a preliminary work on contextualization, which I foster in the sequencing of the readings and in the pedagogical strategies and assignments.

Goals of the Course and Sequencing of the Readings

Undergraduates who read *Les Misérables* for the first time are often familiar with the novel's main child characters from stage adaptations of Hugo's text. While the Broadway show and its 2012 cinematographic adaptation by Tom Hooper draw students to the original text, these versions also render historical and contextualizing work all the more necessary before the novel is read. Because they are familiar with the plot, students do not typically remark on the rarity of having child characters occupy center stage in a nineteenth-century novel. Part of the work of discussing *Les Misérables* in the context of a class on childhood also consists in questioning what *misérable* means as far as child characters are concerned. While the question of social inequality and poverty in Hugo's text concerns both adult and child characters, it does so in quite different ways. Before the novel was published, many debates had raised an unprecedented awareness of children's physical and intellectual development, starting with Jean-Jacques Rousseau's seminal *Émile, ou De l'éducation* (1762).

The class is designed so that students reflect on childhood as a historical construct, one that we subsequently trace and question in the literature of the period. This requires reading assignments that are more historical and theoretical in nature at the beginning of the semester to help students identify relevant historical and conceptual questions present in Hugo's novel. We begin our work on *Les Misérables* around midsemester and spend three weeks on various sections of the text.

I start the semester by assigning "La découverte de l'enfance," a chapter of *L'enfant et la vie familiale sous l'Ancien Régime* (*Centuries of Childhood*), in which Philippe Ariès makes the daring claim that childhood in its modern meaning is a concept that emerged progressively in the seventeenth and eighteenth centuries. While Ariès's claims have sparked a lot of criticism, his text remains seminal in its discussion of childhood as a historically determined concept. As students later read passages from *Émile*, they relate Rousseau's ideals to Ariès's claim about the new importance given to the child as an individual in the modern period. Because Rousseau's text pleads for a more sensitive approach to child rearing while referring extensively to what he saw as the contemporaneous "éducation barbare" 'barbaric education' (301; my trans.), students encounter a good example of the new emotional investment made in the child in the modern period. Jean Itard's 1800 and 1806 reports on the feral child Victor of Aveyron, which we read next, strengthen the students' historical sense of the notion of childhood: Rousseau's ideals preside over Itard's pedagogy, and Victor's case allows the class to discover an early-nineteenth-century pedagogical and ontological experiment.

To prepare students to reflect on the intertextuality of *Les Misérables*, the course then focuses on child characters in children's literature. We first read two tales by Charles Perrault, *Le Petit Chaperon rouge* and *Le Petit Poucet* along with a chapter of Bettelheim on "Little Red Riding Hood." Although the French tales were written in the seventeenth century, their inclusion in the growing corpus of children's literature dates from the nineteenth century.

We spend time looking at nineteenth-century editions of those tales and their illustrations by Gustave Doré, all of which highlight the sexual subtext of *Le Petit Chaperon rouge* and the social implications of *Le Petit Poucet* (Perrault, *Gallica*; the class's Web site). We then read a selection of tales from Madame de Genlis's *Les Veillées du château* (1784) and Arnaud Berquin's *L'Ami des enfants* (1882–83). By their realist ambition, those two texts paved the way for a French classic of children's literature, *Les Malheurs de Sophie*, written by the Comtesse de Ségur and first published in 1858; we read this book in its entirety.

When students approach Hugo, then, many subtexts are present in their minds: from their reading of Ariès, Rousseau, and Itard, they have a sense of the ontological and pedagogical debates of the period preceding the publication of *Les Misérables*; and they are aware of the historicity of childhood as a concept. They have also read fairy tales and analyzed their renditions in nineteenth-century illustrations. They are familiar with the late-eighteenth-century debates on the emergence of realistic tales written for children, and they have read a sample of those tales. *Les Misérables* is a polyphonic novel that marks a point of convergence among these various perspectives, and, as such, the novel is the apex of the course.

Once we have finished our work on *Les Misérables*, we spend the last two weeks of the course on the writers' childhood. We read from eighteenth- and nineteenth-century autobiographical or semiautobiographical texts: Rousseau's *Confessions*, Stendhal's *Vie de Henry Brulard*, Jules Vallès's *L'Enfant*, and George Sand's *Histoire de ma vie*. This last section of the course allows students to explore a different perspective on the topic. We discuss the writers' retrospective gaze on themselves as children, as well as their subsequent attempts at reconstructing that child through writing.

Teaching Hugo's novel in a course on childhood requires focus on segments of the text at the beginning and at the end of the novel. The main sections that I assign are Cosette's encounter with Jean Valjean, "Accomplissement de la promesse faite à la morte," 'Fulfillment of the Promise Made to the Departed' (1: 490–556; 371–424 [pt. 2, bk. 3])) and Gavroche's life in the streets of Paris.[1] While these chapters focus primarily on Cosette and Gavroche, they provide material for a questioning of childhood in a larger sense, through the presence and interactions of several other child characters—Éponine, Azelma, the two younger Thénardier boys, and the bourgeois's son in the Luxembourg Gardens.

Individualized Children: Between Character Psychology and Allegory

Hugo's novel presents contrasting viewpoints on childhood. On the one hand, *Les Misérables* includes child characters that are very individualized for the period. On the other hand, some of these characters are still heavily allegorized (Gavroche in particular), and others occasionally serve as sociological examples to illustrate a larger political problem.

Because they have read chapters of Ariès's book early on in the semester, students are immediately able to link the centrality of child characters in *Les Misérables* to the newfound "importance accorded to the child's personality" that arises during this period (Ariès, "Discovery" 43). The novel contains detailed descriptions of children's daily lives, which we examine in our preliminary work on each section of the book. Examples of these descriptions include child play (Éponine and Azelma in the Thénardier household), child labor (Cosette's daily workload), and infantile vagrancy (Gavroche's everyday existence in the streets of Paris). We also see how child characters are described psychologically and physically; they interact with adults and have an active part in the plot.

Cosette's everyday life at the Thénardiers' inn is depicted in detail, and the narrative voice describes the general functioning of the household through its repercussions on Cosette (1: 490–99; 371–74 [pt. 2, bk. 3, ch. 1]). In order to have students reflect on Cosette's degree of individualization as a character, I have them work in groups to fill in a chart, each group concentrating on a number of chapters from book 3, "Accomplissement de la promesse faite à la morte" 'Fulfillment of the Promise Made to the Departed.' In one column, students list the passages that describe Cosette as an individual (character psychology, narrative importance); in another column, students reflect on the degree of agency attributed to Cosette.

A contrasting portrait thus emerges from this exercise: students remark that we learn about Cosette's feelings either through external descriptions, as in "Cosette songeait tristement" 'Cosette was musing sadly' (1: 500; 379 [pt. 2, bk. 3, ch. 3]), or through an internal focus on her thoughts: "elle . . . eût bien voulu être au lendemain matin," '[she] eagerly wished it were morning' (1: 501; 380 [pt. 2, bk. 3, ch. 3]). We also discuss Cosette's physical and psychological portraits, which Hugo draws in detail. Students remark that although chapters 2 and 8 describe other characters (the two Thénardiers, Éponine, Azelma), they are in fact organized around Cosette. Once we have commented on the literary devices that emphasize her importance, we move on to the second column of the chart and discuss the question of agency. Here it becomes visible that her actions are undertaken as tasks ordered by others (fetching water, making stockings). Cosette is also the object of negotiations between Thénardier and Valjean, and she does not say anything during those negotiations. The dialogues, too, are telling: she rarely speaks unless she is asked a question or given an order. This group assignment frames our discussions of Cosette by prompting students to explore two ways of conceiving her character. While she is highly individualized in comparison to the other child characters that students have encountered before reading Hugo, Cosette lacks agency. This discussion allows students to nuance their perspective on the importance of children in the novel. It also encourages students to approach our subsequent readings of the chapters on Gavroche with a critical mind-set.

Gavroche appears after a long description of "le gamin," which fills most of book 1 of part 3, "Paris étudié dans son atome" 'Paris Atomised' (1: 733–57; 571–91 (pt. 3, bk. 1). The chapters of this section resemble the "physiologies" of the 1830s and 40s. A literary genre in vogue during the July Monarchy (1830–48), "typologies" or "physiologies" were short journalistic texts with little narrative content; they described a social type (e.g., the flâneur, the grocer, the actress) and were sold in installments. The "gamin de Paris" 'Parisian street urchin' was one of the most popular and easily recognizable types of the period and appeared in many of these publications. Because Hugo introduces Gavroche in a pastiche of "physiologies," I choose to start our discussion of Gavroche with an assignment that introduces students to the genre that inspired those chapters.

The *physiologies* writer Jules Janin described the *gamin* in the second volume of the celebrated *Les Français peints par eux-mêmes* (1840–42), a collective work consisting of a series of such journalistic texts. I give students a few excerpts from his 1841 piece, "Le Gamin de Paris." I have the class work in small groups and ask them to compare Janin's and Hugo's texts. Students notice that both writers insist on the contradictory characteristics that define the *gamin* (vice and virtue, cunning and naïveté). Both authors also stress the *gamin's* frequent role in revolts and revolutions; we discuss Eugène Delacroix's *La Liberté guidant le peuple*, whose child figure in the foreground has famously been likened to the character of Gavroche. What's more, students identify the allegorical link drawn between the *gamin* and "le peuple." Because of the character's allegorical value, both Hugo's and Janin's texts struggle with the question of the passing of time: students remark that what becomes of the *gamin* once he is an adult is left unspoken in Janin's text, and Hugo is reluctant to imagine this character as an adult. In those typological chapters, Hugo's text makes it a political question instead—in chapter 12 of book 1 (pt. 3), "L'avenir latent dans le peuple" 'The Future Latent in the People,' the text advocates for education laws and child-protection measures. That Gavroche later dies as a *gamin* is part of the reluctance to imagine this social type as an adult: the *gamin* cannot grow up without losing his special status. As a child, his innocence makes his liminal position charismatic, but as an adult he would be either a drifter, an outlaw, or perhaps a beggar. His youth is also a guarantee of his revolutionary potential, something that both Janin and Hugo insist on.

This does not imply, of course, that Gavroche lacks a psychology of his own or even an individuality. Gavroche's portrait is placed after these "physiological" chapters, and while we are told that he mostly corresponds to that type, the text underscores one important difference: unlike the typical *gamin*, Gavroche has a heart that is "absolument sombre et vide" 'absolutely dark and empty' (1: 755; 589 [pt. 3, bk. 1, ch. 13]). This statement contradicts Gavroche's later actions but ultimately works to give him a psychology, since it allows for character development. Gavroche also has more agency than Cosette, a fact that students remark on as we do a few close readings of the dialogues.

Children of lesser narrative importance than Cosette and Gavroche do not have as extensive a portrait in the text, but they are important to the novel's political statement. The narrative around Gavroche's younger brothers, for example, fulfills a crucial ideological goal. These two children remain nameless in the novel and are described as belonging to "la statistique des 'enfants abandonnés' que la police constate, ramasse, égare et retrouve sur le pavé de Paris' 'the statistics of "abandoned children," whom the police report, collect, mislay, and find again on the streets of Paris' (2: 600; 1214 [pt. 5, bk. 1, ch. 16]). Their very anonymity is significant: invisible, unspoken for, and unaccounted for, they are abandoned by all—including the state. When La Magnon's sons die, the two anonymous children replace them, and Monsieur Gillenormand remains blind to the change: the boys are indistinguishable entities to all the adults who know them. The fact that they remain anonymous throughout the novel stresses a social attitude toward childhood against which *Les Misérables* fights. Students are able to recognize, in the very unrecognizability of the two anonymous Thénardier sons, an invisibility that, according to Ariès, characterized childhood in many premodern representations. On the one hand, we can understand this invisibility as the denunciation of an ancient (and faulty) attitude toward children; Hugo's text pleads for more humanity in the families' treatment of their children as well as for more state intervention when familial care is lacking. On the other hand, though, there is a difference between what Ariès discusses as the premodern child's "invisibility" and the invisibility of these two characters: unlike their premodern peers, these two children are not part of a community. Their invisibility is accrued because no group (be it parents, family, church, or state) claims them as their own. In that perspective, the fate of the two Thénardier sons may indicate that while modernity has brought some children more emotional and familial importance, it might also have worsened the condition of deprived children.

A Polyphonic Novel: Discussing Intertextuality

Hugo's novel draws themes and motifs from many other texts, and our class discussions are partly geared toward recognizing and casting a critical eye on this intertextuality. I choose to focus primarily on fairy tales as a major intertext of the novel, while discussing how several child characters in Les Misérables compare with the feral child Victor de l'Aveyron.

As I have suggested earlier, reading Itard's 1800 and 1806 reports on Victor helps students recognize the medical origin of some of the themes that appear in Les Misérables. Victor's case was famously reported in the newspapers of the early nineteenth century. Found in 1800 in Aveyron, France, Victor was believed to have lived most of his life alone in the woods. He was placed under the care of young Jean Itard, a doctor, in 1800. Itard's reports highly affected the period's representations of childhood: Victor, despite Itard's best efforts, never managed to speak. In his reports, Itard also questions Victor's capacity to cry and laugh, two actions that were understood as important signs of humanity. Like other cases of feral children throughout Europe, Victor's sparked ontological discussions about a child's humanity and possible animalistic traits. In Les Misérables, this ontological question is particularly visible in the section describing Cosette as a child: the text insists several times that she does not cry, despite her fear and the abuse that she endures. Her tears finally appear when she is given the doll, an object that symbolically places her back into humanity and society, preparing her for motherhood — Hugo explicitly describes the doll as a toy designed to foster that transition. The tears, a sure sign of humanity, accompany the child's return to a socialized state.

Other characteristics in the text prompt a comparison between Cosette and Victor: her gaze sometimes makes her look like an "idiote ou un démon" 'an idiot or a demon'(1: 522; 397 [pt. 2, bk. 3, ch. 8]) — Victor was thought by many to be an "idiot" (Itard, "Rapport" 215) — and Cosette's time in the forest awakens a strange instinct in her such that a passerby compares her to an "enfant-garou" 'fairy child' (1: 505; 383 [pt. 2, bk. 3, ch. 5]). Éponine and Azelma speak the "adorable langage des enfants" 'sweet and charming language of children'(1: 527; 401 [pt. 2, bk. 3, ch. 8]), but Cosette utters very short and simple sentences—when she is not, like Victor, silent and "pétrifiée" 'motionless' (1: 503; 381 [pt. 5, bk. 1, ch. 16]).

Some episodes in the novel involving child vagrancy—Cosette's encounter with Jean Valjean, Gavroche's meanderings in the streets of Paris—are reminiscent of fairy tales. Perrault's and Grimm's tales were republished extensively in the nineteenth century, in formats usually designed for a young public. Cosette's walk in the woods and her subsequent encounter with Valjean bear resemblance to the plot of *Le Petit Chaperon rouge*, which students have already read for class. I now prompt them to identify elements of *Le Petit Chaperon rouge* in "Accomplissement de la promesse faite à la morte" 'Fulfillment of the Promise Made to the Departed,' and together we recognize the pastiche at work here: while *Le Petit Chaperon rouge* is a tale about premature sexual awakening, the encounter between Cosette and Jean Valjean in *Les Misérables* has a very different outcome. Valjean's appearance in the woods resembles that of the wolf in the tale, but his role is ultimately closer to that of the rescuing huntsman in Grimm's version of the story. (This episode does not appear in Perrault's version of the tale. Students, however, are aware of Grimm's version because they read a chapter on that subject in *The Uses of Enchantment*.) Students also remark that although those chapters borrow narrative events from the tale—a questionable mother figure sends a young child on an errand in the woods, where she meets an older male character—the narrative voice prevents the reader from identifying Valjean as a predator: "Il y a des instincts pour toutes les rencontres de la vie: l'enfant n'eut pas peur" 'There are instincts for all the crises of life. The child was not afraid' (1: 510; 387 [pt. 2, bk. 3, ch. 5]). I also ask students whether other characters in these chapters resemble fairy-tale figures, and we spend time discussing Mme Thénardier as an "ogresse": she is indeed a combination of a fairy-tale stepmother ("une maîtresse farouche," 'a ferocious mistress' [1: 499; 379]) and a masculine ogre ("elle avait de la barbe" 'She had a beard' [1: 494; 375 (pt. 2, bk. 3, ch. 2)]). Cosette's situation is very reminiscent of Cinderella's: forced into servitude by an evil stepmother, she also lives with two malevolent sister figures. Like Cinderella too, her daily life consists in tirelessly performing household duties, a routine destroyed by a character external to the family (the fairy in *Cinderella*, Jean Valjean in *Les Misérables*).

When examining the chapters on Gavroche, I prompt students to compare him with the Petit Poucet, another child character whom his parents reject and who saves his brothers while he finds his way in an unfamiliar environment. Students remark on the correlation between *Les Misérables* and the tales' narratives; they generally discuss this in relation to the realist mode of the novel, which renders the narrative more tragic than its original fantastic counterparts. The pathos created by such episodes is a rhetorical move destined to awaken the reader to the real miseries suffered by children during the time of the novel and at the time of the writing of *Les Misérables*.

Conclusion: Éponine

As we trace the genealogy of these representations of childhood, we come to see Éponine's character as having a complicated relation to many of the notions examined in class; because she defies categories, Éponine is the object of our final discussions on the novel. A pretty and beloved little girl in the first episodes that describe Cosette's life, she subsequently becomes unrecognizable. Neither a child nor a young woman, she dresses as a man. An "infortunée enfant" 'unfortunate child' who does not fit into any category (2: 511; 1141 [pt. 4, bk. 14, ch. 7]), Éponine is perhaps the most *misérable* of them all, because no identifiable value accompanies her misfortune and her death. Cosette mistakes her for a "jeune ouvrier" 'young working man' (2: 512; 1142 [pt. 4, bk. 14, ch. 7]); to Marius, Éponine is a "forme qui se traînait" 'form . . . dragging itself toward him' (2: 507; 1137 [pt. 4, bk. 14, ch. 6]); and the narrative voice describes Éponine using the pronoun "cela" 'it' (2: 507; 1141 [pt. 4, bk. 14, ch. 6]): ungendered and dehumanized, Éponine in her final moments has become a nameless creature whose death is without meaning. For although she dies saving Marius, she herself prevents any narrative of sacrifice from emerging: as she expires in his arms, she states, "C'est moi qui vous ai mené ici . . . Vous allez mourir, j'y compte bien" 'It was I who led you into this . . . You are going to die, I'm sure' (2: 507; 1138 [pt. 4, bk. 14, ch. 6]). The sixteen-year-old Éponine, like Gavroche, is shot on the barricades; but unlike her brother, her death has no ideological higher value — Éponine is never allegorized. Ending our discussion of *Les Misérables* with this character allows students to reflect on the notions used by the novel in its description of childhood. Éponine holds a powerful place in that regard, one that perhaps questions the validity of the very categories on which the novel builds itself.

NOTE

[1] I assign the following sections on Gavroche in the course: 1: 733–57; 571–91 (pt. 3, bk. 1); 2: 266–96; 934–58 (pt. 4, bk. 6, chs. 1–2); 2: 422–33; 1063–72 (pt. 4, bk. 11, chs. 1–4); 2: 458–62, 469–72; 1094–97, 1104–07 (pt. 4, bk. 12, chs. 4, 7); 2: 499–501, 504–15; 1131–32, 1134–44 (pt. 4, bk. 14, chs. 3, 5–7); 2: 526–38; 1153–64 (pt. 4, bk. 15, chs. 2–4); 2: 570–78, 595–608; 1189–96, 1210–21 (pt. 5, bk. 1, chs. 7–8, 15–16).

Studying Criminality and the Popular Press through *Les Misérables*

Andrea Goulet

In an advanced undergraduate seminar on crime in nineteenth-century French literature, *Les Misérables* takes center stage and can be situated within three sociohistorical contexts: the demographics of postrevolutionary France as they affect poverty and criminality in city and province; laws and reform movements in the criminal justice system as well as in the popular press and literature of the time; and urban topographies of hygiene and violence leading to the Haussmannization of Second Empire Paris. I bring these contexts into the classroom through short secondary readings, brief lectures, and guided student research in *Gallica* (gallica.bnf.fr) and *Médias19* (medias19.org), which serve as support for the primary in-class discussions of Hugo's novel. The goal of discussions and small-group work is to bring students' attention to literary ambiguity and semantic play in *Les Misérables* as well as to nuanced inquiry on questions such as these: What is the role of literature in the elaboration of a nation's legal and penal codes? How do religious and ethical systems of justice intersect with legal and social orders of punishment and reform? What is the relation between individual and collective forms of violence—that is, between individual crimes and political insurrections? How did regime shifts of the nineteenth century affect the spatial organization of crime and punishment in Paris and France? How does Hugo use stylistic devices (e.g., argot, changes of perspective) and metaphorical language (religious symbolism, high and low spaces) to promote social reform? What resonance does the novel have for our own reflections on law, ethics, and criminal justice today?

Setting the Stage: Hugo and the Death Penalty

In order to introduce students directly to Hugo's opposition to capital punishment, I have them first read his short novel *Le Dernier Jour d'un condamné* (1829) in dialogue with an excerpt from Michel Foucault's *Surveiller et punir: Naissance de la prison* (9–23). By emphasizing the mental sufferings of a prisoner facing execution, *Le Dernier Jour* supports Foucault's historical thesis that the first decades of the nineteenth century marked a new age of French penal justice, in which the public display of tortured bodies gave way to less corporealized forms of punishment. But, as Foucault specifies, the years between 1760 and 1840 were an age of jagged evolution, in which progress occurred in fits and starts (22); fittingly, *Le Dernier Jour* retains cruel scenes of ritualized public spectacle in its portrayal of disciplinary process. Hugo's 1829 novel thus sits squarely within a crucial transitional moment, for which the revolutionary democratization of the *guillotine* and its 1832 relocation (from the central Place de Grève to Paris's Barrière Saint-Jacques) serve as symbolic bookends (Gohin, "Réalitiés"; Savey-Casard).

In his 1832 preface to *Le Dernier Jour*, Hugo raises the question of whether the new secrecy of state beheadings actually constitutes progress. For Hugo the move of the guillotine away from public square to hidden quarters is a shameful, cowardly act that exposes the hypocrisy of a law that would murder a man for the crime of murder (391–96). Hugo's argument evokes, naturally, an enduring debate ripe for class discussion; students prepare oral arguments and compare policies in the United States with those of France, which abolished the death penalty in 1981 (Perrot). I highlight Hugo's sustained and public role in the national history of that debate: his allusions in the preface of *Le Dernier Jour* (379) to Cesare Beccaria's 1764 *Des Délits et des peines*; his 1834 *Claude Gueux*, based on a true crime and also arousing sympathy for a condemned man; and his 1848 vote at the Assemblée Nationale for the abolition of the death penalty (and freedom of the press).

"Ah! les misérables!" appears in the last line of *Le Dernier Jour*. Earlier in the text, the poor are described with sympathy, but here the term's opposite meaning ("miscreants") refers to the judges and barbarous crowd at the condemned man's execution, thus allowing us to frame our reading of *Les Misérables* with Hugo's refusal of a clear social or moral distinction between the wretched and the "civilized." A second key point of comparison between the two novels arises in the language used to describe *la guillotine*. In *Le Dernier Jour*, the unnamed instrument of execution is called a machine, perhaps an allusion to its technical advancement over previous methods. But in the context of the 1832 preface, such a progressivist reading is put into question; and indeed, when we trace the semantic field of mechanization and machines throughout *Le Dernier Jour*, we find Hugo's text suggesting instead that the French penal system makes "things" ("choses") out of humans. What happens to that lexical field in *Les Misérables*, written three decades later? In the first pages of *Les Misérables*, the good-hearted Monseigneur Bienvenu suffers from shock at the sight of the guillotine. A guided in-class close reading of the passage reveals a shift from machine to monster, from inert and mechanical instrument of death to personified, flesh-eating ghoul. As seen through the eyes of Bienvenu, for whom divine justice trumps human law, the guillotine calls for a *prise de position* ("taking a stand") regarding the death penalty itself: "La guillotine . . . n'est pas neutre, et ne vous permet pas de rester neutre" 'The guillotine . . . is not neutral and does not permit you to remain neutral' (1: 52; 16 [pt. 4, bk. 14, ch. 6]).

Les Misérables *and the Origins of Crime*

Even before we learn that sympathy for hungry children was at the root of Jean Valjean's act of theft, *Les Misérables* puts forth the thesis that criminality is caused by social injustice rather than evil nature. Bienvenu cites the town of Briançon, where townsfolk provide for poor orphans and, as an implied consequence, no murder has been committed for a century (pt. 1, bk. 1, ch. 3); the outlaw bandit

Cravatte rises to noble action when treated with confidence and respect (pt. 1, bk. 1, ch. 7). Valjean's own story is driven by external circumstances: poverty and orphanhood lead to petty theft, nineteen cruel years of imprisonment toughen his heart, and the ex-con's yellow passport bars him from an honest living. In typical form, Hugo tugs on readers' heartstrings before launching into didacticism; by the time we read that "une statistique anglaise constate qu'à Londres quatre vols sur cinq ont pour cause immédiate la faim" 'English statistics show that in London starvation is the immediate cause of four out of five thefts' (1: 140; 87 [pt. 1, bk. 2, ch. 6]), we are convinced that society is the guilty party. In class, we discuss Hugo's contention that cities produce ferocious men through corruption (1: 136–37; 84 [pt. 1, bk. 2, ch. 6]) in relation to historian Louis Chevalier's claim that the rapid rise of crime in early-nineteenth-century Paris was due to demographic shifts in the poor and working classes. Fantine's moving story of descent from merry *grisette* to toothless whore also supports the theory of criminality as essentially determined by social milieu. Indeed, Hugo's description of prostitution as "civilized" slavery (1: 261; 187 [pt. 1, bk. 5, ch. 11]) and his critique of Javert's discretionary power over Fantine can be understood within the historical context of Napoleonic registration laws and hygiene controls as described by Alexandre Parent-Duchâtelet, who analyzed statistical data and 5,023 birth certificates collected from prostitutes by police between 1828 and 1832 (Nye; Parent-Duchâtelet). If Javert is unable to conceive of a noble heart coexisting with a criminal act ("à ses yeux le vol, le meurtre, tous les crimes, n'étaient que des formes de la rébellion" 'in his eyes theft, murder, all crimes were merely forms of rebellion' 1: 241; 171 [pt. 1, bk. 5, ch. 5]), it is in part because his blind devotion to institutions of justice was itself determined by the environmental circumstance of his birth in a prison.

Still, for Hugo the nature-nurture question of criminality also has a metaphysical dimension. To avoid naively idealizing all members of the downtrodden classes, Hugo cites the existence of unredeemable "monsters" (like Thénardier and the real-life murderer Pierre François Lacenaire) who would unleash chaos even within a just society. The author's metaphorics of the underground combine with his theological grapplings with evil in the image of "le polype monstrueux du mal habitant la crypte de la Société" 'a monstrous polyp of evil that inhabits the crypt of society' (1: 910; 724 [pt. 3, bk. 7, ch. 4]). But when the social *bas-fonds* ("lowest strata") become a demonic cavern of evil, does reformism lose all efficacy? Hugo, the politician committed to progress, will not go that far; his allegory of criminals dwelling in a cave of ignorance calls, still, for social action: "Que faut-il pour faire évanouir ces larves? De la lumière. . . . Éclairez la société en dessous" 'What is required to exorcise these goblins? Light. . . . Throw light on the society below' (1: 913; 727 [pt. 3, bk. 7, ch. 4]).

The truly wicked are rare in *Les Misérables*. Though Thénardier seems born bad, secondary characters from Éponine and Gavroche to Magnon and Montparnasse represent aspects of a population whose criminality has been, at the very least, facilitated by economic inequality and social injustice. When Marius finally learns that Thénardier, whom he had revered as savior of his father, is a "bandit" and a "monster," he is thrust up against the novel's central conflict between two sets of codes: those of the human legal system and those of divine justice (2: 87; 793 [pt. 3, bk. 8, ch. 20]).

Justice, Human or Divine?

Hugo's detailed, research-based depiction of a criminal trial in Arras, at which the esteemed mayor Madeleine will reveal himself as the ex-con Valjean, exposes the injustice of the justice system. Students note the hierarchized layout of the courtroom, the obfuscatory incompetence and corruption of lawyers and judges, and the cruel disproportion between the defendant Champmathieu's crime (the theft of fallen apples) and punishment (life imprisonment for a supposed recidivist). Two grand systems are at play in the trial's somber atmosphere: "cette grande chose humaine qu'on appelle la loi et cette grande chose divine qu'on appelle la justice" 'that great human thing called law, and that great divine thing called justice' (1: 357; 265 [pt. 1, bk. 7, ch. 9]). But despite the crucifix on the courtroom wall (which establishes a contrast between the Restoration's legal system in 1823 and the secularism of Valjean's first trial twenty-seven years earlier under the Directory), God remains absent from the place until Valjean accomplishes his act of Christian self-sacrifice.

The conflict between divine justice and human law structures "Une tempête sous un crâne" ("A Tempest within a Brain")—the chapter in which Valjean struggles with the decision to save Champmathieu at the cost of his own freedom. To remain silent about the wrongly accused defendant would be a moral crime—"un crime bas, lâche, sournois, abject, hideux!" 'a base, cowardly, lying, abject, hideous crime!' (1: 309; 226 [pt. 1, bk. 7, ch. 3]), weighed in the scales of his God-led conscience. But the choice is complicated by his duties toward the town of Montreuil-sur-Mer; unanchored by the mayor's moral and economic leadership, the town's industry could collapse and poverty would lead inevitably to social disorder: "le vol, le meurtre, tous les vices, tous les crimes!" 'theft, murder, all vices, all crimes!' (1: 315; 231 [pt. 1, bk. 7, ch. 3]). An in-class debate (confess or stay silent?) highlights these uses of the term *crime* while helping students track the twists and turns of Valjean's internal conflict.

Hugo continually stages contestations of human and divine law. When the nuns of Petit Picpus bury one of their own within convent walls rather than in the Vaugirard cemetery, they defy the city's health codes enforced by the police commissioner; citing historical precedents of church trumping state, the reverend mother justifies the rebellious act as "défendu par les hommes, ordonné par Dieu" 'forbidden by men, commanded by God' (1: 687; 538 [pt. 1, bk. 8, ch. 3]). The social disorder of the 1832 rebellion creates opportunities for alternative modes of justice, as when Enjolras appoints himself reluctant judge and jury in the unofficial "trial" of Le Cabuc (2: 476; 1115 [pt. 4, bk. 12, ch. 8]) and when Valjean applies the logic of divine grace to his dealings with the captured Javert (2: 617; 1233 [pt. 5, bk. 1, ch. 19]). At the heart of Javert's suicide is this shattering question: "Est-ce qu'il y a au monde autre chose que les tribunaux, les sentences exécutoires, la police et l'autorité?" 'Is there anything else in the world besides tribunals, sentences, police, and authority?' (2: 721; 1321 [pt. 5, bk. 1, ch. 19]). Until then, Javert had conflated eternal justice with contingent social order, seeing himself as the personification of "la lumière et la vérité dans leur fonction céleste d'écrasement du mal" 'light, and truth, in their celestial functions as destroyers of evil' (1: 388; 290 [pt. 1, bk. 8, ch. 3]). But his encounters with Valjean destabilize his faith in a legal system that shifts with the winds of political regimes. Students attend to the irony of Javert's "last will and testament" while considering whether the penal reforms he proposes (improved hygienic conditions, not charging prisoners for their own keep) are undermined by the apparent conservatism of his stated motivations (saving money, keeping order) (2: 729–30; 1328–29 [pt. 1, bk. 8, ch. 3]).

The theme of human versus divine justice returns in the novel's dénouement. Despite decades of social rehabilitation and moral redemption, Valjean considers himself perpetually excluded from human society by virtue of his criminal record, and he fears, rightly, that his confession will cast a shadow of shame over the innocent marriage of young Marius and Cosette. At first, Marius reacts with a righteous, legalistic repulsion: "Marius, sur les questions pénales, en était encore, quoique démocrate, au système inexorable, et il avait, sur ceux que la loi frappe, toutes les idées de la loi. . . . *Il n'en était pas encore à distinguer entre ce qui est écrit par l'homme et ce qui est écrit par Dieu, entre la loi et le droit*" 'Although a democrat, Marius still adhered upon penal questions to the inexorable system, and in regard to those whom the law smites, he shared all the ideas of the law. . . . *He had not yet come to distinguish between what is written by man and what is written by God, between law and right*' (2: 826; 1411 [pt. 5, bk. 7, ch. 2; my emphasis]). And, he asks, would it be right to accept a dowry fortune that might be tainted by criminal origin? This question lies also at the center of Balzac's 1831 story "L'Auberge rouge," which features the discovery that a respected businessman named Taillefer has been hiding a guilty deed from his past. Unlike Valjean, Taillefer has served no prison time; but Balzac's tale has in common with *Les Misérables* a reflection on criminality's connection to the rise and fall of personal fortunes within the context of political upheaval in nineteenth-century France.

Crime, Politics, and Paris Topography

For the monarchist Gillenormand, revolution is a crime. He and his *ultra* royalist cronies refer to heroes of the Napoleonic empire as brigands and bandits, conflating the defeated Colonel Pontmercy with a fugitive from justice (1: 780; 616 [pt. 3, bk. 3, ch. 2]): "Les républicains et les galériens, ça ne fait qu'un nez et qu'un mouchoir" 'Republicans and convicts, like a nose and a handkerchief!' (1: 875; 696 [pt. 3, bk. 5, ch. 7]). The reader, of course, knows otherwise, having witnessed Thénardier's pillaging on the battlefield at Waterloo, breaking both military and ethical codes of honor. Along with the narrator, we see the difference not only between a Valjean and a Thénardier, but between Patron-Minette, the corrupt band of real criminals, and ABC, the idealistic republicans willing to lay their lives down to help the "abaissés" ("downtrodden") and bring true progress to their nation. And yet, part of Les Misérables's dramatic power derives from its bringing together the two groups in the spaces below and above the barricaded streets of Paris. For during times of civil unrest, police patrols are just as likely to suppress noble insurrectionists as assassins (pt. 4, bk. 2, ch. 1). Although Hugo distinguishes between a utopian revolutionary underground and a deeper criminal layer in the chapter "Les mines et les mineurs" (pt. 3, bk. 7, ch. 1), the novel's climactic scenes of the 1832 uprising blur distinctions between crime and social disorder by putting looters next to idealists at the barricades and by having Thénardier cross paths with Valjean and Marius in the subterranean tunnels of the sewers.

Hugo's depiction of the urban landscape has strong symbolic dimensions, but it is also rooted in the history of Paris as a built environment. In conjunction with the "Maître Gorbeau" chapter, in which Hugo reminds readers that "En 1823, le mur d'enceinte existait encore" 'In 1832, the city wall still existed' (1: 561; 461 [pt. 2, bk. 4, ch. 1]), I show students maps of Paris with its successive circular walls. From Philip Augustus's fortifications (1190–1213) to Charles V's fourteenth-century enclosure and the eighteenth-century Wall of the Farmers-General, the city's outward expansion prepares the terrain for a nineteenth-century shift of criminal activity (and a criminal imaginary) from the central Île de la Cité to the terrains vagues ("empty lots") and Barrières that surround increasingly regulated and gentrified areas (Jones; Kalifa, "Crime Scenes"). Hugo situates the shady "masure Gorbeau" ("Gorbeau shack") in a liminal semi-urban space, between the Salpêtrière Hospital and the Bicêtre prison and leading to the Barrière d'Italie—a location that allows for reflection on the sinister associations of crime (for example, a well-known 1829 murder at the site), the cruel enforcement of the death penalty (at the Saint-Jacques barrier), and the mid-century projects of urbanization (1: 561–64; 431–34 [pt. 3, bk. 4, ch. 1]). Class discussion on Haussmann's Second Empire strategy to reduce crime through urban renewal helps students understand Hugo's digressive passages on the capital city's transformation. In the chapter on Paris's 1727 map, Hugo makes a tart jab at Napoleon III's city renovations, by implying that the new Mazas prison is itself a response to so-called progress: "Il y a là aujourd'hui de grandes rues toutes neuves, des arènes . . . une prison, Mazas; le progrès, comme on voit, avec son correctif" 'There are new broad streets, amphitheatres, . . . a prison, Mazas—progress, as we see, with its corrective' (1: 584; 452 [pt. 2, bk. 5, ch. 3]). Designed by the architect Émile Gilbert and inaugurated in 1841, the Mazas prison was erected in the precise quartier of Hugo's fictional Petit Picpus convent—a choice allowing a comment on his century as one in which "Dieu [est] subordonné au commissaire de police" 'God [is] subordinated to the Commissioner of Police' (1: 688; 539 [pt. 3, bk. 8, ch. 3]). The novel values, it seems, Christian purification over hygienic urban reconstruction; and Hugo's pithy "Claustration, castration" 'Incarceration, castration' (1: 657; 513 [pt. 2, bk. 7, ch. 3]) sounds a pre-Foucauldian note on disciplinary regimens in spaces of incarceration.

As peer of France, Hugo made use of his prerogative to inspect a number of prisons and death cells in Paris, Toulon, and Brest (Brombert, *Victor Hugo* 27–28). His suggestion in *Les Misérables* that crowded prisons serve as incubators for criminal plots echoes Eugène Sue's reformist chapters on the merits of solitary confinement in *Les Mystères de Paris* (1842–43). In class we pay particular attention to the prisoners' transfer at the *Barrière du Maine* as described through the prism of Valjean and Cosette's horrified gazes. Rhetorical effects include the dehumanization of the chain gang through impersonal subject pronouns: "Cela grandissait, cela semblait se mouvoir avec ordre, pourtant c'était hérissé et frémissant" 'It grew larger, it seemed to move in order, still it was bristling and quivering' (2: 225; 906 [pt. 4, bk. 3, ch. 8]); and the semantic fields of death ("sépulcral," "faces de cadavres," "cortège," "la tombe" 'sepulchral,' 'faces of corpses,' 'cortège,' 'tomb') and beastliness ("fourmillement," "le mille-pieds," "créatures" 'crawling,' 'the centipede,' 'creatures'; 2: 226–27; 907–08 [pt. 4, bk. 3, ch. 8]).

Prisons, semiurban *barrière* neighborhoods, subterranean lairs, and public execution squares in Paris constitute a complex criminal *bas-fonds* with its own topography, population, and language (Kalifa, *Les Bas-fonds*). The endearing and street-smart *gamin* Gavroche laughs at the guillotine and possesses a knowledge of real-life criminals like Papavoine (executed in 1825) and Lecouffé (executed with his mother in 1824) that replaces school learning. Through Gavroche and Patron-Minette, Hugo gives readers a linguistic lesson in criminal argot, as documented in previous texts like Eugène François Vidocq's 1827 *Mémoires* and the anonymous 1829 *Mémoires d'un forban philosophe* (Rosa, "Essais"). The exposure of "monstrous" slang is justified as socially useful: "étudier les difformités et les infirmités sociales et les signaler pour les guérir" 'the study of social deformities and infirmities and attention drawn to them in order to cure them' (2: 318; 983 [pt. 4, bk. 7, ch. 1]), though the "Argot" chapters testify not only to a documentary impulse we have seen in *Le Dernier Jour* but also to the joy of free play ("Mirlababi surlababo . . ." [2: 332; 995 [pt. 4, bk. 7, ch. 3]]) that recalls the carnivalesque multiplicity of registers in a novel like *Notre-Dame de Paris*.

Truth and Fiction: Crime and the Popular Press

Hugo's Romantic representations of the urban conditions of crime and justice may belong to what we now consider high literature, but in nineteenth-century France these representations were not strictly differentiated from the lurid illustrations and criminal *faits divers* that peppered the pages of popular press journals, which today's students can access through university libraries and online sites (Cragin). A useful resource for teaching the rise of the popular press in nineteenth-century France is the Web site *Médias19*, which links to digitized newspapers like *Le Petit Journal, Gazette des tribunaux, La Justice*, and *Le Petit Parisien* and to biographies of dozens of journalist-authors like Balzac, Élie Berthet, Fortuné du Boisgobey, and Émile Zola. The interconnectedness of crime fiction and crime "reality" becomes evident when we read the *faits divers* above a newspaper's *rez-de-chaussée* (the bottom-center part of the first page) along with the *romans-feuilletons* that appear below the dividing line (Thérenty, Thiesse). Indeed, lines between fact and fiction are blurred by news reports that do not adhere to codes of neutral objectivity that we associate with journalism today. An example: the 8 June 1838 report in *La Presse* (available on *Gallica*) of a merchant-woman's murder relies on crowd gossip for its sensationalistic and editorializing account. Details of this "horrible assassinat" 'horrible murder' entered Sue's 1842–43 *Les Mystères de Paris* and were later fictionalized in 1884 as *L'Affaire de la rue du Temple*, by Constant Guéroult, and rereported by Pierre Bouchardon in 1929.

In *Les Misérables*, Hugo comments on journalistic integrity through his double narration of Valjean's recapture after the Champmathieu trial. After the Waterloo digression, the narrator returns to the intradiegetic present with transcriptions of dated, published accounts in the *Drapeau blanc* and *Le Journal de Paris* (1: 472–75; 359–60 [pt. 2, bk. 2, ch. 1]). We read these (fictionalized) news reports carefully, with an eye to discrepancies with the earlier narration: in the mediated popular press versions, the police are given credit for unmasking Madeleine's identity; Fantine is called a concubine; and the king is praised for his clemency toward the hardened criminal. What ideologies are being served by the slanted language of the popular press? Why does Hugo include these reports, with their exaggerations, distortions, and outright falsehoods? Later, Hugo employs the same stereophonic strategy: the nine-page description of a heroic rescue by the self-sacrificing prisoner we know to be Valjean is followed by a curt report in the Toulon newspaper (1: 489; 373 [pt. 2, bk. 2, ch. 3]). Attending to these chapters encourages students to think critically not only about historical reportage but also about our own media outlets (Fox News, MSNBC) and current events. It also links social questions of criminality to *Les Misérables*'s philosophical reflections on truth and lies: when a nun's well-intentioned dishonesty (Sister Simplice's white lie to Javert [pt. 2, bk. 8, ch. 5]) is presented as ethically superior to a police commissioner's blind adherence to truth, readers must also question the kind of black-and-white thinking that perceives honor on the side of respectable society and dishonor on the side of incarcerated populations.

These issues raised by Hugo's novel can inform student research projects, which I assign to students working in pairs. Using library and online sources, students choose a topic related to nineteenth-century criminality and the popular press: a famous criminal case (such as Jean-Baptiste Troppmann, Pierre François Lacenaire, or Marie Lafarge); a *fait divers* as reported in various newspapers and fictional accounts; the figure of Vidocq; women and crime; the guillotine and the death penalty; the history and fictionalization of a specific carceral space (the bagne of Toulon; the Salpêtrière; the "Biribi"). The students prepare a bibliography and a short oral presentation in which they are asked to analyze not only objective "facts" but the ideological and literary underpinnings of the language used to report them. Thus, even when we seem to have left the realm of fiction, we are reminded that our understanding of nineteenth-century (and today's) criminality is always already a question of representation.

Les Misérables and
the Literature of Paris

Cary Hollinshead-Strick and Anne-Marie Picard

Because we are especially interested in the ways the city of Paris and its literary representations shape one another, when we teach *Les Misérables* we read "Corinth" (pt. 4, bk. 12) through "Javert off the Track" (pt. 5, bk. 4). The barricade fighting and the trek through the sewers are Parisian in location, history, and imagery, and our course shows how they connect backward to François Villon and François Rabelais, and forward to Karl Marx, Charles Baudelaire, Arthur Rimbaud, Georges Perec, and Mehdi Charef. Between Rabelais and Hugo, our readings vary, from a selection of Mazarinades (which we teach by glossing Christian Jouhaud) to fables by Jean de La Fontaine (glossing Michel Serres), Molière's *Le bourgeois gentilhomme* (glossing Roger Chartier), Madame de Lafayette's *La Princesse de Clèves* (sometimes read alongside Norbert Elias), and the beginning of Helen Maria Williams's *Letters Written in France*.

After *Les Misérables*, frequent selections include the beginning of Marx's *Eighteenth Brumaire of Louis-Napoléon Bonaparte*, Baudelaire's "The Eyes of the Poor," Rimbaud's poems related to the Commune, André Breton's *Nadja*, Ernest Hemingway's *A Moveable Feast*, selections from Perec, and Charef's *Tea in the Harem*. Marx's *The Eighteenth Brumaire of Louis Bonaparte*, which says that Napoleon is to Napoleon III as tragedy is to farce, can also serve as an introduction to the section of *Les Misérables* we read, since the chapter begins thus:

> Les Parisiens qui, aujourd'hui, en entrant dans la rue Rambuteau du côté des halles, remarquent à leur droite, vis-à-vis la rue Mondétour, une boutique de vannier ayant pour enseigne un panier qui a la forme de l'empereur Napoléon le Grand avec cette inscription:
>
> NAPOLÉON EST FAIT
> TOUT EN OSIER
>
> ne se doutent guère des scènes terribles que ce même emplacement a vues il y a à peine trente ans.   (2: 438 [pt. 4, bk. 12, ch. 1])

> Parisians who, today, on entering the rue Rambuteau from the side of Les Halles, notice on their right, opposite the rue Mondétour, a basket maker's shop, with a basket for a sign, in the shape of the Emperor Napoleon the Great, with this inscription:
>
> NAPOLEON EST FAIT
> TOUT EN OSIER,
>
> do not suspect the terrible scenes that this very place saw thirty years ago.
>   (1082)[1]

These lines set up a number of characteristic approaches to writing Paris on which we focus throughout our reading of Hugo: the precise but semidisappeared location in Paris, the equally specific yet forgotten moment in history, the way that Hugo makes his jokey inscriptions, reproduced *tel quel* in his text, stand as nuggets of historical or philosophical commentary. Usually, we guide students through a careful reading of this passage, noting that the lettering on the street sign described here may refer to Napoleon the great, but that "thirty years ago" calls attention to 1862, the moment of publication, when Napoleon III is in power and Hugo is in exile. The "osier," which once was alive and flexible enough to weave into the image of an emperor, has hardened into a shop sign. The Napoleon that Parisian readers are stuck with is, in fact, a basket case.

To help students get in the habit of looking for precise historical and geographic details and for instances when the text is self-consciously made to function as a device, we ask them to look for other descriptions of shop signs in this chapter and to consider how accounts of inscription and erasure connect the signs to their location and historical moment.

The story of how the Café Corinth got its name, with its emphasis on zigzag and ellipsis, directly follows several pages of description of the labyrinthine streets that make up its neighborhood, which allows us to connect the writing of the novel and the geography of the scene: "Au siècle dernier, le digne Natoire, l'un des maîtres fantasques . . . avait peint par reconnaissance une grappe de raisin de Corinthe sur le poteau rose. . . . De là ce nom, *Corinthe*. Rien n'est plus naturel aux ivrognes que les ellipses. L'ellipse est le zigzag de la phrase" 'In the last century Natoire, one of the whimsical masters . . . gratefully painted a bunch of Corinth grapes on the rose-colored post. . . . Hence the name Corinth. Nothing is more natural to drinkers than an ellipsis. The ellipsis is the zigzag of a phrase' (2: 440; 1084 [pt. 4, bk. 12, ch. 1]). Location (in this case, Les Halles before the arrival of the Rue Rambuteau) and textuality are made to echo each other in the lead-up to the barricade fighting. The focus on ellipses and on lost inscriptions is something we recall once we get to readings from Perec.

We spend a while on "Carpe Horas" 'Seize the Hours,' noticing how the rain as a physical manifestation of passing time has made the prosaic *"carpes au gras"* philosophical, and we note in passing that Hugo turns penury and vestiges of religious practice into fertile ground for uprising, especially among those who read Latin. Grantaire "y était entré à cause de *Carpe Horas* et y était retourné à cause des *Carpes au Gras*" 'had gone in because of *Carpe Horas*, and he returned because of the *Carpes au Gras*' (2: 442; 1085 [pt. 4, bk. 12, ch. 1]). In fact Grantaire, who sleeps through the barricade fighting in a drunken stupor, only to accompany Enjolras in his hero's death, is a character through whom the ordinary is generally made to portend. He eats a bad oyster, but it doesn't matter because though Grantaire doesn't know it yet, he will die before it can make him sick (2: 446; 1089 [pt. 4, bk. 12, ch. 2]). He does point out, though, that a revolution, like an oyster, can go down the wrong way (2: 450; 1092 [pt. 4, bk. 12, ch. 1]), presumably with similarly convulsive consequences for the social body.

The same bohemian logic that makes accidental Latin attract customers who will join an uprising characterizes Hugo's description of the musket shot that whizzes past Marius as he crosses Paris to join his friends. The bullet is "encore de la vie" 'still a sign of life' even as it leaves a hole in a nearby shop sign. "On voyait encore, en 1846, rue du Contrat-Social, au coin des piliers des halles, ce plat à barbe troué" 'This shaving bowl with the bullet hole could still be seen in 1846, in the Rue du Contrat Social, at the corner pillars of Les Halles' (2: 482; 1120 [pt. 4, bk. 13, ch. 1]). The fictional action and identifiable, politically named location are carefully conjoined.

The uprising Hugo chooses for *Les Misérables* is both precise historically and open to expansion as a fictional example of conflict in the interest of progress. Thomas Bouchet's book *Le roi et les barricades* and his contribution to the invaluable volume edited by Alain Corbin and Jean-Marie Mayeur, *La barricade*, sort out the extent to which Hugo's barricade is and is not faithful to what we know of the barricade fighting that took place in Les Halles in 1832. Though we don't assign specific readings from *La barricade*, we do often tell the story of Charles Jeanne's letter about the defense of the barricade at Saint-Merry, which surfaced in 2010 and was passed to Bouchet for editing and publication, casting significant new light on the uprising. Sometimes, if we are looking to emphasize the continuity of barricade practice over time, we assign the beginning of Mark Traugott's *The Insurgent Barricade* as preparatory reading, for its concept of social sorting as a purpose of barricades and for connections between earlier Parisian barricade events and those of 1832. Traugott's maps are useful for showing that, while Les Halles certainly saw barricade construction in the first part of the nineteenth century, Hugo did not choose a particularly established site of construction on which to imagine his.

To differentiate between which history Hugo gets from sources and which he makes up, we spend some time on chronology. Students are often skittish about dates, and nineteenth-century revolutions can be challenging for them to keep up with, whether or not they include uprisings. So we put 1832 on the board, reiterate that *this* is the fictional date of the barricade fighting, and that the reason they don't know about it is because it was a failed uprising. The revolution didn't happen. We sympathize with students about the challenges of keeping track of Hugo's accounts of other barricades from other times as he tells his story, and we point out that the regime changes that frame the fictional time of this very limited section of the novel took place in 1830 and 1848—dates that then look more familiar when students encounter them in scenes like the one in which Feuilly engraves "VIVENT LES PEUPLES!" at the barricade. Hugo specifies that "Ces trois mots, creusés dans le moellon avec un clou, se lisaient encore sur cette muraille en 1848" 'The three words, graven in stone with a nail, were still legible on that wall in 1848' (2: 550; 1177 [pt. 5, bk. 1, ch. 2]). Once students see how metaphorically tied together Hugo's places and characters, plot and principles are, they are less likely to see his digressions as unfortunate and more likely to see how they elaborate on the perspectives suggested by the fates of his characters.

To shore up student confidence about when Hugo's scene takes place, we sometimes pass around other translations of the novel, as well as Web printouts or DVDs whose jacket notes give the wrong date for the "revolution" covered in the book. A book jacket from a 1982 Penguin Classics edition says, "*Les Misérables* is a novel on an epic scale, moving inexorably from the eve of the battle of Waterloo to the July Revolution of 1830." Others refer to the uprising as the French Revolution. It is good to be an expert on a time and place that has been largely forgotten; students feel more secure retaining their one obscure date after having seen that not everyone knows about 1832. They may even get an inkling of the ways Hugo creates readerly complicity by explaining some little-known facts and showing how they became obscured. To emphasize this latter point, we turn to some of Hugo's examples of misinterpreted events, such as Gavroche's return from the rue de l'Homme-Armé. To the sergeant on guard, "Il était clair que l'Hydre de l'Anarchie était sortie de sa boîte et qu'elle se démenait dans le quartier" 'It was clear that the hydra of anarchy had gotten out of its box, and was raging in the neighborhood' (2: 536; 1164 [pt. 4, bk. 15, ch. 4]). As for the neighbors, "L'aventure de Gavroche, restée dans la tradition du quartier du Temple, est un des souvenirs les plus terribles des vieux bourgeois du Marais, et est intitulée dans leur mémoire: Attaque nocturne du poste de l'Imprimerie royale" 'Gavroche's adventure, preserved among the traditions of the quarter of the Temple, is one of the most terrible recollections of the old bourgeois of the Marais, and is entitled in their memory: "Nocturnal attack on the Post of the Imprimerie Royale"' (2: 538; 1167 [pt. 4, bk. 7, ch. 4]). On the one hand, Hugo engages attentive readers with his thoughts on progress by reminding them of failed steps and misinterpreted events on the way to 1848. On the other hand, he chooses dates and places obscure or fictional enough that careless or creative adaptations can make what they will of his tale of insurgency, ensuring its longevity, if not necessarily its accuracy.

Hugo also facilitates adaptation of his story of uprising by taking a long-term and international point of view toward the conflict of 1832. On his way to the barricade, Marius realizes that "La patrie se plaint, soit; mais l'humanité applaudit . . . Et puis, à voir les choses de plus haut encore, que viendrait-on parler de guerre civile? La guerre civile? qu'est-ce à dire? Est-ce qu'il y a une guerre étrangère? Est-ce que toute guerre entre hommes n'est pas la guerre entre frères?" 'The country laments, but humanity applauds . . . And then, looking at the matter from a still higher standpoint, why do men talk of civil war? Civil war? What does that mean? Is there any foreign war? Isn't every war fought between men, between brothers?' (2: 489; 1126 [pt. 5, bk. 13, ch. 3]).

At the barricade, even "la patrie" is traded for the more international "Patria." When teased about the identity of his mistress, Enjolras "murmur[s] in an undertone, 'Patria'" (2: 594; 1213 [pt. 5, bk. 1, ch. 14]). We roll our eyes together over the exaggerated sanctity of the figure, but we point out nonetheless that "Patria" is Latin—a pan-European language—and that this may be why Enjolras is not made to say "France" as Jean Prouvaire did, just before he was shot. Ideally, some students have encountered Benedict Anderson in a communications course and will find the idea of Latin as an international language familiar.

In the chapter called the "Death Throes of the Barricade," Hugo emphasizes that one can't hurry progress:

> Mais toute insurrection qui couche en joue un gouvernement ou un ré-
> gime vise plus haut . . . ce que combattaient les chefs de l'insurrection de
> 1832, et en particulier les jeunes enthousiastes de la rue de la Chanvrerie,
> ce n'était pas précisement Louis-Philippe. La plupart, causant à cœur ou-
> vert, rendaient justice aux qualités de ce roi mitoyen à la monarchie et à la
> révolution; aucun ne le haïssait. Mais ils attaquaient la branche cadette du
> droit divin dans Louis-Philippe comme ils en avaient attaqué la branche
> aînée dans Charles X.   (2: 624–25 [pt. 5, bk. 1, ch. 20])

> Every insurrection that takes aim at a government or a regime aims still
> higher . . . what the leaders of the insurrection of 1832, and particularly
> the young enthusiasts of the Rue de la Chanvrerie, fought against was not
> exactly Louis-Philippe. Frankly most of them honored the qualities of this
> king, midway between monarchy and revolution; none hated him. But
> they were attacking the younger branch of divine right in Louis-Philippe,
> as they had attacked the elder branch in Charles X.   (1239)

Lest students lose sight of the role that the text intends to play in recuperating the worthiness of the fits and starts of progress, the concluding paragraph of the same chapter reminds them, "Le livre que le lecteur a sous les yeux en ce moment, c'est, d'un bout à l'autre, dans son ensemble et dans ses détails . . . la marche du mal au bien, de l'injuste au juste . . . Point de départ: la matière, point d'arrivée: l'âme" 'The book the reader has now before his eyes—from one end to the other, in its whole and in its details . . . is the march from evil to good, from injustice to justice . . . Starting point: matter; goal: the soul' (2: 628; 1242 [pt. 5, bk. 1, ch. 20]). We note that the book *is* the march. It doesn't describe or advocate it; it enacts that march, be it through inscriptions or words in the mouths of *gamins* or little-known history or engaging characters.

In fact, its combination of those elements could be considered a kind of generic *bricolage* particularly appropriate in a scene in which hastily made barricades play such a prominent role. David Charles's essay in *La Barricade* combines history and aesthetics nicely through the concept of *bricolage* applied to Hugo's barricade scene. We gloss his article in class, sometimes assigning strong groups a selection from Claude Lévi-Strauss's *The Savage Mind* to read. Whether or not they have read Lévi-Strauss, we usually split students into groups and ask them to list what goes into the barricade on the Rue de la Chanvrerie (2: 462; 1102 [pt. 4, bk. 12, ch. 4]), what the one at the Faubourg Saint-Antoine in 1848 is composed of (2: 543; 1171 [pt. 5, bk. 1, ch. 1]), and to speculate on what these components have in common. We hope they will notice the humble, the local, the "used for purposes other than the original" quality. This way we can tell them about *bricolage* even if they have not read Lévi-Strauss (and his agenda, glorifying indigenous thought, is similar to Hugo's: glorifying the craft and guile of the dispossessed). It is an aesthetic, a repurposing of the familiar that finds its echoes in Rimbaud when we read his "Les Mains de Jeanne-Marie" 'The Hands of Jeanne-Marie' or "Ce qu'on dit au Poète à propos des fleurs" 'What the Poet is Told on the Subject of Flowers' (both from 1871) in relation to the Commune (Rimbaud 85–114).

One of the main figures of craft and guile on the barricade is, of course, Gavroche. Students usually want to know how old he is. He is twelve (1: 755; 593 [pt. 3, bk. 1, ch. 13]). We try to get students to identify what makes Gavroche useful at the barricade—his petty crime being the first answer. It is because he has loitered that he recognizes and condemns Javert (2: 471; 1111 [pt. 4, bk. 12, ch. 7]) and because he has stolen that he knows the virtues of a broken window better than his elders do (2: 462; 1102 [pt. 4, bk. 12, ch. 4]). Here, we look forward to Baudelaire's prose poem "The Eyes of the Poor" (*Le Spleen de Paris*), in which glasses (*verres*) are homonyms for verses (*vers*) and serve as taunting and poetic manifestation of property. In his series of chapters describing the *gamin* as a social type, Hugo contends that "peindre l'enfant, c'est peindre la ville" 'To depict the child is to depict the city' (1: 754; 592 [pt. 3, bk. 1, ch. 12]), and indeed, Gavroche's language gets to the point even more directly than the inscriptions with which we begin. Gavroche calls Cosette what she is: "Chosette" 'little thing' (translated as 'Mamselle What's-her-name'), which usually elicits classroom debate about Cosette and her role or lack thereof (2: 530; 1159 [pt. 4, bk. 15, ch. 2]). His famous song, with its refrain about "La faute à Voltaire" and "la faute à Rousseau" is probably pretty accurate, given his involvement with a company of educated bohemian revolutionaries, who are more likely to have read Voltaire and Rousseau than he is (2: 597; 1216 [pt. 5, bk. 1, ch. 15]). While students aren't always able to make that connection, they are, with a little prompting, able to see echoes of "Let them eat cake" in the next chapter, when Gavroche's little brothers fish sodden brioche intended for a swan from the Luxembourg's pool. If students miss the future political implications of such a situation, we attend to the slang that the boys picked up from Gavroche: "L'aîné fit deux parts de la brioche, une grosse et une petite, prit la petite pour lui, donna la grosse à son petit frère, et lui dit:—Colle-toi ça dans le fusil" 'The eldest broke the brioche in two pieces, one large and one small, took the small one for himself, gave the large one to his little brother, and said to him, "Poke that in your gun"' (2: 608; 1226 [pt. 5, bk. 1, ch. 16]). A *misérable*, Gavroche is the voice of life as it is in the Parisian streets—small, impertinent, disrespectful of the law. Though he has died, his language persists in the novel and in his brothers' speech. If his words are Parisian street life made text, the sewer, where Valjean and Marius wind up, is the unvarnished material account of lives that have been.

By the time students read Hugo's passage about the haunted corridors of the sewers, "partout la putridité et le miasma; ça et là un soupirail où Villon dedans cause avec Rabelais dehors" 'putrescence and miasma everywhere; here and there a breathing-hole through which Villon inside chats with Rabelais outside' (2: 651; 1261 [pt. 5, bk. 2, ch. 2]), they have read Villon's *The Testament* and can see how his images of illegal activities redeemed or revenged through literature earns him a place in Hugo's scene.

Hugo's elaboration "L'égout, c'est la conscience de la ville. Tout y converge, et s'y confronte. Dans ce lieu livide, il y a des ténèbres mais il n'y a plus de secrets. Chaque chose a sa forme vraie, ou du moins sa forme définitive. Le tas d'ordures a cela pour lui qu'il n'est pas menteur" 'The sewer is the conscience of the city. All things converge into it and are confronted with one another. In this lurid place, there is darkness, but there are no secrets. Each thing has its real form, or at least its definitive form. It can be said for the garbage heap that it is no liar' (2: 651; 1261 [pt. 5, bk. 2, ch. 2]) is reminiscent of Villon's insistence on the mixing of bones regardless of station in life in the charnel houses of the Cimetière des Saints-Innocents (*Selected Poems* 177, 191) and on the importance of compassion in his "Ballade of the Men Hanged" (241). One of the questions that activate student memories of their earlier reading and discussion is, Why Villon inside and Rabelais out? What does that combination suggest about Hugo's reading of the two authors? Usually the sense that crime can land a person who has rejected or ignored laws and is therefore in trouble in the sewer emerges first. And yet Villon is no Thénardier. To move Villon's role from the criminal to the potentially redemptive, we recall Jane Taylor's reading of the "Ballade pour prier Notre Dame" and the "Ballade de la Grosse Margot" as a paired literary questioning of what is forgivable by God (139–62). Though this is an argument we have usually glossed for students instead of assigning it as reading, it is one that helps them think more carefully about why Villon belongs on the inside of the sewer, in the space of "La Boue, mais l'âme" 'Muck, but Soul' (2: 668; 1276 [pt. 5, bk. 3, ch. 1]).

Rabelais on the outside is harder—as the reading from Rabelais itself is. We read the first twenty chapters of *Gargantua* with the introduction to Bakhtin's *Rabelais and His World* early in the semester. Usually students much prefer Bakhtin to Rabelais, so they are ready to talk about the carnivalesque aspect of the sewer description and the fecundity of the low. Gargantua drowning Parisians in urine provides a direct link to ideas of how excrement affects life in Paris and how the city deals with it, and, in some versions of the course, Freud's ideas on the relation between human waste and gold (in "On Transformations in Instinct") are brought into class discussion of Hugo's thoughts on the "vingt-cinq millions (par an)" 'twenty five millions (a year)' that Paris throws into the sea (2: 645; 1256 [pt. 5, bk. 2, ch. 1]).

Even so, the long descriptions of the old sewer, the newer sewer, and the political philosophy of sewage treatment can try students' patience and attention, so we do two things to keep the setting compelling. We look at excerpts from Josée Dayan's television miniseries of *Les Misérables*, in which this scene was filmed in those very sewers, paying attention to how light is used to convey some of the ideas that Hugo explains. We visit the sewers, where the sense of a parallel city strikes students, often shifting their perspectives on daily life in Paris. The narrative of the tour, which mentions Hugo once but has more to do with how the sewers work today, seems to help them think through the uses, both pragmatic and literary, of the underground network of the city they are getting to know.

If fading inscriptions mark the walls of Paris with traces of the events Hugo portrays, the sewer is legible through scraps of cloth. The tour of the present sewer sometimes mentions that after abortion became legal in 1975, far fewer babies were found in the sewer—and sure enough Hugo's description of the old sewer's contents includes "un fœtus livide [qui] roule envelopé dans des paillettes qui ont dansé le mardi gras dernier à l'Opéra" 'a livid foetus turns, wrapped in spangles that danced at the Opéra last Mardi Gras' (2: 652; 1262 [pt. 5, bk. 2, ch. 2]). That which cannot yet come to term, be it an illegitimate baby or an unsuccessful uprising, is evacuated by the sewer. Valjean and Marius have, after all, come from a premature barricade: "Aussi la barricade de la rue de la Chanvrerie n'était-elle qu'une ébauche et qu'un embryon, comparée aux deux barricades colosses que nous venons d'esquisser" 'the barricade of the rue de la Chanvrerie was no more than a rough draft, an embryo, compared with the two colossal barricades we have just sketched' (2: 549; 1176 [pt. 5, bk. 1, ch. 2]). In the sewer made text, bodies are enveloped with cloth marking the social conditions of their loves and of their deaths, such as a foetus in spangles, and the Marquise de Laubespine's embroidered linen indicating that Marat's remains had been by (2: 659; 1268 [pt. 5, bk. 2, ch. 4]). Marius, too, saved from death in the sewer, unwittingly loses his stitched initials to Thénardier, setting up the eventual revelation of what Valjean has done for him.

If our selection begins with willow stiffened into a parody of the emperor, it ends with an inflexible character undone by the iterations of morality, which he is finally unable to bear. Incapable of softening his perspective, Javert pitches himself into the swirl of the Seine, joining the "tutoiement" of matter that has been brewing in the sewers (2: 652; 1262 [pt. 5, bk. 2, ch. 2]).

Both the barricade and the sewer are spaces of dilation. Putting his life in danger allows Marius to experience "une dilatation de pensée propre au voisin-age de la tombe" 'The expansion of thought peculiar to the proximity to the grave' (2: 488; 1126 [pt. 4, bk. 13, ch. 3]). Similarly, in the sewers, Valjean's eyes adjust: "La pupille se dilate dans la nuit et finit par y trouver du jour, de même que l'âme se dilate dans le Malheur et finit par y trouver Dieu" 'The pupil dilates in the night and at last finds day in it, even as the soul dilates in misfortune, and at last finds God in it' (2: 671; 1178–79 [pt. 5, bk. 3, ch. 1]). Dilation, a reflexive, adaptive opening in a time and space of darkness, is Hugo's project in the parts of *Les Misérables* that we cover in our course Paris through Its Books. We hope to achieve some similar intellectual opening without facing such trying conditions.

NOTE

[1] The Fahnestock and MacAfee edition gives the inscription in French and its translation in a footnote: "Napoleon is made / All of willow braid" (1082).

Misery and Militancy: Hugo's Social and Political Engagement in *Les Misérables*

Brian Martin

In its condemnation of poverty, misogyny, and violence, *Les Misérables* is a powerful forum for what francophones call *engagement* (or what anglophones might call *activism* or *militancy*) against human suffering. With his celebrated preface to *Les Misérables*, Hugo defines his novel as a denunciation of the miseries of both his own century and those to follow: "tant que les trois problèmes du siècle, la dégradation de l'homme . . . la déchéance de la femme . . . l'atrophie de l'enfant . . . ne seront pas résolus . . . tant qu'il y aura sur la terre ignorance et misère, des livres de la nature de celui-ci pourront ne pas être inutiles" 'so long as the three problems of the century—the degradation of man . . . the ruin of woman . . . and the atrophy of childhood . . .—are not solved . . . so long as ignorance and misery remain on earth, there should be a need for books such as this' (1: 31; xvii). To highlight Hugo's social and political engagement in the novel, I discuss his denunciation of war and his condemnation of misogyny as two examples of his broader campaign against misery and inequality. With this approach to Hugo's novel, instructors can help students better understand the nineteenth-century specificity and the twentieth- and twenty-first-century vitality of *Les Misérables* as a beacon for political engagement and social justice.

At Williams College, I teach *Les Misérables* in two courses: an introductory course titled War and Resistance in Nineteenth- and Twentieth-Century France, in which I teach Hugo's Waterloo episode (pt. 2, bk. 1) as a paradigm of antiwar discourse, and an advanced seminar titled Desperate Housewives and Extreme Makeovers in the French Nineteenth-Century Novel, in which I teach the novel's entire first part ("Fantine") as a model of Hugo's engagement against the subjugation of women and the poor. In these courses, I ask students to consider how *Les Misérables* bears witness to the miseries of war and misogyny in nineteenth-century France, and how it serves as inspiration for later struggles against human suffering.

I begin these courses by speaking about Hugo's broad political engagement as a writer and legislator (especially from 1848 to 1885) against the death penalty, the exploitation of women, and Napoleonic despotism (under both Napoleon I and III), and his defense of free speech, universal suffrage, public education, and republican democracy. Hugo's political engagement is exemplified in his celebrated speech—often called the *Discours sur la misère*—to the National Legislative Assembly on 9 July 1849, when he called on his fellow members of parliament to provide better public assistance to the poor: "[J]e suis de ceux qui pensent et qui affirment qu'on peut détruire la misère. Remarquez-le bien, messieurs, je ne dis pas diminuer, amoindrir, limiter, circonscrire, je dis détruire . . . Détruire la misère!" 'I am among those who think and affirm that we can destroy misery. Mark you, gentlemen, I do not say diminish, reduce, limit, contain, I say destroy . . . Destroy misery!' (*Œuvres complètes: Politique* 204). Over a decade before the publication of *Les Misérables*, Hugo had urged his colleagues to take political action against human suffering: "[J]e voudrais que cette assemblée n'eût qu'une seule âme pour marcher à ce grand but, à ce but magnifique, à ce but sublime, l'abolition de la misère!" 'I would like this assembly, in one united spirit, to march towards this great goal, this magnificent goal, this sublime goal, the abolition of misery!' (205).

I then ask students to consider the nineteenth-century miseries that Hugo dramatizes in *Les Misérables* as a lens for better understanding our own confrontations with contemporary suffering. Despite the vital role of the novel's numerous adaptations (from film to musical theater and digital media) in bringing *Les Misérables* to new generations, there is also the danger that—amid such adaptations' glamorous actors and lush visuals—students often forget the misery in *misérables*.[1] While many of my students know the musical by Alain Boublil and Claude-Michel Schönberg (1985) and its lavish screen adaptation by Tom Hooper (2012), I ask them to watch scenes from other film adaptations to help them compare nineteenth-century and latter-day miseries, such as Claude Lelouch's *Les Misérables* (1995), in which Henri (a version of Valjean) helps the Jewish refugees Elisa and Salomé (versions of Fantine and Cosette) flee the Gestapo in Nazi-occupied France. I then invite my students to compare the human suffering in *Les Misérables* with contemporary social struggles. When three hundred Bangladeshi factory workers died in a fire (making cheap clothing for Western markets) in 2013, when Ebola orphaned thousands of children in Sierra Leone in 2014, and when thousands of African and Middle Eastern refugees perished in the Mediterranean Sea in 2014 and 2015, journalists from Montréal to New York wrote about a new generation of what they explicitly called *misérables*.[2] My own students have compared Gavroche with protesters of the Arab Spring (2011), Fantine with sweatshop workers in Cambodia and Bangladesh (2013), Valjean with African American victims of police brutality in New York and Missouri (2014), Cosette with Ebola orphans in Liberia and Sierra Leone (2014–15), and the Thénardiers with human traffickers of migrants from Mexico and refugees from Syria (2011–15). While it is important to avoid generalizations, acknowledge cultural differences, and stress historical specificity, such comparisons help students make a personal connection with the text and better understand both Hugo's political engagement in nineteenth-century France and the novel's persistent role in creating empathy, confronting human misery, and fighting social inequality in contemporary culture.

To demonstrate this approach to teaching Hugo's militancy against misery, I will now examine two examples of social engagement in *Les Misérables* that I teach in my courses: the novel's denunciation of war and its condemnation of misogyny.

Hugo's critique of the carnage at Waterloo exemplifies his broader pacifism and indictment of military violence. While Hugo expresses admiration for Napoleonic soldiers like his father (especially in earlier works, such as the 1827 "Ode à la colonne de la place Vendôme"), Hugo is increasingly critical of war, militarism, and Napoleonic despotism. In his 1849 address to the *Congrès de la paix* in Paris, Hugo describes his utopian and pacifist vision for a future "États-Unis d'Europe" 'United States of Europe,' where "les boulets et les bombes seront remplacés par les votes" 'bullets and bombs will be replaced by votes' (*Actes et paroles I* 299–307).[3]

In my course War and Resistance, we begin by comparing the Waterloo episodes in Stendhal's *La Chartreuse de Parme* (with its focus on individual experience) and in Hugo's *Les Misérables* (with its emphasis on mass misery) in order to discuss Hugo's opposition to violence and warfare. We then consider Hugo's antiwar discourse as a model for future pacifist texts, from the Napoleonic and Franco-Prussian Wars to the First and Second World Wars. Before we examine the Waterloo episode in class (through close reading and textual analysis, in small- and large-group discussion), I explain to students (with an introductory lecture, visual images, and handouts) the broader narrative, historical, and biographical contexts for Hugo's account of Waterloo. This approach to teaching Hugo's "Waterloo" can be adapted to introductory courses (for which the manageable reading load is an advantage) and to advanced seminars in both history and literature. For specialized courses on Hugo, the Waterloo episode is also an important example of the Hugolian digression.[4]

Narratively, Hugo's Waterloo contextualizes the relationship between Colonel Pontmercy and "Sergeant" Thénardier, the military fathers of the revolutionaries Marius and Gavroche, who will later become fraternal partisans on the barricades in Paris. Historically, the French defeat to the English and Prussians at Waterloo on 18 June 1815 marked the end of the First Empire (1804–15) and the Napoleonic Wars (1799–1815). Biographically, the Waterloo episode can be considered Hugo's homage to his military father. Having served in the royal and revolutionary armies, Léopold Hugo rose to the rank of general in Napoleon's *Grande Armée* following his service in Bavaria, Naples, and Spain.

Raised as an army brat with his brothers Abel and Eugène, Victor accompanied his father to military posts in France and Italy, where Léopold Hugo formally enrolled his sons in his regiment. During the chaotic and disastrous retreat from Spain in 1812, the ten-year-old Victor witnessed public executions and war atrocities that haunted him and influenced his later engagement against the death penalty (in *Le Dernier jour d'un condamné* and *Les Misérables*) and political despotism (during the Second Empire of Napoleon III). In his "Ode à la colonne de la place Vendôme," in which he honors Napoleonic officers like his father, Hugo describes himself as a child soldier and veteran: "Moi, qui fus un soldat quand j'étais un enfant" 'I, who was a soldier when I was a child' (*Œuvres poétiques* 1: 400). Even though Victor Hugo was neither a combatant nor present at Napoleon's final defeat in 1815, his Waterloo episode in *Les Misérables* is nevertheless a powerful account by a survivor of the Napoleonic Wars.

In his version of Waterloo, Hugo examines the historic and human costs of this epic defeat by dramatizing collective loss and suffering on the battlefield. This stands in contrast to Stendhal's version of Waterloo in *La Chartreuse de Parme*

(1839), which famously centers on individual suffering and confusion. Stendhal's focus on the graphic horrors of warfare and the disillusionment of his young protagonist Fabrice del Dongo was an important innovation in military fiction.[5] Using the techniques of nineteenth-century realism to describe the agonies and atrocities of warfare, Stendhal redefined modern military fiction as a denunciation rather than a glorification of battle. Told through the eyes of a confused and terrified young man, Stendhal's Waterloo emphasizes the individual horror and suffering of war.

In contrast, Hugo's version of Waterloo in *Les Misérables* recounts the battle in epic terms that mythologize Napoleon as a colossus defeated by divine intervention, whose armies suffer massive losses before filling mass graves. While there are several individual figures in Hugo's Waterloo, especially Napoleon and his General Cambronne, they serve as titanic heroes in the face of epic defeat. To demonstrate Hugo's emphasis on epic loss, I ask students to analyze Hugo's narrative technique by close-reading passages (as the following paragraphs will demonstrate) that link Napoleon's defeat to divine intervention and cosmic collapse.

Comparing Waterloo in 1815 with Agincourt in 1415, Hugo contextualizes these French debacles within a broad historical landscape and attributes Napoleon's defeat to the will of God: "S'il n'avait pas plu dans la nuit du 17 au 18 juin 1815, l'avenir de l'Europe était changé . . . [L]a providence n'a eu besoin que d'un peu de pluie, et un nuage . . . a suffi pour l'écroulement d'un monde" 'If it had not rained on the night of June 17 to 18, 1815, the future of Europe would have been different . . . [P]rovidence needed only a little rain, and [a] cloud . . . for the collapse of a world" (1: 412–13; 309 [pt. 2, bk. 1, ch. 3]). The evening rain had made it difficult for Napoleon's men to move cannon on the muddy field. While Napoleon waited for the morning sun to dry out the ground before getting his artillery into position, the Prussians arrived to reinforce their English allies.

In Hugo's Waterloo, Napoleon is thus toppled by divine intervention: "Dans la bataille de Waterloo, il y a plus que du nuage, il y a du météore. Dieu a passé" 'In the battle of Waterloo, there is more than a cloud, there was a meteor. God passed' (1: 449; 340 [pt. 2, bk. 1, ch. 13]). Challenged by God himself, Napoleon cannot win: "Était-il possible que Napoléon gagnât cette bataille? Nous répondons que non . . . Il était temps que ce vaste homme tombât . . . Napoléon avait été dénoncé dans l'infini, et sa chute était décidée. Il gênait Dieu" 'Might it have been possible for Napoleon to win this battle? We answer no . . . It was time for this titan to fall . . . Napoleon had been impeached before the Infinite and his fall was decreed. He annoyed God' (1: 436–37; 329–30 [pt. 2, bk. 1, ch. 9]). For Hugo, the downfall of Napoleon and his empire is a colossal and galactic defeat: "Waterloo n'est point une bataille; c'est le changement de front de l'univers" 'Waterloo is not a battle; it is the changing face of the universe' (1: 437; 330 [pt. 2, bk. 1, ch. 9]). While Stendhal's Waterloo highlights the experience of a lowly individual soldier, Hugo's Waterloo dramatizes the cosmic collapse of a titan and his vast empire.

Beyond divine intervention and epic defeat, Hugo's Waterloo also emphasizes bloodshed, slaughter, and human suffering. Hugo thus generates the reader's empathy by using a narrative technique that moves from Napoleon to his soldiers, from Romantic tragedy to realist carnage, from celestial condemnation to sepulchral decomposition. In his own empathy with Napoleon's three million conscripted soldiers—of whom 450,000 to 1,750,000 died in combat, from wounds, or from disease—Hugo honors their collective misery.[6] To help students understand this narrative shift from Napoleon's epic fall to his soldiers' mutilated bodies, I ask them to analyze (through close reading in class and in their writing) the text's multiple descriptions of mass graves.

Surveying the field, Hugo considers the countless men buried in the Ohain trench, following their disastrous fall into what has become a mass grave: "s'effondrer dans un abîme, tomber, rouler, écraser, être écrasé . . . des hommes sous soi, des chevaux sur soi, se débattre en vain, les os brisés" 'to plunge into an abyss, to fall, to roll, to crush, to be crushed . . . men under you, horses over you, to struggle in vain, your bones broken' (1: 468; 355–56 [pt. 2, bk. 1, ch. 19]). In the ruins of the Château Hougomont, other mass graves are found in the orchard, the courtyard, and the depths of a well that is "plein de squelettes" 'full of skeletons' (1: 408; 306 [pt. 2, bk. 1, ch. 2]), since "Après l'action, on eut une hâte, enterrer les cadavres. . . . Ce puits était profond, on en fit un sépulcre. On y jeta trois cents morts . . . [O]n entendit sortir du puits des voix faibles" 'After the action, there was a haste to bury the corpses. . . . This well was deep, and they made it a sepulcher. Three-hundred dead were thrown into it . . . [F]eeble voices were heard calling out from the well' (1: 409; 306 [pt. 2, bk. 1, ch. 2]). In documenting such atrocities, Hugo honors those who were buried alive, gives voice to those feeble cries silenced in mass graves, and commemorates (through references to the Greeks and Romans) fallen warriors on battlefields stretching back to antiquity.[7]

Hugo's focus on the mass suffering of these military *misérables* is also reflected in Cambronne's defiant cry of "Merde!" 'Shit!' in the face of overwhelming enemy attack and defeat (1: 451; 341 [pt. 2, bk. 1, ch. 14]). Cambronne's "Merde!" represents the vulgar vocabulary of soldiers but is also a sign of resistance and courage, and a symbol of the rotting bodies on the battlefield. This trope of human excrement and waste permeates *Les Misérables*: from the corpses at Waterloo to the Parisian sewers through which Valjean carries Marius to those *misérables* such as Fantine, Cosette, and Valjean who (as workers and servants, prostitutes and prisoners) are treated like refuse in the slums and prisons of nineteenth-century France.[8] In this way, Hugo's Waterloo is not merely a digression in *Les Misérables* but an integral part of this landscape of misery, in which the low are raised high, the suffering are transformed, and the excluded find what Victor Brombert calls Hugolian "salvation from below" (*Victor Hugo* 86–139). As he concludes his Waterloo episode (with the war profiteer Thénardier inadvertently waking the wounded Pontmercy from the dead), Hugo moves from these rotting warriors of the past toward a future generation of soldiers (Thénardier's son

Gavroche and Pontmercy's son Marius) who will continue the fight against misery, poverty, and oppression on the barricades of Paris.

In contrast to the military miseries that students analyze in my war seminar, we examine Hugo's engagement with feminine misery and misogyny in my advanced course on the nineteenth-century novel. Comparing Fantine in *Les Misérables* with Emma in Flaubert's *Madame Bovary* and Gervaise in Zola's *L'Assommoir*, we consider the misogynist effects of marriage, poverty, and prostitution. To frame the discussion of Fantine, I give an introductory lecture on prostitution in nineteenth-century France, in which I discuss studies by Alexandre Parent-Duchâtelet, Charles Bernheimer, and Jann Matlock (*Scenes of Seduction*), as well as a wide range of literary texts on prostitutes, courtesans, and the demimonde, from Balzac's *Splendeurs et misères des courtisanes* to Maupassant's *Boule de suif* and Zola's *Nana*.

In class discussion and in preparation for their written assignments, I ask students to analyze Hugo's emphasis on Fantine's physical decline as the outward expression of her social exploitation. As a young woman, "Fantine était la joie . . . la pudeur . . . l'innocence" 'Fantine was joy . . . modesty . . . innocence' (1: 188–89; 126–27 [pt. 1, bk. 3, ch. 3]), with "la forme d'une nymphe et la pudeur d'une nonne" 'the form of a nymph and the modesty of a nun' (1: 201; 137 [pt. 1, bk. 3, ch. 7]). Highlighting her beautiful hair and teeth, Hugo writes that "Elle avait de l'or et des perles pour dot; mais son or était sur sa tête et ses perles étaient dans sa bouche" 'For dowry, she had gold and pearls; but the gold was on her head and the pearls were in her mouth' (1: 183; 122 [pt. 1, bk. 3, ch. 2]).

Abandoned by her lover, Félix Tholomyès, and forced to raise their child alone, Fantine later loses her factory job, where her coworkers are "jalouse[s] de ses cheveux blonds et ses dents blanches" 'jealous of her fair hair and white teeth' (1: 250; 178 [pt. 1, bk. 5, ch. 8]). Fantine must then resort to self-mutilation by selling her teeth and hair to support her daughter, whom she is proud to have "habillée de mes cheveux" 'clothed [with] my hair' (1: 256; 183 [pt. 1, bk. 5, ch. 10]). This pattern of poverty and decline is perpetuated from mother to daughter, as Cosette is exploited by the Thénardiers and degenerates from a girl who was once "si jolie et si fraîche" 'so fresh and pretty' (1: 225; 157 [pt. 1, bk. 4, ch. 3]) to an abused child servant who is miserably "maigre et blême" 'thin and pale' (1: 225; 157 [pt. 1, bk. 4, ch. 3]).

Devoid of income and support, Fantine is forced into prostitution, sexually exploited, publicly humiliated, and physically assaulted by men like Bamatabois, who mocks her in the street, crying "Que tu es laide. . . . Tu n'as pas de dents!" 'My, but you're ugly! . . . You've lost your . . . teeth!' (1: 264; 189–90 [pt. 1, bk. 5, ch. 12]). Arrested by Javert, Fantine is punished by a misogynist justice system that blames women for being exploited instead of criminalizing the men who abandon, violate, and abuse them. Having emphasized Fantine's outward physical and social decline, Hugo insists on her inner strength and beauty, as she pleads with Javert for the sake of her child: "La grande douleur est un rayon divin et terrible qui transfigure les misérables. À ce moment-là, la Fantine était redevenue belle" 'Great grief is a divine and terrible radiance that transfigures the wretched. At that instant, Fantine had again become beautiful' (1: 268; 193 [pt. 1, bk. 5, ch. 13]).

In his defense of Fantine, Hugo defines prostitution as a form of social misery and economic slavery that is perpetuated by institutional misogyny: "Qu'est-ce que c'est que cette histoire de Fantine? C'est la société achetant une esclave. À qui? À la misère . . . [L'esclavage] existe toujours, mais il ne pèse plus que sur la femme, et il s'appelle prostitution" 'What is this story of Fantine about? It is about society buying a slave. From whom? From misery . . . [Slavery] still exists, but now it weighs only on women, and it is called prostitution' (1: 261; 187 [pt. 1, bk. 5, ch. 11]). Hugo concludes "Fantine" by summarizing this first part of Les Misérables as a tale "d'un forçat et d'une fille publique" '[about] a convict and a woman of the streets' (1: 400; 299 [pt. 1, bk. 8, ch. 5]). Here, Hugo links the miseries of Fantine and Valjean through their shared experience of poverty and persecution. Buried in "la fosse commune" 'the potter's field' (1: 400; 299 [pt. 1, bk. 8, ch. 5]), Fantine joins countless other prostitutes and nameless misérables: "Elle fut jetée à la fosse publique. Sa tombe ressembla à son lit" 'She was thrown into the public pit. Her grave was like her bed' (1: 400; 300 [pt. 1, bk. 8, ch. 5]). Fantine and her grave bedfellows thus recall the past suffering of Napoleon's soldiers who were buried in analogous mass graves at Waterloo. In this way, Hugo draws a connection between the evils of poverty and misogyny and the miseries of warfare and violence.

As I teach in my course War and Resistance, the influence of Hugo's Waterloo and its mass graves can be seen in numerous later texts and contexts, from Jean Cocteau's First World War trench novel Thomas l'imposteur to Elie Wiesel's Holocaust memoir La Nuit. And as I have discovered during more than a decade teaching this course, Hugo's denunciation of war in Les Misérables continues—as Hugo hoped in the novel's preface—to inspire new comparisons and readers. One of the students in my war seminar had been a child survivor of the war in Burundi (1993–2005). Like the Rwandan genocide in 1994, the civil war in neighboring Burundi triggered genocidal ethnic cleansing among Hutus and Tutsis, which forced my student—whom I'll call Mathieu—and his family to flee for their lives. Moved by the childhood misery of Hugo's Cosette and boy soldier Gavroche, Mathieu recalled the suffering of Tutsi children who were butchered and Hutu youth who became child soldiers.[9]

For Mathieu, Hugo's condemnation of military violence in Les Misérables offered a context for articulating his own experiences of war. From the mass graves in the Ohain trench and the Hougomont well to the slaughter of Gavroche on the barricades in Paris, Mathieu found a model for describing the mass graves and carnage of the genocide in Burundi. In a moving final essay, he compared two different sets of misérables. Admitting that "ce texte m'est trop personnel" 'this text is too personal for me,' Mathieu set out to "parler des gens de ce siècle qui jouaient le même rôle que les personnages dans Les Misérables" 'speak about people from this century who played the same role as characters in Les Misérables.' Arguing that "Les Myriels et les Madeleines . . . ne sont pas aussi nombreux que les Cosettes, les Javerts, les Valjeans et les Thénardiers"

'Myriels and Madeleines . . . are not as numerous as Cosettes, Javerts, Valjeans, and Thénardiers,' Mathieu recounted how Burundian *misérables* struggled to survive in a Hugolian universe of violence and cruelty, punctuated by lifesaving acts of generosity, self-sacrifice, and courage.

It is common for all kinds of students to identify with the *misérables* in their own lives and cultures, to find in Hugo's text and life a model for political and social engagement, and, as Isabel Roche writes, "to ask ourselves why Victor Hugo still matters" (2). While students in my war seminar compare Hugo's Waterloo with other examples of military violence, students in my course on the nineteenth-century novel often compare the exploitation of Fantine and Cosette with current questions on misogyny, from prostitution and sexual assault to child abuse and economic slavery. For these students, Fantine's struggle as a single mother forced into prostitution resonates with contemporary issues on teenage pregnancy, working mothers, institutional misogyny, sexual exploitation, and even campus rape.

In asking students to compare Hugo's novel with the *misérables* in their own lives and communities, teachers can help students understand the nineteenth-century context as well as the twentieth- and twenty-first-century legacy of *Les Misérables*. With this approach, students can better comprehend how Hugo's characters have, as Roche argues, "reverberated in the world in ways that take them beyond the page" and "surpassed long ago the borders of their textual representation" (179). By examining Hugo's goal to illuminate what he describes in his preface as the nineteenth-century problem of human degradation, students can also appreciate Hugo's visionary call to combat future suffering. In this way, we can help students see *Les Misérables* as a modern epic and textual model for empathy and solidarity, engagement and activism, misery and militancy.

NOTES

[1] For more on the novel's many adaptations, see Grossman and Stephens, Les Misérables *and Its Afterlives*.

[2] See Desjardins; Gettleman; Truffaut, *"Les Misérables*: Drame au Bangladesh" and "*Les Misérables*: Des millions de migrants."

[3] Philippe Régnier documents Hugo's pacifism at length.

[4] Detailed analysis of Hugo's Waterloo can be found in Descotes, *Victor Hugo* 187–223; Brombert, *Victor Hugo* 86–112; Martin 126–47; see also Lerner's essay in this volume.

[5] This contrast between Hugo's and Stendhal's versions of Waterloo is outlined in Bersani 104; Brombert, *Victor Hugo* 155; and Brosman 95–97.

[6] For more on casualties in Napoleon's armies, see Schom 789; Blond 511.

[7] Brombert speaks of "Hugo's recurrent terror of being buried alive" (128), which Yves Gohin calls "la récurrence de l'image de l'engloutissement" 'the recurring image of engulfment in the novel (*Victor Hugo* 922n1; my trans.).

[8] The scatological dimensions of *Les Misérables* are documented in Brombert 108–12; Desné 325–27; Rosa, "Jean Valjean."

[9] For moving accounts of the genocide in Burundi, see Kidder; and Tuhabonye and Brozek.

"Les horizons du rêve": Hugo's Utopianism

Daniel Sipe

Few historical novels have proposed a more complete, nuanced, or theoretically profound account of nineteenth-century social utopianism than Victor Hugo's *Les Misérables*. From his depictions of the purveyors of various "brands" of utopian social philosophy to his portrayal of the fictional utopian cenacle, Les Amis de l'ABC, we are to understand that these "confesseurs de l'utopie" are no less than "les glorieux combattants de l'avenir" 'the glorious combatants of the future, the professors of Utopia' (2: 622; 1237 [pt. 5, bk. 1, ch. 20]). Utopianism, then, is not only a suitable means of framing the long revolutionary episode that occupies the last third of the novel, it is also an ideal lens through which to contemplate and understand a cluster of key Hugolian concepts and characters.

In this essay, I provide a context and an organizational framework that will allow instructors to describe and analyze various forms of utopian praxis as they are delineated in *Les Misérables*. I document the rise of the phenomenon as it unfolds in a period roughly extending from the French Revolution to the apex of social utopian activity under the July Monarchy. I map out the broader stakes of Hugo's position and suggest strategies for teaching the three primary varieties of utopianism: visionary utopianism, the utopianism of progress, and revolutionary utopianism. In a final section, I offer a theory concerning the role utopianism plays in Hugo's worldview, specifically as it relates to the author's understanding of the forces of history.

In furnishing its astonishing account of utopianism, *Les Misérables* reveals itself to be an inquiry into the nature of our collective imagination, into the possibilities utopianism holds for social transformation, and into the pitfalls of our overreaching desires. Hugo's utopianism will surely spark important conversations about the relation between aesthetics and politics, desire and subjectivity, imagination and social change. These essential matters can incite creative and often passionate responses from students and can bring them closer to the emotional currents that motivate many of Hugo's characters. More broadly, this approach has the advantage of reasserting the importance and historical significance of the utopian imagination to a generation of readers who must contemplate its ebullient (and tragic) forms from across the chasm of the dystopian twentieth century.

When embarking on the study of Hugo's utopianism, instructors should be aware that students do not typically equate the term with the "applied" social systems that proliferated across nineteenth-century Europe. Instead, students tend to fall back on the tradition of literary fantasies depicting perfected societies existing in the margins of the known world. Here you may choose to remind your students that Hugo and his contemporaries were concerned with the radical social transformation of their own world and not with utopian alterity as an ersatz, trope, or ironic critique of societal values and customs.

One effective way of approaching the problematic distinction that the nineteenth century was attempting to make between the literary history of Utopia and the socioscientific forms of utopianism that had mostly replaced them is to propose—somewhat provocatively—that the difference is that which distinguishes stories from systems. Nineteenth-century utopianism is not primarily a literary mode of discourse, and sometimes isn't even a discourse at all. Rather, it's a diverse, multidisciplinary cultural praxis, a vast and ambitious project aimed at interpreting, organizing, and ultimately optimizing the social world. Such is the mind-set of the utopians who populate Hugo's novel and, indeed, who made up the aspiring classes across Europe during his time.

In England, Germany, and France utopian designers such as Robert Owen, Johann Georg Rapp, and Étienne Cabet had developed complex (if ultimately quixotic) blueprints for the rational perfection of social life. These utopian founders, whose role was often equal parts managerial and messianic, built model societies in Europe and America in an effort to prove the viability of their systems. As Michèle Riot-Sarcey has remarked, the problem was ultimately that these elaborate systems had become simple talismans diverting attention from the difficult work of inciting real social transformation. Echoing the previously delineated critiques of Marx and Engels, Riot-Sarcey remarks, "L'idée d'affranchissement l'emporta sur la pratique d'émancipation" 'The idea of liberation prevailed over the practice of emancipation' (98; my trans.) The idealism, struggle, and failure of social utopianism constitute one of the linchpins of Hugo's worldview.

Visionary Utopianism

Hugo was more than a curious observer of utopianism. He believed that the nineteenth century was an immense "chantier" 'construction site' that aspired toward "la conquête de l'idéal" 'the conquest of the ideal' (1: 755; 593 [pt. 3, bk. 1, ch. 13]). It is important to stress that his take on utopianism is thus profoundly self-reflexive. Hugo was convinced that the artist's capacity to envision alternative forms of existence would play a central role in leading society to a new and better world.

One way to approach this topic might be to remind students that Hugo's utopianism is inscribed in a nexus of activity that was driven by the belief that it was possible to engineer a state of universal happiness through the wholesale restructuring of the institutions and representational practices that regulate social existence.[1] In the novel, Hugo imagines a world where poets and social scientists would work together to bring about a "modern ideal": "L'idéal moderne a son type dans l'art, et son moyen dans la science. C'est par la science qu'on réalisera cette vision auguste des poètes: le beau social. On refera l'Eden par A + B." 'The modern ideal has its model in art, and its means in science. It is through science that we shall realize that august vision of poets: social beauty. We shall reproduce Eden by A + B' (2: 626; 1240 [pt. 5, bk. 1, ch, 20]). One might contextualize Hugo's early thinking on visionary utopianism by showing its close connection with the Romantic concept of *sacerdoce*. Widely cultivated and mythologized in works such as Alfred de Vigny's *Chatterton* and Hugo's own "Fonction du poëte," sacerdocy might best represent a movement that called for the recognition of the sacred nature of the artistic imagination. For those of Hugo's mindset, sacerdocy also became an attempt to confer on the artist an anticipatory social function (see, e.g., 1: 903–04; 719 [pt. 3, bk. 7, ch. 1]).[2] Accordingly, in "Fonction du poëte," Hugo enthusiastically urges a new "utopian man" to cultivate and channel the widespread desire for change that reigned in the decades before the 1848 revolution:

> Le poète en des jours impies
> Vient préparer des jours meilleurs.
> Il est l'homme des utopies;
> Les pieds ici, les yeux ailleurs.   (*Œuvres poétiques* 1: 1025)

> The poet, in impious times,
> Comes to prepare better days.
> He is the utopian man,
> feet in the here and now, eyes elsewhere.   (my trans.)

In the poem, Hugo makes clear that he does not envision this impending society to exist in a state of unchanging perfection. Rather, his utopia would be the product of a process of becoming in time. Here one might point out that Hugo's temporal postulation represents a significant departure from tradition. Most previous iterations of literary utopianism use the framework of the fictional account (often in the form of a travelogue) to consider the various aspects of an imagined society in its final state of perfection. As Louis Marin has observed, these tales set out to depict the "iconic"—that is, static—nature of the revealed society, and, in this respect, they represent a form of ironic displacement, a means of evaluating our own customs and institutions in the light of utopian alterity (76). By contrast, Hugo's utopian man explicitly refuses the trope of geographic dislocation that had been a hallmark of the discovered society from Thomas More to Cyrano de Bergerac. Hugo is a utopian in the nineteenth-century sense: he does not desire to leave the present world but to remake it. He understood that utopia was being transformed from a mode of historical thinking, operating along the lines of ironic displacement and opposition, to a mode of historical being, where subjects are conscious of participating in a moment of great social transformation.

One interesting question that will surely arise during discussion of this material is whether the workers' paradise established by Valjean-Madeleine at Montreuil-sur-Mer constitutes a utopia (see 1: 228; 160 [pt. 1, bk. 5, ch. 2]).[3] The town recalls the many real experimental communities that burgeoned at the time, such as Jean-Baptiste André Godin's *Familistère de Guise,* and, in this sense, Montreuil might very well represent a Hugolian prototype of an ideal community. Yet in its ephemeral harmony and devastating end, Montreuil-sur-Mer also suggests how the dream of the timeless, immutable utopia of the genre's literary past persists as a haunting afterlife in the nineteenth-century imagination. As I have argued elsewhere, in nineteenth-century France many utopias are almost schizophrenically hopeful and pessimistic. As swiftly as these ideal societies take shape in the literature of the period, inspire hope and point to a generalized state of longing for radical social transformation, as soon as they begin to delineate a system or espouse the prescriptions of this or that utopian social philosopher, they are demystified, rejected, or symbolically destroyed as if their very contemplation were indissociable from the sentiments of remorse and melancholy (Sipe 18). In *Les Misérables* (and in texts as varied as François-René de Chateaubriand's *Atala* and Charles Barbara's "Le Major Wittington") the depiction of the utopian fiasco points to the failed promise of nineteenth-century social science and its rosy predictions concerning the perfection of social institutions (on this point see Théophile Gautier's preface to *Mademoiselle de Maupin* [Gautier, "Préface"]). These failed societies also demystify the utopian literary genre itself whose images of justice and felicity had become impossible to read without this new self-reflexive sense of irony. As such, the novel forces us to reassess the prophetic, visionary brand of utopianism that Hugo had championed in the years before his exile.

The Utopianism of Progress

In Hugo's day, it was widely held that the cumulative effects of progress might realistically bring about a utopian state. For Hugo's utopians, "ces grands essayeurs de l'avenir" 'these great pioneers of the future' (2: 623; 1238 [pt. 5, bk. 1, ch. 20]), these effects of progress seem almost to coincide: "Voulez-vous vous rendre compte de ce que c'est que le progrès, appelez-le Demain. Demain fait irrésistiblement son œuvre, il l'a fait dès aujourd'hui" 'and if you wish to understand what Progress is, call it Tomorrow. Tomorrow performs its work irresistibly, and it does it from today' (1: 460; 349 [pt. 2, bk. 1, ch. 17]).

In many respects, the utopianism of progress broadly represents the nineteenth century's attempt to instrumentalize the principles of Enlightenment philosophy. One effective way of helping students come to an understanding of the intellectual bonds that link nineteenth-century utopianism to Enlightenment thought is to ask them to consider select passages from the works of social philosophers who were attempting to systematize its theories of progress and perfectibility. For example, utopian optimists such as Nicolas de Condorcet believed that it was possible to arrive at "the true principles of social happiness" by applying the methods of the experimental sciences to social life. Condorcet asserts that his work fits into a growing number of experiments in which "les méthodes des sciences mathématiques, appliquées à de nouveaux objets, ont ouvert des routes nouvelles aux sciences politiques et morales; où les vrais principes du bonheur social ont reçu un développement et un genre de démonstration inconnu jusqu'alors" 'the methods of mathematical sciences, when applied to new objects, opened new roads to political and moral sciences. True principles of social happiness were therein developed and a previously unknown type of proof was discovered' (vi; my trans.).

Although many of Hugo's characters (and, certainly, his narrator) convey a profound belief in the transformational power of science and technology, few do so more clearly than the spiritual guide of Les Amis de l'ABC, Combeferre:

> Il croyait à tous ces rêves: les chemins de fer, la suppression de la souffrance dans les opérations chirurgicales, la fixation de l'image de la chambre noire, le télégraphe électrique, la direction des ballons . . . Il était de ceux qui pensent que la science finira par tourner la position.
> (1: 821 [pt. 2, bk. 4, ch. 1])

> He believed in all the dreams: railroads, the suppression of suffering in chirurgical operations, the fixing of the image in the camera oscura, the electric telegraph, the steering of balloons . . . he was one of those who think that science will at last turn the position.   (650)

If Combeferre's "dreams" are remarkable, it is first because they are hardly dreams at all but realities of nineteenth-century life and thus might be better read as *futuristic emblems* of progress. Students might discuss the consequences of such a position, since it is not so much the products that are dreamlike; their producers and users believed that such things portended a larger utopian transformation of society.

Combeferre's unflappable faith in technology will provide an opportunity to explore further Hugo's conception of the relation between progress and utopia. Students can be asked to think about why, in a novel that develops a sophisticated and nuanced reading of utopianism, the first specific mention of the concept of utopia appears to be a dismissive comment on technology: "une mécanique bonne à pas grand'chose, une espèce de joujou, une rêverie d'inventeur songe-creux, une utopie: un bateau à vapeur" 'a machine of little value, a kind of toy, the daydream of a visionary, a utopia—a steamboat' (1: 179; 118 [pt. 1, bk. 3, ch. 1]). Does the steamboat represent a pointless mise-en-scène of progress, a utopia in the pejorative sense that might amount only to the solipsistic dream of a delusional inventor? This is not an unimportant observation since it suggests that Hugo is keenly aware that true progress is hardly a function of technology. Rather, it is a concept that holds that technological advancement must necessarily be accompanied by moral and social progress: "La philosophie doit être une énergie; elle doit avoir pour effort et pour effet d'améliorer l'homme . . . Le progrès est le but; l'idéal est le type" 'Philosophy should be energy; it should find its aim and effect in the improvement of mankind. . . . Progress is the aim, the ideal is the model' (1: 665; 519–20 [pt. 2, bk. 7, ch. 6]). Might we then read the steam engine and the momentous changes it will bring about as a utopia in the sense that it represents a form of progress whose social benefits have yet to be realized?

Here one might consider adopting a wider perspective to help students understand the imbrication of these concepts. In Hugo's day, utopia itself had come to represent a kind of techne, a set of laws, operations, and techniques aimed at producing and regulating an idealized social sphere. It is useful to remind students that social scientists such at Charles Fourier and Claude Henri de Saint-Simon envisioned society to be an infinitely complex but nonetheless knowable mechanism of competing needs and desires. Fourier went so far as to propose a complicated formula for dividing society into groups, or "Phalansteries," of compatible personality types of which he was certain there were exactly 810 (Fourier 310). *Les Misérables* fittingly evokes the emergence of this generation of "systems-makers" who designed and promoted new forms of work and polity, elaborate blueprints of ideal worlds whose imminent realization they believed to be a mere question of rational organization and political will.[4]

Revolutionary Utopianism

After promoting himself as one of utopianism's greatest champions in the decades preceding the revolution of 1848, Hugo becomes in *Les Misérables* one of its great historians. In anticipating the precipitous collapse of social utopianism around midcentury, Hugo's failed utopian uprising of 1832 shows how attempts to bring these visions to fruition had spiraled into violence and insurrection. Instructors might ask students why, when afforded the benefit of hindsight, Hugo would persist in defending the principles of utopianism. Why not conclude with Baudelaire that 1848 marked both the spectacular apex and laughable demise of utopian optimism in France? "1848 ne fut amusant," the poet would quip in his journal, "que parce que chacun y faisait des utopies comme des châteaux en Espagne" '1848 was entertaining if only because everyone was making utopias like castles in the sky' (Baudelaire, "Journaux intimes" 680; my trans.). With this in mind, perspicacious readers will have noted that there is an anachronistic quality to the revolutionary moment highlighted by Hugo. In choosing 1832, Hugo reveals that he is engaged in more than the archaeological task of reconstructing a failed politics. One might ask students to think about this choice by suggesting that the novel helps us understand that these failures — so common to the nineteenth-century utopian experience — are often relegated to the liminal spaces of history. Is it for this reason that the suicidal uprising sparked by his utopian conspirators takes place not during one of the century's canonized historical moments (1830 or 1848, for example) but in the ellipses of history? Significantly, Hugo does not dismiss these interstitial moments but endows them with a profound historical significance, which I describe below.

Instructors who want to explore in detail Hugo's conception of revolutionary utopianism should turn to the chapter "Les morts ont raison et les vivants n'ont pas tort" 'The Dead Are Right and the Living Are Not Wrong' (2: 618; 1234 [pt. 5, bk. 1, ch. 20]). Here Hugo's narrator passionately condemns the radicalization of social utopianism while recognizing revolution as an undeniable (if unsavory) agent of progress: "L'utopie d'ailleurs, convenons-en, sort de sa sphère radieuse en faisant la guerre. . . . Elle se sert de la mort, chose grave. Il semble que l'utopie n'ait plus foi dans le rayonnement, sa force irrésistible et incorruptible" 'Utopia, moreover, we must admit, departs from its radiant sphere in making war. . . . She uses death, a solemn thing. It seems as though Utopia had lost faith in the radiation of light, her irresistible and incorruptible strength' (2: 622; 1237 [pt. 5, bk. 1, ch. 20]). Hugo's archetype of this radicalized iteration of utopianism is the dying *conventionnel* who unrepentantly explains to Myriel the necessity of regicide and terror (1: 81; 39 [pt. 1, bk. 1, ch. 10]). Later, among the group of young idealists who will form the core of Les Amis de l'ABC, Enjolras will incarnate this revolutionary spirit.

In the end, the only viable mode of utopianism for Hugo is the visionary. Here instructors might consider pairing the discussion of "Les morts ont raison" with the important chapter "Les mines et les mineurs" 'Mines and Miners' (pt. 3, bk. 7, ch. 1), whose theme of excavation develops one of Hugo's major metaphors for the intellectual work of utopianism. Unlike his ill-fated insurrectionists who try to force the hand of change, Hugo's utopian miners, "ces pionniers souterrains" 'these subterranean pioneers,' often advance the cause of progress in obscurity (1: 904; 719 [pt. 3, bk. 7, ch. 1]). While Hugo establishes a hierarchy among his miners (some are closer to "breaking through" than others), he is also quite clear on one point: these miners and the passages they create are tied together by utopia: "Les utopies cheminent sous terre dans ces conduits. Elles s'y ramifient en tous sens" 'Utopias travel underground through these conduits. They branch out in every direction' (1: 903; 718). If Hugo reads the works of thinkers such as Descartes and Voltaire as utopian, it is because he is interested in considering ideas in their "embryonic" state, that is, before they have become part of our social reality. Inasmuch as these emergent ideas represent possible futures, Hugo's mine, "cet immense système veineux souterrain du progrès et de l'utopie" 'this immense underground venous system of progress and utopia' (1: 904; 720), becomes a place where the difference between utopia and progress is a matter of degrees, or, rather, of proximity to reality.

Because its outcomes are uncertain, utopia occupies an equivocal space between the forces of progress and Hugo's "dark miners," who work to undermine the system. Students might explore the consequences of this conception. Why are Hugo's utopians so closely associated with the forces of social degeneration? How, in their efforts to better society, do his utopians compare with the novel's other altruists and humanitarians? Is their sacred mission to advance the cause of progress justified, even when it is marked by a series of violent "convulsion[s] vers l'idéal" 'convulsive movement[s] towards the ideal' (2: 628; 1242 [pt. 5, bk. 1, ch. 20])?

Dark Matter: Utopia and Representing Change

Although he recognized that momentous upheavals such as Waterloo and the revolution often inaugurate new eras or end those that had run their course, Hugo was adamant that such events were merely symptomatic of a larger process of social transformation, one that operated on a cosmic, if not divine, scale. Here instructors will want to inform students that the effect of this perspective is to assert a new kind of historiography, one that minimizes the tradition of Plutarchian "great-man" narratives in favor of social historicism, where the cumulative effect of the actions of anonymous individuals becomes the preponderant force of history (cf. Hugo's diametrical reading of the importance of Napoleon and the unknown Cambronne at Waterloo in pt. 2, bk. 1, chs. 13, 15). One might suggest that Cambronne is exactly the kind of figure that represents what Hugo would metaphorically call a *petite feuille*: "il n'y a ni petits faits dans l'humanité, ni petites feuilles dans la végétation" 'there being neither little facts in humanity nor little leaves in vegetation' (1: 180; 119 [pt. 1, bk. 3, ch. 1]). For Hugo, the image that emerges from the sum of these not-so-insignificant things is that of a society engaged in the slow, halting shift from absolutism and aristocratic privilege to republicanism and meritocracy (see, e.g., 2: 628; 1242 [pt. 5, bk. 1, ch. 20]).

This is where utopianism comes into play in Hugo's exploration of historical experience. For the author, the key to unraveling history's complexities lies in our understanding of the invisible force exerted on social life by the utopian imagination. In the "circulation féconde des intérêts et des idées" 'the fruitful circulation of interests and ideas' that constitutes our social existence, utopianism acts somewhat like the *dark matter* that motivates these dynamic forces (2: 573; 1196 [pt. 5, bk. 1, ch. 7]). Therein are revealed the levers that dominate nineteenth-century life—history, progress, and revolution—and with them Hugo's compelling theory of the human condition. By this I mean that, for Hugo, the opacity of experience often stems from the fact that it coalesces in the sediment of our marooned desires. It is in examining the nature of our collective fantasies that we might hope to come to a greater understanding of our condition: "Nos chimères sont ce qui nous ressemble le mieux" 'Our chimeras are most like us' (1: 872; 693 [pt. 3, bk. 5, ch. 5]). Hugo alerts us to the manner in which utopia, like dark matter, exercises a distorting effect on history. History, in its retellings, does not (cannot?) take into account the manner in which utopian fantasies invisibly shape our quotidian—a shaping that is, for Hugo, undeniable: "Et rien n'est tel que le rêve pour engendrer l'avenir. Utopie aujourd'hui, chair et os demain" 'There is nothing like dream to create the future. Utopia today, flesh and blood tomorrow' (1: 816–17; 646 [pt. 3, bk. 4, ch. 1]).

In another fundamental way, *Les Misérables* must also be read as Hugo's attempt to deconstruct the terms of this "utopia today." It is against the backdrop of an absent utopian world that the novel's historical drama plays out. A staunch defender of his progressive ideals after the collapse of the utopian-minded Second Republic, the banished author devotes significant portions of *Les Misérables* to parsing out the legacy of nineteenth-century utopianism at a time when most had come to the bitter realization that "Aucun paradis ne devient terrestre à l'époque où nous sommes" 'No paradise comes to earth in our day' (1: 768; 606 [pt. 3, bk. 3, ch. 2]). Here *Les Misérables* intersects with other important historical novels of the time such as Gustave Flaubert's *L'Éducation sentimentale* and Émile Zola's *Le Ventre de Paris*. One of their commonalities is that these works do not simply espouse or reject utopianism as a political or philosophical position on the necessity of social transformation. They also represent an attempt to recall the impact of the social utopian movements that pervaded France during the first half of the nineteenth century.

In the end, students should understand that Hugo's mature treatment of utopianism is significantly complicated by the fact that the author is writing from a position of retrospection and exile in which he must take stock of the debacle of social utopianism while simultaneously asking what (if anything) might be salvaged of its visionary spirit. In depicting the vertiginous rise and fall of these applied utopian systems and their supporters, *Les Misérables* captures brilliantly the mixture of hope and skepticism, of radicalization and co-option that characterizes nineteenth-century utopianism. Classroom discussions directed toward exploring how these movements embody the inherent tension between these countervailing forces will go a long way to helping students understand Hugo's social philosophy. The latter encourages us to embrace the quixotic nature of utopian praxis, even when its effects remain obscured or unrealized. Here the novel's likable but doomed utopians, these forgotten martyrs of progress, come to represent an aesthetic of hopefulness that sustains Hugo's somber masterpiece, reclaiming it for the purpose of his "modern ideal."

NOTES

[1] For a more complete picture of nineteenth-century utopianism and a broader context for the discussion of Hugo, see my *Text, Image, and the Problem with Perfection in Nineteenth-Century France*.

[2] For additional perspectives on "l'artiste civilisateur" 'civilizing artist,' see Hugo's preface to *Les Rayons et les ombres* (1840).

[3] For an enlightening analysis of the utopian elements in Hugo's novel and of Montreuil-sur-Mer as a utopia, see Grossman, *Figuring Transcendence*.

[4] On the importance of these systems in 1831–32, see 2: 123; 821–22 (pt. 1, bk. 2, ch. 3). For 1817, see 1: 178; 118 (pt. 1, bk. 3, ch. 1). Among the group of insurgents that make up Les Amis de l'ABC, esp. in the figures of Jean Prouvaire and Combeferre, see also 1: 822–23; 651–52 (pt. 3, bk. 4, ch. 1).

Les Misérables and the French Revolution: How to Keep That "Unfamiliar Light" Aflame

Julia Douthwaite Viglione

Il était en quelque sorte, lui, le dernier chaînon du genre humain qu'ils touchassent, il les entendait vivre ou plutôt râler à côté de lui, et il n'y prenait point garde! (*Les Misérables* 2: 28 [pt. 3, bk. 8, ch. 5])

He was in some way the last link of the human race that they touched, he heard them live or rather breathe beside him, and he took no notice!

(744)

The course I describe here juxtaposes Hugo's novel with works produced during and after the French Revolution in order to explore the treatment of republican values in *Les Misérables*. It also questions the call for empathy found in Hugo's preface and in the epigraph above, where the hero Marius suddenly realizes the suffering of his next-door neighbors. As readers of Hugo in the twenty-first century, we dare to hold the author accountable for the quintessential modern experience that he serves up in this book—that is, how he makes us into what Susan Sontag calls "spectators of calamities taking place in another country" (18).

By studying sources on the French Revolution during the first seven weeks and focusing on *Les Misérables* in the remaining eight weeks of the semester, our goal is to animate discussion of three themes inherited from the decade 1789–99 and to show how Hugo integrated them into the plots of his novel. The themes include the revolutionaries' desire to create a more just nation, the post-revolutionary generations' desire to reconcile past and present, and the hope of inspiring fraternity among humankind. Students are expected to engage with all course materials not only in daily discussions that are oriented by questions circulated in advance but also through the creation of a twelve-page research paper in French.

The three revolutionary themes behind this book can be identified in the preface: "Tant qu'il existera, par le fait des lois et des mœurs, une damnation sociale créant artificiellement, en pleine civilisation, des enfers, . . . des livres de la nature de celui-ci pourront ne pas être inutiles" 'So long as there shall exist, by reason of law and custom, a social condemnation which, in the midst of civilization, artificially creates a hell on earth, . . . there should be a need for books such as this.' By stressing the *artificial* nature of poverty and injustice, the author suggests that it is possible to destroy bad laws and create better ones. The temporal modifier "so long as there shall exist" expresses the hope of putting old problems to rest.[1] In indicting what he calls the "social asphyxia" that suffocates the poor, Hugo demands compassion. With such an ambitious agenda, one expects this hefty tome to pack a powerful emotional punch and possibly even some policy advice.

The first half of the course introduces students to revolutionary history through some unusual sources, including C. Calvet's *Histoire de France: Cours moyen*.[2] This slim volume is well organized, easy to use, and includes maps and images of key events. During the middle of the Third Republic (1870–1940), Calvet's manual would have been required reading for pupils ages twelve to sixteen in public lycées. Unless, that is, it was outlawed by local clerics or others offended by his views (Garcia and Leduc; Sauvage). Calvet's enthusiasm for the republic dominates the narration, as when he slams Louis XVI's regime for propagating "le despotisme, l'arbitraire; l'absence de libertés" 'despotism, arbitrary [price manipulations]; absence of freedoms' (159; my trans.). His description of Thermidor should also spark debate, for Robespierre's downfall is attributed not to violence but rather to restraint, as "un dernier exemple d'obéissance à la loi" 'a last example of obedience to laws' (193; my trans.). By studying such an ideologically charged history book alongside literature, students will see how political opinions can color interpretation.

Literary sources include a taut detective story set during the Terror, a ribald dialogue in the *poissard* genre, and an Oriental allegory warning against ministerial manipulation. Honoré de Balzac's mystery "Un épisode sous la Terreur" ("An Episode Under the Terror") starts on a snowy night in January 1793 when a mysterious stranger follows an elderly nun home from a bakery where she spent her last pennies purchasing illegal hosts for mass. The cat-and-mouse game between the stalker and the terrified cleric cleverly exploits anxieties felt during the Terror to build suspense. The surprise ending suggests that even the steeliest regicide may earn atonement: a theme not unrelated to Hugo's "unfamiliar light." The *poissard* pamphlet is Bellanger's *Le Falot du peuple* (*The People's Lantern*), a sixteen-page conversation among fishmongers who debate the king's misdeeds during the 1792–93 trial. I suggest reading *Le Falot* to accompany Hugo's treatment of the *gamin* ("street urchin") Gavroche because there is a direct lineage between him and the fishwives. Not only does Hugo consider the *gamin* "le fils des Halles" 'son of the marketplace' (1: 747; 586 [pt. 3, bk. 1, ch. 9]), he also infuses some of the dialogues among underworld characters with traits attributed to the working-class *poissardes* of *Le Falot*: insolence, wit, and irony.[3] *L'Histoire véritable de Gingigolo* comments on the fragile legitimacy of kingship through its bizarre plot of a king whose head is sliced off and replaced with other heads—first a dopey sheep, then five querulous ministers—before regaining his original head and the love of his people at the end. Instructors might teach it as an allegory of conflict resolution and contrast it to Marius's struggles with his three father figures: Colonel Pontmercy, Monsieur Gillenormand, and Jean Valjean. Artists clearly drew inspiration from the first revolution to make sense of later revolts: a point made by the curators of *Le Peuple de Paris au XIXe siècle*, wherein portraits of *sans-culottes* of the 1790s are juxtaposed to working-class combatants of the 1830s (Musée Carnavalet 13–32, 159–61, 198–99).

History may also be brought to life through emotional moments in film and music. D. W. Griffith's *Orphans of the Storm* presents a hilarious cameo of

Robespierre "the pussyfooter" and casts burly, bearded men to play the female militants from Les Halles (*les poissardes*), thus leveraging viewers' fears of the unwashed masses and their leaders for an anti-Communist message. Another "must-see" is the tense dinner scene in Andrzej Wajda's *Danton*, where a fleshy Danton played by Gérard Depardieu stuffs himself with heavy food and wine while a pale, thin, and abstemious Robespierre warns him against mobilizing the masses against the state. Juxtaposing aristocratic "excess" against Jacobin "restraint," this scene reveals how friendships were swept aside by the zero-sum game of the Terror. An example of hard choices made in polarized times can be found in two Beatles songs of 1968: "Revolution 1" and the better-known "Revolution." Students may be surprised to learn why John Lennon's change in wording, from supporting violence to demanding peaceful change, generated outrage among the Left ("Number 13"). By exposing students to these thorny choices and studying how media have portrayed armed revolt over the years, we can heighten students' awareness of the potency of "revolution."

Although ambivalent on the use of violence for political ends, Hugo nevertheless stressed his admiration for 1789, for example, in *Littérature et philosophie mêlées*, where he described the revolutionary era as an abyss separating modernity from what has come before (42). But his appreciation of what that modernity might mean varies. In the two novels where he addresses the revolution most directly—*Les Misérables* and *Quatrevingt-treize*, published eleven years later—one finds tortuous accounts of individual soul-searching among the wreckage, as well as exalted visions of a better world yet to come. In *Les Misérables*, numerous philosophical digressions invite a contemplative response to the revolutionary past, and melancholy cloaks the short-lived revolt. Well before the battle takes place, readers suspect that the rebels may be fighting a losing cause, because the lead-up is punctuated by numerous warnings about their youth and naïveté (pt. 3, bk. 4, ch. 1). In *Quatrevingt-treize*, the revolutionary struggle tears apart the family bonds between its three protagonists, and Hugo warns about dogmatic attachment to ideologies inherited from 1789 through the visceral scenes of hand-to-hand combat and executions by guillotine. Yet there is something sublime about the murder-suicide of Cimourdain and Gauvain at the end, and a suggestion of something divine in their sacrifice for the Republic.

The "unfamiliar light" in the title of this essay forms one of the most explicit yet overlooked connections between the revolution and *Les Misérables*. It refers to "The bishop in the presence of an unfamiliar light" (1: 76–89; 35–45 [pt. 1, bk. 1, ch. 10]), where Msgr. Bienvenu begrudgingly offers last rites to a dying pauper known only as "the conventionist G—." After a couple of hours spent debating the Catholic Church's role in perpetuating the injustices that resulted in revolutions past, the bishop is dumbfounded to realize not only that the conventionist G— is his intellectual equal but that he may possibly be his spiritual equal as well. Bienvenu falls to his knees at this moment, bows his head, and asks for a blessing. But we never know what happens next because G— dies. This memory

haunts Bienvenu; henceforth, every allusion to G— sends him into "a strange reverie" (1, 88; 45 [pt. 1, bk. 1, ch. 10]). This scene shows how the author's dream of
promoting compassion and respect, even among people as opposed as a church-
man and an anticlerical republican, motivates the plot from the beginning. Our
students will understand the difficult work assumed by deputies during the Convention (1792–95): they will appreciate the humanitarian principles behind legislation passed in those years, as well as the crises that made "terror" the order
of the day (Tackett; Livesey). Without that crucial knowledge, one cannot grasp
how this tête-à-tête changes the bishop for the better. As Hugo notes: "À partir de
ce moment, il redoubla de tendresse et de fraternité pour les petits et les souf-
frants" 'From that moment he redoubled his tenderness and brotherly love for
the weak and the suffering' (1: 88; 45 [pt. 1, bk. 1, ch. 10]).

"The bishop in the presence of an unfamiliar light" displeased Hugo's readers;
it likely helped keep *Les Misérables* on the Church's index of banned books from
1864 to 1959. Although important enough to warrant a frontispiece in the 1907
English translation, the chapter is omitted from the 2007 abridgment and the
productions of *Les Mis* on stage and screen.[4] Why is this passage so unpopular?
One might point to its irreverence toward the Catholic doctrine of infallibility,
but I think Hugo's portrait of a secular sage was even more irksome. As Victor
Brombert aptly notes: "[T]he real surprise is not that the bishop goes down on
his knees in front of the old Conventionnel; it is that the Conventionnel speaks
the language of religious mysticism. . . . The dying Jacobin uses with no problem
words such as sacre, ciel, infini, Dieu" (*Victor Hugo* 120–21). This is arguably
the most thought-provoking moment in *Les Misérables*. It gives us reason to
suspect that the beginning of the novel, not the end, holds the key to Jean
Valjean's destiny. Redemption must extend to all humanity, not just the exceptional Christian.

As seen in the 1789 publication of the *Declaration of the Rights of Man and
the Citizen* and the 1790 Festival of the Federation, the early revolution rode on
hopes of leveling the hierarchy and creating new social bonds (Calvet 168–75).
This attitude is captured in Hugo's treatment of the *gamin*—described as "[c]et
enfant du bourbier est aussi l'enfant de l'ideal" 'a child of the gutter [who] is
also the child of the ideal'—and in the build-up to the barricade scene (1: 747;
587 [pt. 3, bk. 1, ch. 9]). Describing the atmosphere in Paris in early June 1832,
Hugo notes: "Un certain frisson révolutionnaire courait vaguement. Des souf-
fles, revenus des profondeurs de 89 et de 92, étaient dans l'air. . . . C'était comme
une marée montante compliquée de mille reflux" '[A] vague revolutionary thrill
was noticeable. Gusts from the depths of '89 and '92 were in the air. . . . It was
like a rising tide, complicated by a thousand ebbs' (1: 816; 646 [pt. 3, bk. 4, ch. 1]).
Also sympathetic is the narrator's declaration that the revolution "a créé l'homme
une deuxième fois, en lui donnant une seconde âme, le droit" 'created man a second time, in giving him a second soul, his rights' (2: 334; 997 [pt. 4, bk. 7, ch. 3]).
Fraternity among the downtrodden emerges in the many vignettes of hands
touching hands, where coins, crusts of bread, and clothing change hands between

the poor and the poorer. Consider the piteous sight of two small boys holding each other by the hand described as "en haillons et pâles; ils avaient un air d'oiseaux fauves" 'pale and in rags; they looked like wild birds' (2: 599; 1218 [pt. 5, bk. 1, ch. 16]), and the charity displayed by Gavroche, when he steals a thief's purse and throws it over the fence to a poor old man on the other side (2: 245; 923 [pt. 4, bk. 4, ch. 2]). But beyond these gestures of ordinary kindness, there is no social net to rescue the wretched in *Les Misérables*. After Gavroche dies from a gunshot wound, the people he once helped will likely starve.

Revolutionary memories can also turn the reader's stomach, as when we encounter the filthy shroud used to wrap the sickly corpse of Jean-Paul Marat in the sewer. Noting that no one saw fit to preserve it, Hugo asks, "Fut-ce mépris ou respect? Marat méritait les deux" 'Was this contempt or respect? Marat deserved both' (2: 659; 1268 [pt. 5, bk. 2, ch. 4]). Or consider the nightmarish section called "Patron-Minette," where the reader has the sensation of falling into a pit, spiraling past both Robespierre and Marat before landing among society's hopeless dregs (1: 906; 721 [pt. 3, bk. 7, ch. 2]). Hugo seems to be sizing up the past from different angles: weaving optimism, repulsion, and martyrdom into the memory of events.

In describing a battle that took place forty-three years after 1789, Hugo shows another step in that great human epic. The battle—which lasted about twenty-four hours on 5–6 June 1832—inches forward over about 430 pages while Hugo pulls all the characters in.[5] But the rebels' humiliating failure and the vision of all those beautiful young cadavers are hard to square with the earlier optimism. Moreover, Hugo downplays the realpolitik of the warfare by localizing it in one neighborhood and calling it, in the longest section of the scene, "[l]a Guerre entre quatre murs" 'the war between four walls' (2: 541–644; 1169–1255 [pt. 5, bk. 1]). He evades political accountability by minimizing the role of the skilled workers who drove this insurrection and by insisting on the noble deaths of the martyred students. With eyes fixed on a future when it will all make sense, he intones, "[c]e livre est un drame dont le premier personage est l'infini. L'homme est le second" '[t]his book is a drama whose first character is the Infinite. Man is the second' (1: 653; 509 [pt. 2, bk. 7, ch. 1]).[6] Jumping over long stretches of time allows Hugo to distance himself from 1832. Just as apologists for the Terror made allowances by likening it to a storm, a volcano, or other cataclysm, Hugo infers that construction will inevitably follow destruction.[7]

The threat of violence also hangs in the air, at home and abroad. After depicting the sorry state of the urban poor, Hugo warns of their future revenge: "Ce petit grandira" 'This little fellow will grow' (1: 737; 579 [pt. 3, bk. 1, ch. 4]). Just as we admire Enjolras for the beautiful words that energized the Friends of the ABC in 1832, Hugo praises Danton for his oratory in the 1790s, exclaiming: "Le cri: *Audace!* est un Fiat Lux. . . . L'aurore ose quand elle se lève." 'That cry of boldness is a *Fiat Lux!* . . . The dawn dares when it rises' (1: 753; 592 [pt. 3, bk. 1, ch. 11]). Scoffing at restraint, Hugo retorts: "Tenter, braver, persister, persévérer, s'être fidèle à soi-même . . . voilà l'exemple dont les peuples ont besoin et la lumière qui les électrise" 'To strive, to brave all risks, to persist, to persevere, to be faithful to oneself . . . such is the example nations need and the light that electrifies them' (1: 753; 592). Yet this commitment to populism eventually fades from sight. Although the pursuit of Jean Valjean by police inspector Javert sprawls over hundreds of pages, right does not really triumph over wrong (Javert's final memo notwithstanding). Even the most visible symbol of left-wing sympathies—Marius's heroic father—fails to maintain a hold on the boy's heart.

The revolution's global reach and Hugo's hopes for America—which he describes as pregnant with the potential for emancipation—emerge in *Littérature et philosophie mêlées* (214) as well as in *Les Misérables*, which describes the spirit of '89 as electrifying the campaign against slavery: "[I]l chuchote le puissant mot d'ordre: *Liberté*, à l'oreille des abolitionnistes américains groupés au bac de Harper's Ferry" '[I]t whispers the mighty watchword *Liberty* in the ears of the American abolitionists gathered at Harper's Ferry' (1: 752; 591 [pt. 3, bk. 1, ch. 11]). We should note, however, that the author's commitment to racial equality evolved over time: in the colonial novel of his youth, *Bug Jargal* (1826), black insurgents in the Saint Domingue revolution are portrayed as murderers of innocent white planters, while in his later works he adopts an abolitionist stance.[8]

We end the semester with a study of Jean Valjean's death, at which he feels the spectral presence of Msgr. Bienvenu, and "[l]a lueur des deux chandeliers l'éclairait" 'see[s] a light from the candlesticks' (2: 886; 1462 [pt. 5, bk. 9, ch. 5]). This light emanates from a divine source: it signals the hero's salvation and the peace he feels after entrusting family secrets to his heirs. It has nothing to do with "la lumière qui électrise" 'the light that electrifies' political action (1: 753; 592 [pt. 3, bk. 1, ch. 11]). The claims of positive social change laid out in the preface are forgotten. Consider Valjean's dying speech: he talks of love and forgiveness, but also dwells on the "honest money" (more precisely, the 600,000 francs) that he leaves behind and the industry secrets that made his factory such a success (2: 884; 1460 [pt. 5, bk. 9, ch. 5]). Through their tears, Marius (now named Baron Pontmercy) and wife Cosette fall on their knees, "overwhelmed" and "choked with tears" (2: 886; 1462). Perhaps those are tears of joy for their newfound financial security as well as grief for his passing. As Brombert notes, "[N]ot a word is said about social conditions, while private property is justified, indeed sanctified" (*Victor Hugo* 135).

What to do with this ending? One could explain it as a result of Hugo's milieu (Brombert, *Victor Hugo* 135–39), sidestep it by labeling Hugo a "divided person" (Ewing 46), or turn it into a discussion of privilege. Although economic privilege is at stake here rather than racial privilege, the basic principles could easily be extended to the United States. Consider Nicholas Kristof's bleak survey of poverty in the American West; it concludes on a decidedly Hugolian note: "the essential starting point is empathy" (11). One might track that issue through study of an essay in the anthology *White Privilege*, where one reads that "[E]veryone knows that money brings privilege. But the myth persists that all have access to that power through individual resourcefulness. This myth of potential economic equality supports the invisibility of the other power systems that prevent fulfillment of that ideal" (Wildman and Davis 109). These readings allow students to see how by narrowing his vision to one exceptional person Hugo brushes the unfairness of capitalism and privilege under the rug.

If the author's social agenda washes away by the end and leaves us with a conventional tableau vivant of a teary-eyed bourgeois family, recent adaptations have done even more to muffle the political potential of *Les Misérables*. Critiqued for its "push-button emotionalism" and "lurid melodrama" on opening night, the musical version has nevertheless been packing theaters around the globe since 1985 (Nightingale and Palmer 30). Can one blame Tom Hooper, director of the 2012 film, for following such a lucrative lead?

The most radical choice for teachers might be to invite students to rewrite the end of *Les Misérables*. Maybe they could make it answer to the preface. Marius might remember his father's sacrifice or see the ghosts of Enjolras or Éponine lighting a path forward. Creativity may be the best way to restore urgency to *Les Misérables*, because it prompts students to realize the potential of brotherly love, if only in the classroom. What happens next will be up to them.

NOTES

[1] The wording echoes Manette's prophecy against the Evrémonde family in *A Tale of Two Cities*, wherein Manette denounces them "to Heaven and to earth" and looks forward "to the times when all these things shall be answered for" (Dickens 344).

[2] Besides Calvet's book, sources could include "Un Épisode sous la Terreur" (Balzac), *Le Falot du people* (Bellanger), and *L'Histoire véritable de Gingigolo*.

[3] On the *poissarde*, see Douthwaite 17–58.

[4] For evidence on the suppression of this section, see Gefen's *Les Misérables* 22–24. In his edition, Gefen presents the first two chapters of "Un Juste," the first book of "Fantine," in two small excerpts: "M. Myriel" and "M. Myriel devient Monseigneur Bienvenu" and then moves directly to book 2, "La Chute," and the introduction of Jean Valjean into the story. See also Nightingale and Palmer 6–11, 22–23, and Seebacher.

[5] The battle runs from pt. 4, bk. 1, ch. 1 to pt. 5, bk. 1, ch. 24 (2: 123–645; 821–1255).

[6] The death count on the barricades of June 1832 remains a subject of contention; see Harsin 60; Nightingale and Palmer 12–15.

[7] As a deputy, Hugo's wobbly adhesion to revolutionary politics also infuriated critics (Harsin 282). On disaster rhetoric, see Ashburn-Miller.

[8] That the author's abolitionist stance was not appreciated among all Americans is evident in the scathing critique by Latrobe.

Les Misérables and Adaptation Studies

Bradley Stephens

Les Misérables can be seen as "a user's guide to how texts travel across time, media, and place" (Stephens and Grossman 5). The global popularity the novel achieved when published in 1862 has been maintained and enhanced thanks to a wealth of international adaptations on screen, on stage, in print, on radio, and now online. From the lights of Hollywood to the spectacle of London's West End and the fervent visuals of Japanese manga, *Les Misérables* is one of literature's most adapted works of fiction and has a rich history that reaches back to the novel's own time. While Alain Boublil and Claude-Michel Schönberg's stage version, the world's longest-running musical, is the best-known of these adaptations, some eighty percent of screen and radio versions were made before that show's London debut in 1985. If we include televised and animated adaptations in that select media sample, there have been at least eighty versions to date. This figure is subject to upward revision as we uncover more adaptations outside Europe and America—it is double those in the same media of Gaston Leroux's *The Phantom of the Opera* and around four times as many as Charles Dickens's *Oliver Twist*, which are both now megamusicals, and over six times as many as Leo Tolstoy's *War and Peace*.

Victor Hugo's novel therefore provides a revealing focal point with the field of adaptation studies, which continues to step beyond "the rather limiting framework of novels-into-film" and to think more about "adaptation as process" (Cutchins et al., "Introduction" xi). On the one hand, the critical perspectives afforded by adaptation studies achieve their depth of focus by acknowledging adaptation as a multimedia phenomenon that covers a variety of forms, from established media such as theater to today's digital platforms. On the other hand, they take on intellectual breadth by exploring the circumstances in which adaptations are created and understood. The relation between an adaptation and its source may be described as exploitative, contemplative, revisionist, or reverent, but it rarely fits easily into such descriptors and consistently calls for less categorical readings of how and why a work is adapted. Indeed, the idea that an adaptation should only be studied through its faithfulness to its source has been displaced by a more dynamic network of determining factors, including "social change, narrative form, cultural difference, commercial imperatives, power relationships and so much more" (Whelehan). For instructors working across different languages and cultures, the appeal is especially considerable given the dialogue between adaptation studies and translation studies (see Krebs). Such a network is fully active in what might be termed the multimedia "afterlife" of *Les Misérables*, the contexts and diversity of which have been integral to the cultural renown of Hugo's novel.

If students are to probe this adaptive legacy as fully as possible using the theories and methodologies of adaptation studies, they need some prior knowledge of the novel itself, be it selective or extensive. I use adaptations of *Les*

Misérables in both a graduate survey course titled Cultural Encounters and an advanced undergraduate course titled *Les Misérables*: Readings and Receptions. The former examines how cultures interact with one another through various lenses such as globalization, diaspora, translation, and adaptation. Targeted reading of *Les Misérables* is therefore required for the two sessions on adaptation. Formative moments in Jean Valjean's narrative arc are pertinent choices: central both to the plot and to Hugo's moral vision, they consistently figure in adaptations of the novel. They may be grouped as follows: part 1, book 2 (Valjean's time in Digne); book 7, chapter 3 (his crisis of conscience during the Champmathieu affair); book 8 (his promise to Fantine with regard to Cosette); and part 5, book 3 (his flight through the Parisian sewers). At a combined length of less than 150 pages, these episodes also constitute a manageable amount of reading for the time available, leaving sufficient space for the students to study at least two adaptations in different media.

For the latter course, in contrast, students look specifically at the novel for the first half of the semester before studying its reimagining through a broader range of media in the second half. As a result, they will have a much wider familiarity with the book itself before moving on to its adaptations. Students read the novel during vacation before the semester begins, and to this end I created a reading guide through the course's virtual learning environment (VLE) to help them navigate the sprawl of Hugo's text. This includes a summary of the novel's five parts (and its digressions, so that these need not be read in their entirety); distinct but interrelated topics for discussion (the spiritual, the sociopolitical, and the historical), which I frame within Hugo's Romantic worldview and his idea of an interconnected world; and an encouragement to approach the novel as they might when watching the entirety of a television series, working progressively through (and taking pleasure in) different episodes (further suggestions for working through the novel's length can be found in Ginsburg's essay in this volume).

This undergraduate course nonetheless has the same learning aims as the graduate option: to conceptualize adaptation as both creative interpretation and material object in order to analyze the works in a more astute manner than the strictures of fidelity discourse (a mode of criticism that focuses on how closely an adaptation models itself on its source) allow. To fulfill those goals, undergraduates complete a two-step preparatory exercise through the course's VLE two weeks before the first seminar. In the first week, they think of an adaptation they know (other than the musical) and ask themselves how they have assessed that work's value. They post their ideas online, fostering some initial group exchange and illustrating the extent to which material is continually being adapted around them. Such exchanges are light in nature and do not encroach heavily on other study commitments. Novels turned into films or television shows are the most cited examples, such as *Harry Potter* or *Game of Thrones*, although transfers from other media onto screen do receive attention, including video games like *Angry Birds*, Shakespeare's plays, and superhero comics. Variants of the question, Which version do you think is better? inexorably appear, but such reliance on hierarchical evaluation establishes a useful benchmark that the students will reassess later in the course as a means of measuring how their understanding has changed.

In the second week, the students read Robert Stam's introduction to *Literature and Film: A Guide to the Theory and Practice of Film Adaptation*. In this clearly organized and widely respected audit of adaptation studies, Stam's approach primarily initiates book-to-film analyses, but his attention to the importance of form and context ultimately allows for a broader media literacy. He opens by underlining the shortcomings of fidelity criticism, which sees difference only in terms of loss. This discourse's main focus is that an adaptation is never going to be the original novel, and so it paints adaptations either as unimaginative copies or as disrespectful departures. Discrediting such conceit and its implicit logic of an indomitable literary canon, Stam synthesizes the conceptual and methodological models that are needed in its place—moving from "the rather subjective question of the *quality* of adaptations" to "the more interesting issues of (i) the theoretical *status* of adaptation, and (ii) the analytical *interest* of adaptations" (4). Resisting the will to taxonomize adaptations that drives a number of other studies,[1] his overview prepares students for approaching versions of *Les Misérables* not as imitative replicas of Hugo's novel, but as acts of self-expression through interpretive readings of that text. Citing Mikhail Bakhtin, Gérard Genette, and Julia Kristeva, among others, Stam outlines a detailed framework in which to think about an adaptation's production and reception. He identifies intertextuality as the defining condition for adaptation—"the endless permutation of textualities rather than the 'fidelity' of a later text to an earlier model" (8)—then posits comparative narratology as the most fruitful method for any investigation: "[seeing] story as a kind of genetic material or DNA to be manifested in the body of specific texts" (10).[2] The essay is divided into different sections that mark logical breaks for student reflection. At the same time, students can observe how the most productive approaches draw on multiple ideas, from Derridean semiotics to Judith Butler's theory of performativity, encouraging a versatile use of secondary sources for their own research.

During the first seminar's in-class discussion of Stam's paradigms, the relevance of *Les Misérables* can be specified through Hugo's own voice. Hugo conceived of authorship as an autonomous rather than a deferential position with clear structural parallels to the act of reading: writers and readers alike generate meaning for themselves rather than passively imitate or receive an assumed message. At first glance, Hugo's novel is more popular than it is canonical, enjoying sensational commercial success but receiving a mixed and often dismissive response from critics when it first appeared in 1862. Consequently, it might seem more easily wrestled away from the qualitative assessments impelled by notions of fidelity than works such as Flaubert's *Madame Bovary*, whose artistic merits are perceived to surpass Hugo's and to be harder to emulate. But since Hugo's towering reputation as one of France's "great men" can generate a culture of ardent worship, the lure of fidelity criticism and adherence to a canonical standard remains. The temptation to fall into "Hugolatry" has to be countered by emphasizing the extent to which Hugo himself embraced adaptation as an integral aspect of his artistry.

Les Misérables borrows different literary narratives and modes in its composition, including stories and parables from the Bible (e.g., the likening of Valjean's suffering before Champmathieu's trial to Jesus's anguish in the Garden of Gethsemane [pt. 1, bk. 7, ch. 3]); Homeric epic (e.g., the "modern reenactment of the Iliad" during the Battle of Waterloo [Brombert, *Victor Hugo* 94]); Romantic melodrama (e.g., coups de théâtre such as Fantine's arrest for assaulting Bamatabois, in pt. 1, bk. 5, ch. 12); and the urban fiction of Balzac and Sue (whose wildly popular *Les Mystères de Paris* was alluded to in one of Hugo's original titles for his novel, *Les Misères*). Hugo's son Charles would go on to adapt *Les Misérables* for a stage version in 1863, although this was not the first time that Hugo had been involved with an adaptation of his fiction, having written the libretto for Louise Bertin's 1836 opera of *Notre-Dame de Paris*. Most important of all, as Hugo wrote to his Italian publisher, Daelli, in October 1862, "[c]e livre n'est pas moins votre miroir que le nôtre" 'this book is no less your country's mirror than ours': he wanted his readers to recognize their own reflection and to personalize the story in a novel that in his eyes was not simply French, but belonged to all of humanity (*Les Misérables* [1985] 1154; my trans.). Other musings, such as his speech to the 1878 International Literary Congress, underscore his commitment to empowering the reader over the author, since "l'intérêt public est notre préoccupation unique" 'the public interest is our sole concern' (*Œuvres complètes: Politique* 995; my trans.). Through such references to his notion of the "thoughtful reader" or *lecteur pensif*, students realize that Hugo invites readings (and, by extension, adaptations) that are fluid and personal rather than fixed and dutiful.[3]

It is also important to establish some working criteria for inclusion in the corpus of adaptations to be studied. No adaptation to date has attempted to represent every line of Hugo's 1,500-page epic: the digressions alone pose a challenge for other media in their verbal density and philosophical complexity, while even lengthy versions such as Josée Dayan's 2000 television miniseries and a BBC Radio serial from 2001 had to be partial in their coverage, given that their respective running times of over six hours equal the time it takes the average reader to get through around just twelve percent of the novel. Nevertheless, students note that there is a quantitative difference between examples that espouse *Les Misérables* and works that aim for a fuller but inevitably abridged retelling. Acts of citation, such as Ultimate Improv's use of the song "One Day More" from the musical for "Les Misbarack" to support the 2008 Obama presidential campaign, can be juxtaposed with more wide-ranging recuperations, such as Teddie Films' 2013 music video "Dream and Shout," which restages Tom Hooper's entire 2012 film musical through a parody of a Britney Spears and will.i.am dance-pop duet. Both *YouTube* videos rely on a similarly appropriative logic (and both are only a few minutes long to show in class), but only the latter meets the criteria in Linda Hutcheon's seminal theorization of adaptation studies. She argues that "defining an adaptation as an extended, deliberate, announced revisitation of a particular work of art does manage to provide some limits: short intertextual allusions to other works or bits of sampled music would not be included" (170). I add prequels, sequels, and spin-offs to this category, not out of any conviction that such modes are of no interest to adaptation studies, but for the practical purposes of further limiting what could otherwise be a huge body of works.

With these ideas and approaches in place, students can analyze an illustrative range of the novel's adaptations. The data set I use to map the contours of this adaptive history in a class presentation is divided into sections based on different media, with each section incorporating examples from different generations and cultures—from a ten-part comic parody in *Le Journal amusant* that began appearing just months after the first volumes of *Les Misérables* were published (*Le Journal amusant*) to a recent hidden-object video game called *Jean Valjean*, in which players become the hero in his journey from the *bagne* to the barricade (for iOS, Android, PC, and Mac). Students would have difficulty accessing a number of these examples, including animated films such as *Jean Valjean Monogatari* (1979), since they have come from my own research, but an ever-growing selection is available online, either for purchase or free (e.g., video-sharing Web sites and public archives). The following should be relatively easy to find for students and instructors alike (works not subtitled or translated into English are marked with a dagger):

Film and Television

Director	Year
Raymond Bernard	1934
Richard Boleslawski	1935
Tatyana Lukashevich	1937† (titled *Gavrosh*)
Lewis Milestone	1952
Jean-Paul Le Chanois	1958
Marcel Bluwal	1972†
Glenn Jordan	1978
Robert Hossein	1982
Bille August	1998
Josée Dayan	2000
Tom Hooper	2012 (adaptation of Boublil and Schönberg)

Stage and Musical Theater

Writer	Year	Title
Henry Neville	1868	*The Yellow Passport*
Boublil and Schönberg	1985	*Les Misérables*
Jean Bellorini	2010†	*Tempête sous un crâne*

Print

PUBLICATION	DATE
Le Journal amusant	6 Sept. 1862–4 Apr. 1863† (see Cham)
Classics Illustrated	1961 (see Sundel and Nodel)
UDON Manga Classics	2014 (see Silvermoon and Lee)

Radio

DIRECTOR	DATE	PRODUCED FOR
Orson Welles	1937	
Sally Avens and Jeremy Mortimer	2001	BBC Radio
Philip Glassborow	2001	Focus on the Family
François Christophe	2012†	France Culture Radio

Digital

TITLE	DATE	DEVELOPED BY
ArmJoe	1998	Takase
"Dream and Shout"	2013	Teddie Films
Les Misérables: Jean Valjean	2014	Anuman Interactive

To heighten their awareness of the transmedial, transhistorical, and trans-cultural nature of adaptation, students need to ask themselves how, when, and where the novel is being adapted. As opposed to looking exclusively to Hugo's novel as the source of an adaptation's meaning, these questions point toward the significance of both format and context as agents of authorship that fashion how an adaptation can be read.

The specific affordances of these media can be highlighted by splitting the students into groups to scrutinize how adaptations in different forms dramatize one of the novel's key moments, which I singled out earlier. The verbal signifiers and interiorized trajectories of literary fiction are marshaled in "A Tempest within a Brain" by Hugo's descriptions of Valjean's "burning" mind: "une sorte de convulsion de la conscience qui remue tout ce que le cœur a de douteux" 'a convulsion of the conscience that stirs up everything dubious in the heart' (1: 307; 224 [pt. 1, bk. 7, ch. 3]). Short extracts or demonstrations from five adaptations can be allocated to allow for sustained group work. Boleslawski's 1935 film takes advantage of cinema's visual literalism and material mise-en-scène to capture this tumult, which of course can vary in scale for television versions. The camera looks up at Valjean (Fredric March) from inside his fireplace as he hunches against the mantelpiece, fretting over the "long road" to Arras as light flickers across his troubled face to imply the instability of his thoughts. The frame cuts out to a wide shot of the room as he storms across to his closet to seize his old rags and then back to the fireplace to burn this evidence of his past, spatially evoking the oscillations of his mind, before one of Myriel's candlesticks suddenly falls as a sobering reminder of his conscience. On stage, the musical relies on the physical immediacy and dramatic spectacle of live theater to render this predicament. A spotlight falls on the tormented hero, isolating him in the darkness as the alternating tempos and lyrics to his solo "Who Am I?" express his swinging thoughts: "If I speak, I am condemned. / If I stay silent, I am damned!" The courtroom surroundings eventually move into place around Valjean during the song's rousing crescendo, and the intensity and elevation of the final high B communicates the moral superiority he has achieved in declaring his true identity.

Arresting visuals become paramount in the 2014 manga version (Silvermoon and Lee), where dialogue is condensed into succinct speech balloons in which Valjean ponders his future: "I strive to be a good man, but what is good in this situation?" In one of the sequential frames, the monochrome images divide Valjean's face into two halves to symbolize his moral fracture, while in another frame he stares at one of his candlesticks in the foreground, whose candle has nearly burned out in a visual suggestion of his increasingly urgent dilemma. Conversely, the 2001 BBC Radio series uses the auditory sensibilities of the so-called "blind medium" to take its listeners inside Valjean's troubled mind (Avens and Mortimer). The narrator tells us that Valjean has fallen into "a bad night's sleep" in which "he is confronted with all the splintered voices of his soul": citations of echoing dialogue from previous episodes with Myriel, Petit Gervais, Fantine, and Javert all fortify the moral stakes and are layered upon the soundtrack's faint jarring chords in order to immerse the listener in a besieged conscience. A siege mentality reigns in the "beat 'em up" video game *ArmJoe*, whose fan-made origins affirm the participatory nature of digital media in which audiences take ownership of content. No specific chapters from the novel are staged: players can just as freely choose Valjean to demonstrate his strength of will against other characters as they can choose Marius to assert dominance over him as Cosette's protector. However, the inclusion of "Judgment" as an unbeatable supercharacter or "final boss" manifests the moral forces that win out in the Champmathieu affair. The different characteristics of these five versions stress their creative rather than simply their derivative status as adaptations.

Having examined how these adaptations necessarily reshape Hugo's novel when exercising their own aesthetic strategies, students more perceptively articulate the changeable dialogues that *Les Misérables* initiates with successive generations. By transforming postrevolutionary French society into a universal allegory for the human condition, the novel has a clear capacity for giving expression to sociocultural anxieties and aspirations. This ability may be concisely teased out in student discussion and assignments by referring to four different versions from the 1930s: Bernard's French film; Boleslawksi's Hollywood film; Welles's American radio dramatization; and Lukashevich's Soviet film. Even the most rudimentary knowledge of world history allows students to pick up on the resonances between Hugo's story and the thirties' climate, unsettled as it was by the Great Depression and the political polarities of extremism and radicalism in Europe. The totalizing reach of Hugo's social vision, weaving together individual fate and collective plight, enables *Les Misérables* to channel the altruism of Roosevelt's New Deal in America, the tensions between the *haute bourgeoisie* and the Front Populaire in France's Third Republic, and the revolutionary communism of Stalinist Russia.

Both historical situation and cultural context weigh heavily on these adaptations. The extent to which threads from Hugo's narrative are frayed or entirely cut out quickly becomes a topic of discussion, as does the potential influence of previous adaptations and contemporary aesthetic trends. Both Boleslawski and Welles marginalize the ideology behind the 1832 insurrection at a time when revolution had become increasingly associated with the Soviet Union, while Lukashevich centers on Gavroche as an emblem of popular revolt, excluding Valjean's acquisition of wealth and Cosette's rags-to-riches fairy tale. Alongside these references, Bernard's film neatly illustrates the significance of intertextuality as a critical tool. The scene of General Lamarque's funeral, for example, reveals the director's debt to more than Hugo's poetic imagination alone. The high contrasts, slanted frames, and sharp angles recall the visual signatures of German expressionism, complete with the matte backdrops, intricate miniature work, and grand exterior sets that stand in for nineteenth-century Paris and that owe much to Pathé-Natan Studios' emulation of the Hollywood studio system. That system would the following year cast the bankable March as Valjean, who was a handsome actor with a reputation for feted adaptations, whereas Bernard eschewed Hollywood glamour for Harry Baur. The theatrically trained Baur's rough features and heavyset frame brought both everyday normality and emotional gravitas to the lead role, reminding students of how actors themselves enrich an adaptation's intertextuality.

Furthermore, the sound era meant that Bernard could distinguish himself from Henri Fescourt's silent film version (which had appeared less than a decade earlier) through more than visuals alone. Fescourt's adaptation matches Bernard's film in terms of narrative coverage, but Bernard utilizes dialogue and sound to his full advantage, collaborating with the playwright André Lang on the script and persuading the celebrated Swiss composer Arthur Honegger to write the film's majestic score. Bernard's film also confirms how the figurative historical and cultural currencies that *Les Misérables* can trade in are equaled by the literal capital it can generate, both in investment (which gave Bernard enviable means as a director) and revenue. Rightly predicting the film's success, Pathé's boss, Bernard Natan, "felt that a new take on this tried-and-true property could both inspire the populace in the midst of the Depression and be an impressive national export," revitalizing the French film industry (Koresky).

In these ways "adaptations not only make commercial sense, but they continue to make cultural sense" (Griffiths et al. 127), and students can better grasp the appeal of adapting a novel like *Les Misérables* and of using its adaptations for critical inquiry in the arts and humanities. Moving forward, the widespread availability of digital platforms can encourage instructors to ask their students to adapt *Les Misérables* for themselves as part of a practice-led teaching approach, in which students would learn firsthand about the possibilities of adaptation and make their own original contributions to the novel's enduring legacy.

NOTES

1 Cartmell and Whelehan helpfully summarize these systems of classification, from models based on degrees of fidelity to those based on genre (*Cambridge Companion* 2).

2 For a fuller discussion of Stam's pedagogical importance, see Hudelet.

3 For an overview of Hugo's appeal to the reader's creativity, see Stephens and Grossman, esp. 8–14.

Reading *Les Misérables* with
High School Students

André Iliev

I teach Hugo's *Les Misérables* in the French-American School of Chicago, in a bilingual program that prepares students for the International Baccalaureate, A1 standard or higher level.[1] The students are tenth graders or older and they have already been introduced to French Romanticism; they have achieved some level of critical thinking as well as a good understanding of different narrative forms and some basic figures of speech. The novel is taught in the context of social Romanticism—a concept that combines the Romanticism practiced by authors such as Alfred de Musset and Alfonse de Lamartine with the realism of authors such as Guy de Maupassant and Honoré de Balzac. The hybridity of this form is a source of difficulty for the students. In teaching the novel, my goal is to help them understand this form and its historical importance as an instrument of change.

Our study of the novel focuses on three main characters: Fantine, Cosette, and Jean Valjean. We study their main personality traits and their evolution through selected passages.

The study of these characters is preceded by two periods of preliminary work. The first one is dedicated to elucidating the differences between Romanticism and classicism by reading and discussing four types of texts: classical tragedy, classical comedy, Romantic drama, and Romantic novel. The extracts are approximately five hundred words each. The second period is devoted to discovering Hugo's own brand of Romanticism by analyzing extracts from the poems "Ce siècle avait deux ans" (*Feuilles d'automne*), "Réponse à un acte d'accusation," and "Mélancholia" (*Les Contemplations*). The students are asked to reflect on three questions:

> Which elements of Romantic drama did you find in these poems?
> How do these texts illustrate the revolutionary commitment of Hugo?
> Why can you assert that these poems are both a poetic and a social manifesto?

The class is divided into three groups, each group working on one question. At the end of the period, the answers can be summarized in chart 1. After completing this chart, the instructor may point out that the first row represents the elements of Romanticism in the studied poems. The second and the third are an outline of Hugo's major innovations to this movement, especially his interest in characters representing a particular contemporary social class. At the end of the second period of preliminary work, the students can define Hugo's art in

Chart 1

	POEM 1: "Ce siècle avait deux ans"	POEM 2: "Réponse à un acte d'accusation"	POEM 3: "Mélancholia"
Elements of the Romantic drama	The topic is related to historical events. The main topic (Hugo's birth and early childhood) is closely related to Napoleon's life, which represents a second topic.	A two-act progression: the first describes the literary world before Hugo; the second, the one after Hugo. A heterogeneous universe: he visits, as in a documentary film, symbolic places of historical reality of the seventeenth century.	The action takes place in a contemporary setting; sublime and grotesque elements are used simultaneously.
Hugo's revolutionary commitment	Hugo insists on the importance of the Romantic poet by evoking his birth among other events that would change European history. He begins his poem by using the present continuous (imparfait), a tense that is used to announce a past event that may have an impact on later events.	Hugo animates the text from one end to the other and justifies the proud motto he had given himself, "Ego, Hugo," by multiplying statements in the first person, apostrophes, and vivid exclamations. He appears as a military leader reigning over his verses ("bataillons d'alexandrins"). He is finally a "bandit" but is full of generosity and sympathy for the oppressed and the marginalized.	Hugo appears as an intermediate between God and the children. He redefines labor conditions and condemns child exploitation. Despite his revolutionary engagement, which may appear as leftist, he promotes deism.
Hugo's poetic and social manifesto	Hugo describes himself as feeble ("débile"), announcing his interest in the disadvantaged. He uses banal metaphors ("table toujours servie"). He uses twelve-syllable verses reminiscent of classical aesthetics.	A literary stance: Hugo makes clear his literary preferences, rejecting classicism but not all the classic writers; thus, he advocates tolerance. He addresses the specific issue of vocabulary by giving examples of the mixture of sublime and grotesque. He rejects the negative influence of politics on the poetry.	A social stance: according to Hugo, the role of the Romantic poet is to defend the oppressed. Hugo invites the reader's sympathy through a precise but subjective description of the main characters.

relation not only to classicism and Romanticism but also to critical realism, and they can therefore begin the study of the characters of *Les Misérables*.

During the following six periods, students will deepen their analysis of Hugo's art by focusing on its social aspect through three extracts from *Les Misérables* discussed below. To perform this analysis, the students will apply a grid of four readings to each extract. The first reading is a cursory one. At the end of this reading, the instructor may help the students with the following questions:

> What is the theme of the text? Can it be related to the work from which it is extracted, to the title of the work, the author, the period?
>
> What are its genre (poetry, drama, novel) and type (argumentative, narrative, descriptive)?
>
> What is its tone or literary register (comic, tragic, lyrical, pathetic, ironic, epic)?
>
> What is its interest (historical, philosophical, sociological)?
>
> What resonances does it awaken in the reader (emotion, interest, passion, reflection, questioning)?

The second reading is dedicated to the study of the lexical level. This step may include

> a word classification to find the lexical fields;
>
> a study of the forms, colors, movements, organization of space, and the symbolic or emotional values of these elements;
>
> a study of the organization of these elements in different forms (parallel, recall, opposition);
>
> the establishment of lexical networks in order to identify the topics (intellectual, emotional, symbolic) of the text;
>
> the study of the register of speech: lyrical, elegiac pathos, irony, comic;
>
> the study of the grammatical structures and their meaning in the text.

The third reading focuses on imagery, while the fourth reading articulates the overall significance by gathering the results of previous research, comparing them to the context, and examining the text from an aesthetic (classic, Romantic, baroque) and ideological (rationalism, Romantic sentimentality, desire to provoke) perspective.

The obtained results will be organized in a detailed plan containing three arguments, each of which will be supported by three elements from the text. The first three readings will be done during the first period. The second period will be dedicated to the fourth reading and discussion. Then, the students will be assigned a commentary as homework.

With this background, the students can easily understand the first text to be taught, an extract from "Entrée en scène d'une poupée," beginning with "Au moment où Cosette sortit, son sceau à la main" up to the end of the chapter (1: 503–04 [pt. 2, bk. 3, ch. 4]). Students are first asked to outline the representation of Cosette's emotions and then we focus on the symbolism of the child and the doll.

Students notice easily that Hugo represents Cosette's confused and conflicting feelings. The young child, conscious of her misery, is afflicted but she also experiences an almost devotional delight when she discovers the doll. The author uses an internal point of view to describe the emotional uproar that assails the young girl. The theme of sight corroborates this analysis: the lexical field of perception is accentuated; the scene of the discovery of the doll is represented through the child's eyes. The students will also notice the expression "lever les yeux," which connotes an upward motion, marking an aspiration toward an ideal. The terms that refer to perception ("vu," "vision," "ses yeux," "croyait voir") are supplemented by terms such as "apparaissait," "considérait," "s'éblouissait," which suggest a heightening of this sense.

Students will notice the lexical field of religion, which makes the contemplation of the doll a mystical experience, giving the scene an atmosphere of safety and protection, as if the doll provoked a feeling of happiness and relief in the child. The students can identify expressions such as "paradis," "Père éternel," "adoration," that illustrate the "divine" aspect of the doll. Students also notice the elements of the marvellous that transfigure this "shack" ("barraque") into a "palace" ("palais") that only a "princess" may deserve. This soothing world of naive fairy tales is the product of the imagination of a child who wants to escape the bitter drudgery of her life of slavery to the Thénardiers. And yet, despite the contemplation of the doll, which arouses in her a tender and innocent dream, the child remains conscious of her misery, as is illustrated by terms such as: "morne," "triste," "malheureux," and "accablée." This conflicting duality is expressed in the oxymoron "sa sagacité naïve" that highlights the painful awareness of the child of her misery, but that also shows her pathetic hopes, which give her the status of a tragic heroine.

By using a circular structure, Hugo emphasizes the rapidity of Cosette's enchantment and disenchantment, which arouses the reader's empathy. From the first reading of the text, students should note that it begins and ends with the image of the bucket ("son seau à la main" / "emportant son seau") symbolizing her hard and exhausting work; the expression "tout à coup" denotes a radical break with the quiet moment of reverie. Students may also notice the use of the derogatory expressions "péronnelle" and "petit monstre" that bring Cosette back to her sad reality. Overcome by her exhausting work, Cosette is described as "morne et accablée," which presents her as dull and worn just like an old garment. Hugo depicts her as an abyssal being through a lexical field consisting of words such as "profondément," "englouti[e]," and "abîme." To this idea of descent into hell is opposed the upward movement aroused by the contemplation of the doll as Cosette has to raise her eyes ("lever les yeux") to see her; the doll is also elevated by the use of the term "reine."

A more symbolic reading of the passage reveals two beings who embody two opposite realities. Indeed, if the beautiful doll is the epitome of opulence and provides soothing and protective joy, Cosette is the emblem of a child degraded by the life that has befallen her, so that her miserable condition echoes her affliction, as is made clear by the word "malheureux."

The omniscient point of view reveals the criticism of the author, and students will notice the group of adjectives that emphasize the ameliorative aspect of the doll, which contrasts with the child's misery.

After this study, students will be able to notice that, unlike other Romantic authors, Hugo describes with precision and great detail a character that is radically different from himself in order to awaken the consciousness of the reader to a particular social problem. They will understand that a literary movement considered fundamentally personal and intimate can exceed the strict framework of the personality of the author and have a social dimension without losing its subjectivity. They will also note that if the poem "Mélancholia" is about a social group, in this extract Hugo evokes a particular character while also representing a social class.

At the end of their work, the students should be able to conclude that by creating a diptych portrait, Hugo criticizes the inverted values of a society in the grip of materialism. This critique takes place through a particular kind of lyricism where the author speaks on behalf of a character representing a social class: a fundamental device of social realism.

For the second extract, the study of Fantine, students read part of the chapter "Suite du success" from "Fantine, depuis la veille" to the end of the chapter (1: 230–32 [pt. 1, bk. 5, ch. 10]). They then discuss how, through the character of Fantine, the author denounces the condition of lower-class women in the nineteenth century. They are divided into groups; each group looks for textual support for one of the following elements: material poverty, physical and moral decline, social hostility, and pathos. The outcome of their work can be summarized in a chart that will be completed by the end of the second period dedicated to the study of the passage (chart 2).

During the periods dedicated to the study of the first passage, the students have understood the essential elements of social Romanticism; in analyzing this passage they will focus on the means used by this particular literary movement. Students will notice that Hugo uses metaphors, understatements, and internal perspective to reinforce the subjective point of view, but he also uses numbers, adverbs, and enumeration that make the text appear more objective. They will conclude that it is this constant movement between objectivity and subjectivity applied to a character different from the author that creates the particularity of social Romanticism and differentiates it from both traditional Romanticism and critical realism.

The third and last passage to be discussed is from the chapter "L'Évêque travaille," beginning with "Jean Valjean ouvrit les yeux" to the end of the chapter (1: 162–63 [pt. 1, bk. 5, ch. 10]); it is supplemented by the last three pages of the following chapter (the aftermath of the encounter with Petit Gervais; 1: 170–73). This is the passage dealing with Jean Valjean's metamorphosis: the encounter with Monseigneur Bienvenu turns him from a hideous and vengeful convict to a man willing to do good. Our focus will be on the impact of the religious figure on the hero.

Students will notice that Monseigneur Bienvenu represents first and foremost God and religion. The bishop grants Valjean forgiveness and a second chance ("Je vous achète votre âme. Je la retire à l'esprit de perversité et je la donne au bon Dieu"; 1: 163). He is the intermediary between God and Jean

Chart 2

Argument	Quotation	Identification of the device	Analysis
Material poverty	"une loque qu'elle appelait sa couverture, un matelas à terre et une chaise dépaillée"	Accumulation of pejorative terms	Emphasis on poverty.
	"Elle avait perdu la honte, elle perdit la coquetterie"	Parallelism	Shows personal and moral loss due to poverty.
	"vieux et usé," "se déchirait," "sales"	Lexical field of poverty: Fantine's clothes	Illustrates the marks of poverty as far as Fantine's appearance is concerned.
Physical decline	"Fantine jeta son miroir par la fenêtre"	Symbolic act	She despises her image because of her physical decline.
	"les yeux très brillants," "Elle toussait beaucoup"	Lexical field of illness	Announces fever and respiratory problems related to tuberculosis, an illness associated at that time with poverty and a fatal outcome.
	"[U]n sourire sanglant. Une salive rougeâtre lui souillait le coin des lèvres, et elle avait un trou noire dans la bouche."	Periphrasis	Indirect reference to the loss of her teeth due to poverty.
Moral decline	"en vendant le reste"	Litotes from an internal point of view	Evidence of Fantine's bitterness and irony toward her own destiny.
	"bonnets sales," "ne raccommodait plus son linge," "ses talons s'usaient"	Enumeration	Shows Fantine's loss of dignity and self-respect.
	"bête farouche"	Metaphor	Illustrates Fantine's loss of humanity.
Social hostility	"ne lui laissaient aucun repos"	Hyperbole	Insistence on Fantine's moral exhaustion due to harassment by creditors.
	"Elle les trouvait dans la rue, elle les retrouvait dans son escalier"	Parallelism	Shows the pervasiveness of creditors.
	"Elle se sentait traquée"	Metaphor	Hugo compares Fantine to a hunted animal and reveals her fear.
Fantine's sense of imprisonment	"dix-sept heures par jour"	Numbers	Shows with precision the extreme length of Fantine's working day.
	"Dix-sept heures de travail et neuf sous par jour"	Numbers	Illustrates the gap between the working hours and the derisory payment.
	"travailler," "travail," "jour," "journée," "sous," "francs"	Lexical fields of money and labor	Show Fantine as a victim of work (lack of money and time) and remove any prospect of a better life.
Pathos	"Depuis longtemps elle avait quitté sa cellule du second pour une mansarde fermée d'un loquet sous le toit"	Sentence introduced by an adverbial expression insisting on time	Emphasis on Fantine's resignation about her decline that arouses the reader's compassion.
	"ne peut aller au fond de sa chambre comme au fond de sa destinée qu'en se courbant de plus en plus"	Parallelism	Marks the link between material and personal decline and presents Fantine as a victim of social injustice.
	"Cellule," "mansarde . . . sous le toit," "galetas"	Lexical field of housing	Shows the poverty of Fantine's immediate environment.

Valjean. Students will see how later in the novel Jean Valjean uses religion to serve others.

Monseigneur Bienvenu is also the embodiment of the good, associated with a symbolic light, related to religion but mostly to morality—the values of goodness and virtue. Jean Valjean, in contrast, is associated with darkness, since he is evil. Hugo allows the reader to see this clash of opposites, through the image of blindness: "L'évêque lui avait fait mal à l'âme comme une clarté trop vive lui eût fait mal aux yeux en sortant des ténèbres. . . . Comme une chouette qui verrait brusquement se lever le soleil, le forçat avait été ébloui et comme aveuglé par la vertu" (1: 170 [pt. 1, bk. 2, ch. 13]).

The symbolism of light continues with the image of the flaming torch, symbolizing the way forward toward the Good, and its relay: the bishop did a good deed and now he gives over to Jean Valjean: "Il [Jean Valjean] voyait dans une profondeur mystérieuse une sorte de lumière qu'il prit d'abord pour un flambeau. En regardant avec plus d'attention cette lumière qui apparaissait à sa conscience, il reconnut qu'elle avait la forme humaine, et que ce flambeau était l'évêque" (1: 172).

Students will see the purification of Valjean through faith represented first by the bishop himself who grants pardon to Jean Valjean, then by the symbol of the light, and finally by Jean Valjean's prayers: "un homme dans l'attitude de la prière, à genoux sur le pavé, dans l'ombre, devant la porte de Monseigneur Bienvenu" (1: 173). The students will easily understand that this man is none other than Jean Valjean.

Monseigneur Bienvenu has played a key role in the metamorphosis of Jean Valjean. Monseigneur Bienvenu appears to be the best man in the world; he is idealized throughout the part of the novel dedicated to him. Through him, students will understand Hugo's social Romanticism's perception of religion: a saving and deeply humanist religion, opposed to a legal and political system devoid of humanity. They will examine the difference between this view and that of critical realism, which devalues religion.

The last period will be dedicated to a reflection on the following topic for the final assignment:

> Selon le réalisateur et scénariste polonais Andrzej Wajda, "L'artiste romantique doit se transcender. Il lui faut être plus qu'un créateur. Il lui faut être la conscience de la nation, un prophète, une institution sociale" (evene.lefigaro.fr/citations/andrzej-wajda). Vous commenterez cette citation en vous basant sur des exemples de vos lectures en général et sur les textes étudiés des *Misérables* de Victor Hugo.

This way of teaching parts of *Les Misérables* provides teachers with tools to introduce students to the essential elements of social Romanticism, a movement often neglected at the expense of traditional Romanticism and critical realism, a movement that, by its deep humanity and unwavering commitment to the disadvantaged, may generate interest in students living in a world where social inequalities are more and more present.

NOTE

[1] Because this essay is designed specifically for high school teachers of French, quotations from Hugo's text are not translated.

CRITICAL PERSPECTIVES

Teaching *Les Misérables* through the Lens of Gender and Sexuality

Dorothy Kelly

"The social question" of poverty in *Les Misérables* discloses new meanings when examined through the lens of gender and sexuality. Hugo's explicit criticism of the suffering of women in society and the embodiment of this suffering in his female characters reveal the social enforcement of normative gender roles and their violent effect on their female victims. Pierre Bourdieu's concepts, as well as Michel Foucault's, form the theoretical basis of this approach to gender in *Les Misérables* and bring out the ways in which the social construction of gender roles forces women into certain practices and excludes other, preferable choices from the realm of possibility. In *Les Misérables*, students can see how this exclusion is represented by theft, a major theme in the novel, symbolized in Jean Valjean's theft of bread, as society "steals" possibilities of action and being from women, when other options and identities they might prefer are unavailable to or taken from them. In *Les Misérables*, the woman who remains after this social "theft" is a symbolic ghost, a living being whose life has been stolen.

This understanding of theft and "ghosting" can expand to represent the general social violence inflicted on the "miserable ones," when misery affects the gender, sexuality, and identity of men as well. Thus gender can serve as a different entry point into the social questions raised by the text; it can be used to introduce Bourdieu's and Foucault's ideas of symbolic violence, social discipline, and punishment; and it can also be used when teaching an abridged version of the text, because it can focus on the main characters (with the exception of the important segment of the text on the convent, which could easily be given as a supplement to students).

To provide some background on Hugo's views on the status of women, one could begin before reading the novel with three short excerpts from other works by Hugo (discussed by Savy, "Victor Hugo") that tie together the situation of poor women, the symbolism of ghosts, and the effects of poverty. Students could begin by reading the first twelve lines of the poem "Melancholia" in *Les Contemplations* (1856; 1: 203–04). Here an abject, impoverished woman holding her child is described as a specter who laments her fate in the midst of the city crowd and receives insults in return; this introduces students to Hugo's vision of the spectral identity and sad plight of the poor woman in the modern city (Agnès Spiquel suggests that ghosts in Hugo are predominantly women [100]). The second text consists of a few sentences from "Sur la Tombe de Louise Julien" ("Over the Tomb of Louise Julien"), in which Hugo describes how this woman was imprisoned for political reasons, became ill in jail, was exiled, and died (*Actes et paroles II* 92). Of her tomb he says: "Ah! Une telle tombe n'est pas muette; elle est pleine de sanglots, de gémissements et de clameurs" 'Ah, such a tomb is not mute; it is full of sobs, moans, and outcries' (89; my trans.). One could point out to students that these ghostly moans and sighs from the dead woman's tomb are conveyed to us by Hugo's voice; he will do the same in *Les Misérables* through the representation of ghostly women (and men).

The third preliminary text is a brief and well-known excerpt from *Choses vues* that describes a poor man who has just been arrested, significantly, for having stolen a loaf of bread. As the soldiers lead him away, he glares at a rich woman in a carriage who is oblivious of his existence. Hugo writes of this man: "Cet homme n'était plus pour moi un homme, c'était le spectre de la misère, c'était l'apparition brusque, difforme, lugubre, en plein jour, en plein soleil, d'une révolution encore plongée dans les ténèbres, mais qui vient" 'This man was in my view no longer a man, he was the specter of misery, he was the brusque apparition, shapeless, lugubrious, in broad daylight, under the sun, of a revolution still plunged in shadows, but coming' (130; my trans.). This image depicts the poor who lurk in the depths and who, ghostlike, threaten to rise in revolt. Thus students have before them a trio of texts that bring out the theme of the ghosting of women and men and its importance in the social discourse of Hugo, who decries misery in general, be it that of spectral women, men, or children.

Students turn to *Les Misérables*, to the lives of the nuns in the Petit Picpus convent, to begin the discussion of social theft from women and the ghosting of the individual. The section on the convent is long, but a few select passages suffice to provide students with an understanding of Hugo's representation of the social construction of women, shown in the discipline of the convent. A passage by Foucault on physical and psychological discipline that is fairly accessible to a wide range of students is the chapter in *Discipline and Punish* titled "The Means of Correct Training." This Foucault text prepares students to understand how discipline shapes human subjects.

One could then begin by discussing the role of the convent and nuns in the plot. Clearly, the convent is in some ways a positive institution, a place that provides a safe haven for Cosette and Valjean (Savy, "De Notre-Dame" 89), one that can foster thought through prayer: "Mettre, par la pensée, l'infini d'en bas en contact avec l'infini d'en haut, cela s'appelle prière" 'To place, by process of thought, the infinite below in contact with the infinite above is called "prayer"' (1: 662; 517 [pt. 2, bk. 7, ch. 5]). Religious institutions could be good social systems to promote equality if they were "volontaires" 'voluntary': "Le monastère est le produit de la formule: Égalité, Fraternité" 'The monastery is the product of the formula "Equality, Fraternity"' (1: 661; 516 [pt. 2, bk. 7, ch. 4]). Furthermore, some of the nuns in the text are admirable characters, such as Sister Simplice, who sacrifices her good conscience by lying to save Valjean. However, Hugo also uses the nuns to criticize the effects of the harsh discipline of convent life on women specifically: it takes away—"steals"—their freedom and rigidifies behavior into reiterated and deadening physical and mental practices, and here Foucault could again be used. There are many examples of this discipline that one could give to students: some women are forced to join the convent (1: 657; 513 [pt. 2, bk. 7, ch. 3]); the nuns must wear hair shirts for part of the year and must limit their speech (1: 622; 483 [pt. 2, bk. 6, ch. 2])—one could discuss how taking away the voice is a symbolic act; and their following of such strict practices becomes "machinal par l'habitude" 'mechanical from habit' (1: 625; 485 [pt. 2, bk. 5, ch. 2]).

One could then ask students to think of convent discipline as theft in a more broadly symbolic way that represents the plight of women in general in this text, which will be studied through the characters of Fantine, Éponine, and Cosette. The example of convent discipline points to the way in which the imposition of social practices in general (like the specific rules of convent life) constructs identities, specifically gendered identities, and here selections from Bourdieu's *Masculine Domination*, such as the chapter "Anamnesis of the Hidden Constraints," could form the basis of discussion. (Judith Butler's introduction to *Bodies That Matter* could also prove useful in understanding iterative practices that produce gender, although her work is more difficult.)

Drawing on examples from Kabyle society, Bourdieu reveals the process through which gender, once constructed, "excludes from the universe of the feasible and thinkable everything that marks membership of the other gender" (23). This quotation introduces the idea of the elimination or theft of choices from women when gender expectations preclude them. Study would then turn to the nun's spectral identity, created by convent discipline, as an image of the theft of their very lives from them. Particularly striking is Jean Valjean's first vision of one of the nuns just after he scales the wall to the convent. In this lugubrious scene, Hugo portrays both the harsh disciplinary religious practices and the symbolic death that they bring:

> Il crut voir à terre, sur le pavé, quelque chose qui paraissait couvert d'un linceul et qui ressemblait à une forme humaine. Cela était étendu à plat ventre, la face contre la pierre, les bras en croix, dans l'immobilité de la

mort. . . . Il était effrayant de supposer que cela était peut-être mort, et
plus effrayant encore de songer que cela était peut-être vivant.

(1: 597–98 [pt. 2, bk. 5, ch. 7])

He thought he saw something stretched out on the pavement, which
appeared to be covered with a shroud and resembled a human form. It
was lying face down, with arms outstretched in a cross, in the stillness of
death. . . . It was terrifying to suppose that perhaps it was dead, and still
more terrifying to think that it might be alive.   (463)

This section on convent practice is replete with images of death and of living death, and one could assign students the task of taking note of them as
they read.

One theme that expands from the description of the spectral nature of the
nuns to the other ghostly characters in the novel is the loss or lack of identity.
When nuns take their vows, they give up their family names (1: 660; 515 [pt. 2,
bk. 7, ch. 4]) and become, in a sense, orphans "adopted" into an artificial familial
structure of mothers, sisters, and fathers, brides. It is significant that one of the
first things seen by Jean Valjean when he enters the convent garden is a statue
with no identifying face, because it has been mutilated, erased (1: 594; 460
[pt. 2, bk. 5, ch. 6]). In the rest of the novel, the multiplicity of names assumed
by several characters (which Ubersfeld thoroughly traces) underscores the mal-
leability of identity and its social roots. "Un nom, c'est un moi" 'A name is a me'
claims Jean Valjean (2: 811; 1398 [pt. 5, bk. 7, ch. 1]).

To link ghostly identity more closely with gender and sexuality, discussion
could explore how it is not just general, familial identity that is taken from the
women in the convent (and from other characters in the novel) but also their
sexuality. Convent life subsumes sexuality into spirituality in "ce sérail d'âmes
réservé à Dieu. La nonne était l'odalisque, le prêtre était l'eunuque . . . Claustration, castration" 'this harem of souls set apart for God. The nun was the odalisque, the priest was the eunuch . . . Incarceration, castration' (1: 655, 657; 511,
513 [pt. 2, bk. 7, chs. 2, 3]). The word "castration" clearly expresses that a part
of the gendered and sexed being of women has been taken from them, a similar
situation for Fantine and Éponine.

After finishing discussion of Hugo's asexual "harem" of women reserved for
God, the class could move to the opposite type of woman, Fantine, the prostitute. Discussion could begin with her strange "birth": she emerges, like the impoverished man in *Choses vues*, from the shadowy depths of the people: "Sortie
des plus insondables épaisseurs de l'ombre sociale" 'Sprung from the most un-
fathomable depths of social darkness' (1: 183; 122 [pt. 1, bk. 3, ch. 2]). The nuns
give up their familial identity; Fantine never had one. She gets her name from an
anonymous passerby, as if she were born from the faceless social throng in the
streets. It is significant that Hugo compares her to Galatea (1: 187; 125 [pt. 1,
bk. 3, ch. 3]): although referring specifically to the context in Virgil, the name

also conjures the story of Pygmalion, in which Galatea is a statue come to life. Here in Fantine's case, it is a woman created not by an artist but by society itself.

One could then ask students to reflect on the various ways in which Fantine embodies Hugo's socially created "misérables": she is first female, and also poor, illegitimate, and uneducated. This social state limits and dictates the possibilities open to her, as Bourdieu describes, and which Hugo presents to the reader from the point of view of Tholomyès. On the day he leaves Fantine, after calling her a phantom (1: 201; 137 [pt. 1, bk. 3, ch. 7]), he says in their group of friends that he is an illusion for her, and that she doesn't really hear what he says. He then bemoans the fact that "Les filles sont incurables sur l'épousaille" 'Women are incurable on the subject of weddings' (1: 201; 137 [pt. 1, bk. 3, ch. 7]), implying that she mistakenly harbors the idea of marrying him, another illusion. As the narrator said of these working girls earlier: "On les accable avec la splendeur de tout ce qui est immaculé et inaccessible" 'They are overwhelmed with the splendor of all that is immaculate and inaccessible' (1: 182; 121 [pt. 1, bk. 3, ch. 2]). The reader is made to see that her social status makes a life of marriage with Tholomyès a desirable but "inaccessible" option for her, outside the realm of possibility.

Discussion could then move to the question of class and gender more generally: Fantine's poverty and the lack of social capital provided by a bourgeois upbringing block the most desirable possibilities of fulfillment available to a woman because they are beyond her reach. Society, in a sense, symbolically steals this desired future from her, just as, more concretely, poverty makes her sell (thus essentially "stealing") her most valuable cultural capital (which has real value in the marriage and prostitution "markets"): her golden hair and her pearly teeth, which Hugo calls her dowry (1: 183; 122 [pt. 1, bk. 3, ch. 2]), and then her body itself. If convent cloistering is castration, then we see the same symbolic castration of Fantine in these excised body parts. Society has taken from her the best of what she was, both in her body and in her character since she has "tout perdu" 'lost all'; as the narrator says, "il ne reste plus rien à Fantine de ce qu'elle a été autrefois" 'Fantine has nothing left of what she had formerly been' (1: 261; 187–88 [pt. 1, bk. 5, ch. 11]); she is a slave (1: 261; 187 [pt. 1, bk. 5, ch. 11]), sold to society, and finally a ghost of her previous self, in Hugo's remarkable expression, a "triste spectre paré" 'a sad, overdressed specter' (1: 264; 190 [pt. 1, bk. 5, ch. 12]). Fantine is a "fantôme" 'phantom,' as Tholomyès describes her (1: 201; 137 [pt. 1, bk. 3, ch. 7]).

After studying Fantine's ghosting by poverty, students could then compare and contrast her with Éponine. Like Fantine, Éponine is forced by poverty into a degraded life. Described at first as a spoiled child, she reemerges later in Paris as a spectral form, as if poverty had turned her into a ghost as well. When she stands up to her father and his criminal accomplices, her spectral nature disturbs them, as Hugo compares her to "L'impassible linéament spectral rôdant sous un suaire, debout dans sa vague robe frissonnante, et qui leur semble vivre d'une vie morte et terrible" 'the impassive spectral figure prowling beneath a shroud, standing in its hazy trembling robe, and seeming to them to live with a dead and terrible life' (1: 363; 1021 [pt. 4, bk. 8, ch. 5]). Her impoverished circumstances also make of her a "jeune fille avortée" 'a misshapen young girl' (2: 19; 736 [pt. 3, bk. 8, ch. 4]), which suggests (particularly the French word) that she is arrested in her development; in another example she is similarly a "larve" 'larva' ("sprite" in the translation): in this case the two senses of the French word "larve," both the underdeveloped stage of an insect and of a ghost, have meaning (2: 27; 743 [pt. 3, bk. 8, ch. 5]).

One could then give students passages from the text that describe Éponine's masculinity. The following quotations show how, on the one hand, her arrested development and life of poverty seem to have masculinized her. She now has "une voix de vieux homme" 'the voice of an old man' (2: 18–19; 736 [pt. 3, bk. 8, ch. 3]), making her similar to the impoverished Fantine, whose voice, close to death, was "si rauque que les deux femmes crurent entendre une voix d'homme" 'so hoarse and rough that the two women felt they were hearing a man's voice' (1: 343; 254 [pt. 1, bk. 7, ch. 6]). On the other hand, Éponine and her sister seem to have no gender at all: "ni des enfants, ni des filles, ni des femmes . . . Tristes créatures sans nom, sans âge, sans sexe" 'neither children, nor girls, nor women . . . Sad creatures without name, age, or sex' (2: 21–22; 738–39 [pt. 3, bk. 8, ch. 4]). If the convent takes the nuns' sexual life from them, the Thénardier girls have their genders changed or stolen by poverty. One could give examples of the way in which the Thénardier parents also transgress normative gender identities, however in a comically odd way: la Thénardier is a giant masculine woman compared to her smaller mate.

Although in some ways Éponine's ghosting resembles that of Fantine, in others she differs greatly. When Éponine dresses in male garb, her genderless form convinces people of her masculinity, and she uses this trick to her own ends. Her masculinity and cross-dressing make possible her active involvement in life. Rather than passively acquiescing to her condemnation, like Fantine, who "plia sous cet arrêt" 'bowed to that decree' (1: 252; 180 [pt. 1, bk. 5, ch. 8]), Éponine forcefully intervenes to change the course of events, sending messages that change people's lives and standing up to a group of dangerous criminals, thus symbolically rejecting a more traditional and passive female role.

Discussion of women ends with Cosette, who presents an ambiguous final example of the spectral female. She begins life as an adored child, but is then reduced to spectral form as the battered and hungry waif who walks through the night to get water and who appears to be an "enfant garou," translated as "a fairy child" (1: 505; 386 [pt. 2, bk. 3, ch. 5]), but which is also in French a kind of ghost child in limbo who has died without being baptized (Drouet 96–97). Thus she represents again a ghostly *misérable* whose life has been stolen by the Thénardiers. However, from this oppressed but sometimes rebellious child who herself "stole" and played with the Thénardiers' doll against their orders, Cosette turns into Gavroche's thing, a "Chosette," translated as "What's-her-name" but also meaning "Little Thing" (2: 530; 1159 [pt. 4, bk. 15, ch. 2]), also "sa chose," translated as "his property, but more literally "his thing" that Marius enjoys having by his side (1: 365; 1023 [pt. 4, bk. 8, ch. 6]). She loses her will to Marius: "Il y avait de Marius à elle un magnétisme tout-puissant, qui lui faisait faire, d'instinct et presque machinalement, ce que Marius souhaitait" 'There was an all-powerful magnetism flowing from Marius to her, which made her do, instinctively and almost automatically, whatever Marius wished' (2: 847; 1429 [pt. 5, bk. 9, ch. 1]). Cosette says to him: "Eh bien, est-ce que je suis quel-qu'un?" 'Well, am I anybody?' (2: 815; 1401 [pt. 5, bk. 7, ch. 1]).

Class discussion can explore this ending for Cosette. It is true that her new life is good. However, even though her lot is improved, she now becomes the good wife, sheltered by and spectrally "disappeared" into her place in the home, the normative role allotted to bourgeois women in the course of the nineteenth century. She becomes the elegant doll she so much admired, a future predicted for her by the narrator who calls dolls "tout l'avenir de la femme" 'the whole future of woman is there' (1: 528; 405 [pt. 2, bk. 3, ch. 8]), even though Hugo himself had relationships with feminist and independent women (Savy, "Victor Hugo" 9). Valjean gives her the life that Fantine wanted.

Class discussion turns finally to Jean Valjean and his similarity to women in the novel, starting with the nuns and with his burial and near death in a nun's coffin: his literal burial parallels their "enterrement des âmes toutes vives" 'the live burial of the soul' (1: 657; 513 [pt. 2, bk. 7, ch. 3]). Like the nuns' "claustration" ("incarceration"), prison incarceration has been Valjean's lot, deemed "cette affreuse mort vivante . . . qu'on appelle le bagne" 'that terrible living death . . . called prison' (1: 310; 227 [pt. 1, bk. 7, ch. 3]). As in the case of the identity of the nuns and women, here society, the law, steals identity from the prisoner, as we hear from Marius: "le forçat n'est plus, pour ainsi dire, le semblable des vivants. La loi l'a destitué de toute la quantité d'humanité qu'elle peut ôter à un homme" 'the convict is no longer, so to speak, the fellow of the living. The law has deprived him of all the humanity it can take from a man' (2: 826; 1411 [pt. 5, bk. 7, ch. 2]). If society formed Fantine as Pygmalion formed Galatea, prison society formed Valjean: "Le bagne l'avait façonné"; in English "prison training," but also more literally "prison had shaped him" (1: 148; 93 [pt. 1, bk. 2, ch. 7]). One might again discuss Foucault and the discipline of social policing that takes away a certain kind of liberty, which imprisonment literally takes away.

Valjean's sexuality, like that of the nuns, has been taken from him, a symbolic "castration" like theirs. As a young man, he had to work to support his extended family and thus was never able to experience love. Several other male characters seem to have no sexuality: Enjolras, Javert, and Mabeuf. These three characters either revolt against the social order or cannot fit or succeed in it. This outsider status coincides with their state of nonnormative, "absent" sexuality and contrasts with Cosette's comfortable bourgeois life. It might be good to discuss with students that Hugo himself ironically enjoyed a rather scandalous sex life and to ponder with them its relation to the fate of his characters.

Comparison of Valjean with the women in the text then continues when Valjean, like Éponine, assumes different gender roles, specifically familial roles in his relationship with Cosette. He assumes nearly all possible family roles: "Père étrange forgé de l'aïeul, du fils, du frère, et du mari qu'il y avait dans Jean Valjean; père dans lequel il y avait même une mère" 'A strange father forged out of the grandfather, the son, the brother, and the husband that existed in Jean Valjean; a father in whom there was even a mother' (2: 523; 1154 [pt. 4, bk. 5, ch. 1]). This is similar to the roles that he plays in his biological family. Also significant is the name that he takes, "Madeleine," which represents the fallen woman redeemed; this name thus shows how "Madeleine" later completes the work of Fantine, the fallen woman, when in his role of "mère," as Cosette's adoptive "mother," he redeems himself by saving his "daughter."

Unlike the nuns and Fantine, Valjean does not accept his imprisonment and fate and continually tries to escape. He overcomes the harm done to him by society by educating himself and, instead of continuing to inflict the same harm on others, he helps them at the risk of his own well-being. Éponine, that other defiant androgynous being, does the same when she sacrifices herself for Marius. These two odd, nonnormative, spectral beings, robbed by society but seeking to change things and save others, embody much of the moral value in the novel. One might think of them as exiles from the center who act to change the way things are, like Hugo himself who was, as Jann Matlock notes, "exiled into ghostliness" from France for part of the time that he was writing this novel, and at the time when he was interested in ghosts and turning tables while in exile ("Ghostly Politics" 67). One might finish with the fact that Hugo linked the degraded status of women to exile in "À Celle qui est voilée": "Et femme, c'est-à-dire, exil?" 'And woman, that is to say, exile?' (*Les Contemplations* [1856] 2: 274).

Infinity and Home:
Exploring Moral Action in *Les Misérables*

Joseph Mai

I have taught *Les Misérables* most gratifyingly in the context of an assembly of seven honors students known as the Dixon Fellows. The students become "fellows" through a competitive process, and work informally with a professor on some question or text (in this case *Les Misérables* in translation). One of the explicit goals of the program is "to enable [the Fellows] to assume a position of leadership and responsibility in their communities and in the world" ("Dixon Fellow Program"). Taking the task seriously, I admit, creates a particular regime of reading, one that plays directly into Hugo's hands, given his rousing defense of the moral and social utility of his novel in the 1862 preface: "tant qu'il y aura sur la terre ignorance et misère, des livres de la nature de celui-ci pourront ne pas être inutiles" 'so long as ignorance and misery remain on earth, there should be a need for books like this.' Much of our discussion focuses on what we might mean by a book for which there "should be" a moral "need," or one that is "not useless," as Hugo puts it. At first, perhaps naively, students embrace the image of morality that emerges from the book, but they ultimately approach it more critically, albeit with a persevering admiration. Here I will concentrate on three aspects of the compelling problem of moral responsibility: first, the relation between conscience and action; second, the limits of altruism through the figure of the home; and third, ambiguities in Hugo's moral "system" through a discussion of the character Marius. The tutorial-like experience consists in a reading of the entire novel in chronological order over two semesters, with biweekly discussions driven by students' interest.

Infinity and Action

One of the first questions the fellows raise, during their reading of the book's opening passages on Bishop Myriel, is whether or not Hugo was religious. By considering three interrelated characters, the bishop, the senator, and the member of the Convention, they gain an insight into how Hugo in fact argues for neither religion nor atheism but for a notion that he calls "the infinite." Since the bishop's constant generosity and apparent selflessness come as a shock to most of his diocesan community, he seems like a rather disruptive religious representative, at least for organized religion. The senator enjoys needling the bishop with arguments for atheism and a naturalist materialism of the survival of the fittest. Myriel does not bother arguing against this "philosophie après boire" 'after-dinner philosophy' but merely points out that it can only be enjoyed by the rich and sounds more like the rationalization of tyrants than a foundation for ethical behavior (1: 56; 28 [pt. 1, bk. 1, ch. 8]).

A better sense of Hugo's theological and moral views comes during the meeting between the bishop and the Conventionnel G., a "monstre" living in the diocese, whom the bishop visits only because he is dying (1: 76; 35 [pt. 1, bk. 1, ch. 10]). The conventionnel turns out to be a "lumière inconnue" 'an unfamiliar light' who exposes the bishop's own prejudices concerning the revolution and the ancien régime, in part by recasting the death of Louis XVII as the death of a child rather than regicide and setting it alongside the numerous sufferings of the people (1: 76; 35 [pt. 1, vol. 1, ch. 10]). G. gives a rather contradictory definition of God: "l'infini est. Il est là. Si l'infini n'avait pas de moi, le moi serait sa borne; il ne serait pas infini; en d'autre termes, il ne serait pas. Or il est. Donc il a un moi. Ce moi de l'infini, c'est Dieu" 'The infinite exists. It is there. If the infinite had no *me* the *me* would be its limit; it would not be the infinite; in other words, it would not be. But it is. Then it has a *me*. This *me* of the infinite is God' (1: 87; 43 [pt. 1, bk. 1, ch. 10]). This variant of the ontological argument works from the notion of the infinite and then ascribes to it a face—an impossible to describe, contradictory, but necessary image. Later in the book Hugo will call the infinite "l'absolu dont nous sommes le relatif" 'the absolute of which we are the relative' (1: 662; 517 [pt. 2, bk. 7, ch. 5]). From the conventionnel the bishop learns that he himself holds prejudices and is attached to certain social hierarchies, which prevents him from perceiving how society can be improved for all. He gets, then, from the conventionnel a consciousness of being relative, of being only a part of an infinity that cannot be contained in class, religion, self, or any other societal limitation. Hugo's novel likewise attempts to paint a portrait of individuals in relation to the infinite rather than in relation to the contingent laws of society, self-interest, and materialism that rule their lives.

This critique prefigures the philosophy of Emmanuel Levinas, who has elaborated a twentieth-century ethical philosophy according to which Infinity is opposed to what Levinas calls totality. Whereas totality takes the self as a stable entity and its preservation as the primary motivation for action, infinity preexists and radically destabilizes the individual. Infinity calls for action that is first oriented toward the other, most directly in response to the vulnerability of the other person. *Les Misérables* is filled with this type of ethical alternative. I should note that Levinas's philosophy influences some of my teaching and inspires some of the subjects we discuss during the fellowship. However, the project does not focus on Levinas and students do not read more than an occasional quote. In the same way, we consider other moral philosophies, such as utilitarianism and consequentialism. In any case, Hugo's ethical outlook seems hard to pin down with one ethical theory or another.[1]

The individual perceives the infinite in conscience. Moral laws and consequences count significantly in *Les Misérables*, but they are less essential than the consciousness of others that inspires moral actions in the first place. Though they are unique and complex individuals, the characters of *Les Misérables* are first and foremost defined by their relation to the infinite. The self of the infinite—and Hugo famously tells us that *Les Misérables* is a "drame dont le premier personnage est l'infini" 'a drama whose first character is the Infinite' (1: 653; 509 [pt. 2, bk. 7, ch. 1])—expresses itself through them, exercising its will through humankind (the second character) to become present in the world. Valjean's selflessness is innate, but he has learned selfishness—an opposition to society, his enemy—through the experience of imprisonment. He does not come to his moral conversion through rational arguments; rather, it appears in front of him in an exposure to goodness from Bishop Myriel. After giving him the candlesticks and his freedom, the bishop tells him "vous n'appartenez plus au mal, mais au bien" 'you no longer belong to evil, but to good' (1: 163; 106 [pt. 1, bk. 2, ch. 12]).

The immediate obedience to conscience drives virtuous action in a highly spontaneous way, often independently of reflection. In the Champmathieu sequence, Hugo presents an ineluctably linear narrative in which Valjean learns about the situation of Champmathieu, buys a horse, rides to Arras under difficult circumstances, and confesses to the court. This narrative is preceded by what the narrator calls "le poème de la conscience humaine," in which Valjean wrings his hands over every possible implication of the act. His interior debate continues through the night and following day, until he finds himself in the courtroom, in a chapter playfully titled "Un lieu où des convictions sont en train de se former," translated as "A Place for Convictions" (1: 356; 265 [pt. 1, bk. 7, ch. 9]). Students enjoy unpacking the polysemy here: Champmathieu is about to be legally convicted but then is saved by Valjean, who will be convicted in his stead; but more important, it is here that Valjean's conviction is formed, as his conscious mind catches up to the moral action he has spontaneously initiated.

Operating in this way, consciousness of the infinite has a profound effect on how one looks at freedom. Levinas captures the paradox in the following way: "To philosophize is to trace freedom back to what lies before it, to disclose the investiture that liberates freedom from the arbitrary" (84–85). In other words, as one becomes a subject to goodness (what "lies before"), one attains a great deal of autonomy with regards to the world. Myriel's conscience gives him the freedom to ask the regicide conventionnel for his benediction. Valjean, belonging to the good, plows through all obstacles. What appears as Jean Valjean's autonomy is sourced in his conscience, which gives him the conviction and, somehow, the ability to perform courageous actions despite overwhelming circumstances.

Such conviction makes a character hostile to oppressive social hierarchies and constrictions. At this point in the discussion, however, Hugo, unlike many moral theorists, descends deeply into the ambiguities of concrete reality in a way that awakens students' critical minds. For Hugo's resistance to social repression is so strong that he does not seem entirely against breaking some rules and producing some negative consequences. Contrary to the rather sentimental image one gets from the stage musical and film adaptations of *Les Misérables*, Hugo is indeed not necessarily against stealing from stingy shopkeepers or shooting some national guardsmen; however piously, some of his most admired characters violate the moral prohibition to kill. I don't believe Hugo condones these actions. He states explicitly that they are morally ambiguous, sometimes wrong, but he seems willing to look past some bad side effects in order to burst through the laws that obscure life's moral dimension.

The question of acceptable violence is central to discussions of violence represented in the novel, but it is also extremely relevant to the fellows' contemporary situation. That these ambiguities are as salient today as they were in the 1860s was made clear by a passionate discussion about the parallels between *Les Misérables* and recent social unrest. For someone teaching in the United States during the fall semester of 2014, it was difficult to ignore the many parallels between the narrative and another story of a hulking petty criminal and the rather limited and authoritarian policeman who pursues him, this time in Ferguson, Missouri. Without here emphasizing the several uncanny resemblances between *Les Misérables* and the Ferguson case (including biographical details of the individuals involved, Hugo's condemnation of racial prejudice, even a negative mention of the slave-holding states of South Carolina—where I teach—and Missouri), it is worth noting that Hugo would not fully condemn, for example, the destruction of business property that occurred in the demands for democratic change. In fact Hugo would likely have condoned, if ambiguously, much harsher and more violent actions. These discussions relate literature to the students' lives and complicate their original acceptance of Hugo's version of infinity. Suddenly action becomes problematic, and students begin to read Hugo as a more complex, indeterminate author.

Self-Sacrifice and the Home

Students are generally more open to the idea of self-sacrifice than they are to the idea of sacrificing others. We approach the theme of self-sacrifice through the concept of the home, once again suggested by Levinas, who sees the home as a place of minimal material protection against the elements, a place to which one withdraws to a welcoming and safe life, and from which one can venture into the larger world (153–74). At first glance this might look like look a typical bourgeois position: the property owner is the best suited to contribute to society and thus to shape the law. Hugo's position is very different for two reasons. First, as we shall see in the case of Gavroche, "having a home" is by no means a question of legal proprietorship. Second, all Hugo's moral heroes, of the bourgeois class or not, are precisely those who, having a home, are willing to risk it to follow their conscience. This leaves several attitudes one might have toward homes, of which I will emphasize three here: the struggle to obtain one, the desire to maintain one, and the willingness to share or relinquish one. Those characters who are willing to share or relinquish their home seem to be the most compelling ones, since this willingness indicates freedom with regard to the self.

First, one must have a home if one is to play a role in society, and involuntary homelessness is exclusion. During his trial, Champmathieu tells the jurists (Bamatabois, the elector and "property owner" who had harassed Fantine, among them) the following: "Vous êtes bien malins de me dire où je suis né. Moi je l'ignore. Tout le monde n'a pas des maisons pour y venir au monde" 'You must be very smart to tell me where I was born. Me, I never knew. Everybody can't have houses to be born in' (1: 367; 274 [pt. 1, bk. 7, ch. 10]). Champmathieu's origins, identity, and participation in society are in doubt because of his lack of a home. He is approaching the fate of the numerous orphans and abandoned children in the book, on their way from homelessness to prison. Their homelessness is produced or at least encouraged by society: "La misère offre, la société accepte" 'misery makes the offer; society accepts' (1: 261; 187 [pt. 1, bk. 5, ch. 11]). Orphans, prostitutes, prisoners, and their like struggle to find homes, and until they do they lack social identity.

Being without a home does not necessarily make you a victim, for some are homeless by design in order to evade responsibility. Thénardier, "l'aubergiste," preys on the precarious and itinerant (where he also recruits his fellow criminals) and changes domiciles and identities to protect his criminal life: his homelessness is a refusal to participate responsibly in society. At the other extreme, the root of Javert's overly rigid police worldview is his birth in a prison to criminal parents. Nowhere in the novel is there mention of his house or apartment: he invades the spaces of others, lurks in the street, and retreats only to the police station. He goes there even to compose his "suicide" note, a simple list of improvements to the city's prisons rather than an explanation or a cry for help (perhaps a home would have opened up different choices). Voluntary homelessness, for these characters, is a way of refusing to participate in the call of conscience.

Through the stories of Fantine, Mabeuf the churchwarden, and the two boys abandoned by Thénardier, students explore the extremely tenuous line that separates those who have a home from the homeless. Perhaps the most creative and brazen character in the novel, in terms of homemaking, is Gavroche, an abandoned child himself, who generously shares his home with two other street kids (who also happen to be his brothers). Gavroche's transformation of Napoleon's dilapidated elephant at La Bastille, a forgotten relic of the Egyptian campaigns, illustrates how little material comfort it takes to make a home. Only a flimsy copper trellis cage separates the boys from the teeth of the rats (who have already eaten the cats Gavroche had adopted). Gavroche turns out his candle in the night with an odd expression that may reveal something of Hugo's humanism: "Les enfants, il faut dormir, mes jeunes humains" 'Children, we must sleep, my young humans' (2: 292; 962 [pt. 4, bk. 6, ch. 2]). For Levinas, one becomes human when another lifts one up to a vertical stance. Gavroche gives his brothers a lift into humanity by pulling them into the elephant, just as Valjean takes Cosette's bucket in the woods or carries Marius through the sewers.

Sometimes becoming a subject to the goodness of infinity requires more than sharing but actually risking a home or even choosing homelessness. The Bernardines of the Petit Picpus monastery choose to separate themselves from society in a habitation of extreme impoverishment. Their choice makes the convent "un des appareils d'optique appliqués par l'homme sur l'infini" 'one of the optical appliances man turns on the infinite' (1: 653; 509 [pt. 2, bk. 7, ch. 1]), a space outside society in which the suffering and exclusion of others are contemplated and remembered. There are other characters that have more established, even bourgeois homes, whether they have gained them through struggle (Valjean and Cosette) or have inherited them (Tholomyès, Bamatabois, Gillenormand, Marius, the father in the Luxembourg gardens episode, and many more). Here the question is whether a character has enough of a conscience to make material sacrifices in the name of generosity, or whether care for the home will give them a rigid attachment to law and social hierarchy. Bamatabois and Gillenormand obviously fall into the latter category. But Valjean, as Madeleine, also comes close to enjoying success so much that he misses Fantine's exclusion from his own factory. Later he risks overinvesting in his new home with Cosette. It is only the encounter with the nuns and their profound humility that keeps him from returning "tout doucement à la haine" 'gradually back to hatred' (1: 724; 569 [pt. 2, bk. 8, ch. 9]). After observing their abnegation he chooses "la plus divine des générosités humaines, l'expiation pour autrui" 'the most divine of all human generosity, expiation for others' (1: 727; 571 [pt. 2, bk. 8, ch. 9]). This is a self-abnegation in the service of others, only briefly tested later when Valjean must give up his home by entrusting Cosette to Marius.

Marius and the Critical Reader

Gavroche, Valjean, Eponine, Enjolras, and other characters act spontaneously as subjects to the good. They are inspiring and heroic but sometimes hard to identify with for readers who do not find themselves in such extraordinary circumstances. Mario Vargas Llosa refers to them as "monsters." But one of the most fascinating discussions I have had with the fellows involves Marius, a character that stands out because he is unexceptional and imperfect, indeed still a student, just as they are. The last part of our discussion looks more closely at this "mediocre and nondescript figure," who also happens to be the "most 'realist' character in the novel in that his actions are ambiguous and not obviously predictable" (Vargas Llosa 59).

Marius's ambiguities can be found, for instance, in the devolution of his moral certitude. He begins life as the spoiled grandchild of the snobbish M. Gillenormand, with the run of a wealthy bourgeois home. When he discovers his father, just after the latter's death, his moral bearings shift completely, both politically (becoming a Bonapartist) and personally (beginning his quest to help Thénardier). Until this point, one might say that his moral philosophy is paternalistic: he is following uncritically the model laid out for him by his grandfather and then his father. But Marius quickly loses confidence when Enjolras destroys his defense of Bonapartism with just a few words. The result is a relative vacuum of moral convictions, a blank slate that will lead to inappropriate responses and lack of spontaneity. The reader becomes suspicious of Marius's intelligence when he insists on helping the obviously sleazy Thénardier or when he allows the attack on Valjean to continue dangerously in the Gorbeau slum. Vargas Llosa calls him "naïve rather than intelligent, egotistical rather than generous, more passive than active . . . paralyzed by indecision" (58). Marius's moral autonomy comes to him abruptly and as a deep problem that is nearly impossible to work through.

Part of the problem is that Marius can rely only on the ponderous strategy of reasoning out complex moral situations rather than acting in them. We explore this in a close reading of the chapter titled "Cinq de moins, un de plus" 'Five Less, One More' (pt. 5, bk. 1, ch. 4), where Marius must decide which of five men chosen to leave the barricades—in order to live and care for their family—will be left behind, since there are only four National Guard uniforms for them to disguise themselves and escape. He is so petrified by the decision that he is reduced to counting the men over and over again, just to make sure there are indeed five, and then staring down and counting the four uniforms. How can he decide life and death for another? The movement of fate once again intervenes, bringing Valjean at just that moment: "un uniforme tomba, comme du ciel, sur les quatre autres" 'a fifth uniform dropped, as if from heaven, onto the four others' (2: 562; 1187 [pt. 5, bk. 1, ch. 4]). The numbers in the chapter title seem to mock whatever moral calculations Marius may have been making and substitute the very different mathematics of destiny.

Perhaps worse than being indecisive, Marius often comes off as selfish, especially in his attitude toward the home. Marius starts with a home that he gives up in rejecting paternalism but then regains a home thanks to Valjean. And yet, once he has returned to Gillenormand's house and inherited Valjean's fortune, he obtusely rejects Valjean, whom he has in typical fashion misread as having stolen Madeleine's money and murdered Javert. His late embrace of Valjean at the very end of the book strikes many as too slow, as if his lack of moral intuition has caused him to turn again to a bourgeois and selfish view of the home. These ambiguities figure prominently in the final chapter, which famously describes Valjean's abandoned, unmarked grave in a corner of Père Lachaise. Why end on this figure of neglect? How do we interpret the absence of Marius (and Cosette) in this last chapter?

But a more critical reading tempers the students' judgment of Marius. Some in the group feel that the narrator is arranging the action so much that it exceeds their willingness to suspend disbelief. We are happy that Valjean arrives at the barricade, but his almost magical appearance only avoids rather than solves the difficulties of navigating moral autonomy, in which reasoning certainly must play some role. The same critical readers consider Hugo's choice to close the book on Valjean's grave to be open to a number of interpretations, both negative and positive, which we work out in discussions by imagining a number of predictive narratives concerning Marius, Cosette, and their home. Some speculate that they are back at their impressive house, enjoying the money, perhaps a family, and general domestic tranquility and have simply forgotten the grave. Some say that the neglect proves that they have dedicated their lives to the poor and are working hard on social issues. Marius is sometimes described as a lawyer defending innocent criminals or as a politician working to improve the lives of children or women. Cosette is volunteering in orphanages. Others imagine that they have lost everything, or that they are exiled on some island for having been too vocally critical of the government. Interestingly, none of them really see Marius returning to the barricades or engaging in violent disobedience. Mostly they see the couple as functioning in society but dedicating much of their lives to its improvement. As these predictive narratives demonstrate, students are not wholly dismissive of Marius: they also recognize in him at least a strong desire to be a subject to moral goodness, even if his "evolution" is simply "not completed in one day" (Grossman, Les Misérables 115). In fact, many of their narratives imply a broader and more effective, if less heroic, social activism on the part of Marius than what Valjean was able to achieve through extreme self-abnegation.

The Usefulness of Reading

At the end of the year we return to both the preface and the goals of the program that framed our reading, and the fellows write an informal paper in which they address the moral utility of the book and the moral "system" they find within it. As many of these reports demonstrate, they are generally sympathetic to the ideas of infinity and the consciousness of others portrayed throughout the book. They think of Myriel, Valjean, and even Gavroche and Enjolras as models that spontaneously sacrifice their self-interest for the betterment of others. Many come out of the experience admitting that the book inspires them to get out of their houses and accept risk for moral actions. But they are not entirely convinced that these forms of radical freedom are feasible choices in many of the morally salient situations they themselves are likely to encounter. Many, for instance, doubt whether their conscience is always reliable and believe that more reflection is necessary even at the expense of action. Many balk at the partially condoned violence or at the extreme self-denial they find in the book. These varied reactions suggest that reading Les Misérables was not "useful" in the sense that it provided fellows with clear and set moral precepts, but clearly "not useless" either, for it served as a vast training ground for exploring complex moral questions and sounding their previously held opinions and intuitions.

NOTE

[1] For connections between Hugo and Levinas, see Bradley Stephens in *Victor Hugo, Jean-Paul Sartre, and the Liability of Liberty* (ch. 2), echoing and extending a line of thinking of Jacques Neefs in his essay "Penser par la fiction."

What the Novel Omits from the Musical: Teaching 1848 and the Misfortunes of Progress

William Paulson

One of the most difficult tasks in teaching *Les Misérables* to students who come to it through its modern adaptations is enabling them to comprehend the novel's deep connections to the historical and ideological conflicts of nineteenth-century France. This is a crucial aspect of the novel in that Hugo presents the plight of the *misérables* as requiring political action, and postrevolutionary French history generates much of his political lexicon. To today's students, however, most of this political-historical language initially feels both foreign and dead, and it can strike many of them as all the stranger an intrusion in the book since the musical (and the films) seem to get along well without it. Indeed, among the novel's features most often cut in adaptations are almost every detail pertaining to the specificity of history and ideology in nineteenth-century France. In the musical, for example, vague references to "the King"—whom American audiences can imagine as a sort of George III with no Atlantic Ocean to distance him—replace any concrete sense of the stakes of the 1830s uprisings against the July Monarchy or of Hugo's intransigent stand against "Napoleon the Little" at the time of the novel's publication.

It is thus both refreshingly counterintuitive and pedagogically useful to be able to turn the tables and use a key element added to the musical and not present in the novel as a point of entry into one of the knottiest historical and ideological problems of the text: the relation of *Les Misérables* to the revolution of 1848, specifically to the June workers' uprising and its violent suppression, in which Victor Hugo, as a recently elected member of the French National Assembly, was involved.

In the musical, two songs—"Turning" and "Empty Chairs at Empty Tables"—lament the dead of the barricade. (They were not part of the original French concept album but have been present in the English-language version of the musical since its opening in London.) To what do they correspond in the novel? In the case of "Turning," sung by "women of Paris," they correspond to nothing. "Empty Chairs," sung by Marius, could be said to have limited novelistic counterparts in two brief passages that describe Marius as both vaguely remembering and forgetting his friends and their death on the barricade (2: 740; 1338 [pt. 5, bk. 5, ch. 2] and 2: 763–64; 1358 [pt. 5, bk. 5, ch. 7]). Though an element of memory is involved, the emphasis lies far more on forgetting; the deaths on the barricade, for Marius, are marked more by a sense of unreality than by a sense of loss. There is no act (or even speech) of commemoration.

I will cite here only the more developed and lyrical of these passages, the one that might, at a stretch, be considered a novelistic source for the song of remembrance and lamentation in the musical. Yet even here, doubt and forget-fulness seem to triumph over conviction and memory:

> Par moments, Marius prenait son visage dans ses mains et le passé tu-multueux et vague traversait le crépuscule qu'il avait dans le cerveau. Il revoyait tomber Mabeuf, il entendait Gavroche chanter sous la mitraille, il sentait sous sa lèvre le froid du front d'Éponine; Enjolras, Courfeyrac, Jean Prouvaire, Combeferre, Bossuet, Grantaire, tous ses amis, se dres-saient devant lui, puis se dissipaient. Tous ces êtres chers, douloureux, vaillants, charmants ou tragiques, étaient-ce des songes? avaient-ils en ef-fet existé? L'émeute avait tout roulé dans sa fumée. Ces grandes fièvres ont de grands rêves. Il s'interrogeait; il se tâtait; il avait le vertige de toutes ces réalités évanouies. Où étaient-ils donc tous? était-ce bien vrai que tout fût mort? Une chute dans les ténèbres avait tout emporté, excepté lui. Tout cela lui semblait avoir disparu comme derrière une toile de théâtre. Il y a de ces rideaux qui s'abaissent dans la vie. Dieu passe à l'acte suivant.
> (2: 763–64 [pt. 5, bk. 5, ch. 7])

> At times Marius covered his face with his hands, and the vague past tu-multuously crossed the twilight that filled his brain. He would see Ma-beuf fall again, would hear Gavroche singing under the hail of bullets; he felt the chill of Eponine's forehead against his lip; Enjolras, Courfeyrac, Jean Prouvaire, Combeferre, Bossuet, Grantaire, all his friends, would rise up in front of him, then dissipate. All these beings, dear, sorrowful, valiant, charming, or tragic—were they dreams? Had they really existed? The uprising had cloaked everything in its smoke. Great fevers have great dreams. He would question himself; he groped within himself; he was dizzy with all these vanished realities. Then where were they all? Was it really true that all were dead? A fall into the darkness had carried off everything, except himself. It all seemed to him to have disappeared as if behind a curtain at a theater. There are such curtains that drop in life. God is moving on to the next act.   (1358)

This entire passage fits the progression of the verbs in the phrase listing the names of the dead: "se dressaient devant lui, puis se dissipaient" 'would rise up in front of him, then dissipate.' It begins with evocative memories ("[h]e would see Mabeuf fall," etc.) but then shifts to, and through, a series of terms that serve to strip the dead of their human features, effacing distinctions between human beings and actions or events: "Tous *ces êtres* chers . . . toutes *ces réalités* évanouies . . . *tout* fût mort? . . . avait *tout* emporté . . . *Tout cela* lui semblait avoir disparu . . ." 'All *these beings* . . . all *these vanished realities* . . . all were dead? . . . had carried off everything . . . *It all* seemed to him to have disap-peared . . .' (emphasis added). It is no surprise that after this moment there is no further mention of Marius's dead friends in the novel.

The only other passage in the novel evoking any of these dead is even more negative: a laconic exchange between Marius and Gillenormand, on the initiative of the latter, in which Marius tells his grandfather that his friend Courfeyrac has died—he does not say how or where—and then makes no protest when the old man reacts by saying "Ceci est bien" 'Very well' (2: 750; 1346 [pt. 5, bk. 5, ch. 4]).

Now one may object that Cameron Mackintosh and his collaborators simply added something foreign to the novel and that it is thus logically as well as chronologically absurd to speak of an omission on Hugo's part. But it is an omission not merely with respect to the late-twentieth-century musical but with respect to a romantic narrative schema that could legitimately be expected in Hugo's work and that, indeed, can be found in other parts of *Les Misérables*: one mourns one's dead and draws inspiration from them while continuing on their path. The two most striking instances of this schema in the novel concern, first, Marius and his father and, second, the men of the barricade and old Monsieur Mabeuf. Young Marius's pilgrimages to his father's grave are accompanied, of course, by Hugo's famous (and partially autobiographical) descriptions of how Marius, inspired by his father, discovers the Napoleonic Empire, thus rejecting his grandfather's reactionary ideology and even becoming receptive to the cause of the revolutionary republic when it is presented to him by the Friends of the ABC. One could reasonably expect the same of Marius in the wake of his friends' death on the barricade: mourning their loss, he would rededicate himself to the cause for which they gave their lives. This is, after all, how the barricade's first dramatic death is treated: after Mabeuf is shot dead while waving the red flag of revolution, Enjolras calls on his comrades to draw inspiration from his sacrifice, proclaiming the old man's bullet-riddled and bloodstained jacket to be "maintenant notre drapeau" 'our flag now' (2: 499; 1134 [pt. 4, bk. 14, ch. 2]). In other words, in adding "Turning" and "Empty Chairs at Empty Tables," the creators of the English-language musical respected and even followed a Romantic narrative paradigm central to Hugo's novel—but omitted by Hugo himself in the fifth part with respect to Marius and the dead of the barricade.

The cause for which the men of the barricade died disappears from the final part of the novel as well. The forgetful half memories of Marius make no reference to the men's political commitment or to the place of their sacrifice in history. Transformed into Cosette's very bourgeois husband, Marius gives no sign of drawing inspiration from his fallen comrades or of rededicating himself to any political action. This is all the more surprising in that Marius is a lawyer, a profession that would lend itself well to joining the cause of "Reform"—the most common label for the political agitation that, following the failure of the early 1830s uprisings such as that of June 1832, sought to transform the July Monarchy. Marius, after all, had been presented from the outset as a fictional character charged with ideological meaning. His awakening to politics draws on key elements of Hugo's mythologized account of his own life, and it is through him that the story of Jean Valjean and Cosette is brought to the barricades. Hugo could easily have extended this political significance by telling his readers that the post-barricade Marius would still support the cause of social justice, thereby honoring both his friends and (in a different way) his father-in-law—but he did nothing of the sort.

Students can thus be productively invited to reflect not only on the relation between the absence of memorialization and the eclipse of the progressive (as distinct from the redemptive) narrative in part 5 of *Les Misérables* but also on the role of 1848 in both the text and the composition of Hugo's novel. As is well known, Hugo largely drafted the first four parts before the February 1848 revolution, presumably expecting to complete it under the regime then in power, the July Monarchy of Louis-Philippe. The historical horizon of expectations, for Marius and for readers who identified with him, would have been a social movement or process of reform capable of realizing what Hugo's *combattants* of June 1832 had sought: some fulfillment of what the French Revolution of 1789 had started. My language here is deliberately vague, because we cannot know how Hugo would have finished *Les Misères* (as the novel was then called) in 1848 or 1849 had no revolution intervened. He had already written Marius's discovery of the virtues of the First Empire and the French Revolution through his father, and he had placed the uprising of June 1832 at the novel's climax—indications that its end might point to a future revolution or republic that would fulfill the promises and sacrifices made since 1789, and especially those of 1832. On the other hand, Hugo himself, named a life peer by Louis-Philippe, was not then a partisan of a republic, and certainly not of the overthrow of the monarchy under which he enjoyed favor and privilege—whence the plausibility of a "reform" option that would advance the cause of social justice without envisaging the July Monarchy's downfall. (It is even possible that the defeat of 1832 might have been interpreted as a lesson to Marius and others that peaceful reform should be chosen over armed insurrection or that poverty and ignorance, rather than monarchy, were the real ills against which to struggle.) Under these circumstances, a Marius who would honor the memory of his friends by taking up some version of their cause through other means, presumably less revolutionary, would have been a plausible figure for the final part of the novel.

In June 1848, Hugo, as a recently elected member of the National Assembly, went to several barricades to demand that the insurrection surrender to the Second Republic and apparently offered words of encouragement (or even command) to those conducting military operations against the workers in revolt (Robb 268–78; Leuilliot, "Les barricades"). Following June 1848, however, Hugo moved politically to the left, and by opposing the coup d'état of Louis-Napoléon Bonaparte on 2 December 1851 and then going into exile, he became the most famous and intransigent opponent of the Second Empire. He returned to his unfinished novel only in 1860–61, writing the last book of part 4 and all of part 5, while adding many elaborations, digressions, and interpretive commentaries to what he had written from 1845 to 1848.

The importance of 1848 in Hugo's twelve-year break from writing *Les Misérables* is underscored by the final part's opening chapter, in which he leaves the gathering storm of 5 June 1832 to describe and analyze at length the barricades of the June 1848 workers' uprising, erected and defended fifteen years after the novel's chronological endpoint (Valjean's death in the summer of 1833). Here the barricade of June 1832 becomes "une ébauche et . . . un embryon" 'a rough draft, an embryo' of those of June 1848 (2: 549; 1176 [pt. 5, bk. 1, ch. 2]). In what reads like a desperate bid to maintain a progressive philosophy of history when many others had questioned or even abandoned it, Hugo asserts that "Juin 1848 fut . . . un fait à part, et presque impossible à classer dans la philosophie de l'histoire" 'June 1848 was . . . a thing apart, and almost impossible to classify in the philosophy of history' (2: 542; 1170 [pt. 5, bk. 1, ch. 1]). One plausible interpretation of this statement is that in order to maintain a "philosophy of history," a configuration in which history is meaningful and purposive, June 1848 must simply be set aside as an exception.

It is as if Hugo could not continue to recount the insurrection of 1832 without justifying (and, to at least a degree, regretting) his complicity in the Second Republic's repression of the 1848 workers' uprising. (He may also have realized that he could no longer motivate readers' interest in June 1832 — as of the novel's publication, a thirty-year-old incident in the early years of a now-vanished regime — without attaching it to the more recent and momentous social cataclysm of the June Days.)

In reprising and finishing *Les Misérables* from 1860 to 1862, Hugo in effect changed his novel's relation to the arc of nineteenth-century French history in two distinct and barely compatible ways.[1] On the one hand, consistent with his own move to the left, he adds the many interpretive digressions that link the tale of his characters much more explicitly to French history since the Revolution of 1789. These include the bishop's conversation with the old revolutionary; the account of Waterloo; the detailed story of Tholomyès and Fantine in part 1, book 3; "Parenthèse" (the discussion of convents); much of the section on the *gamin de Paris*; most of "Les Amis de l'ABC"; "Patron-Minette"; and the chapter on Louis-Philippe together with much of the surrounding material in "Quelques pages d'histoire."[2] The effect of these sections is to reinforce the sense that the June 1832 revolt, the novel's dramatic climax, was a way station on the path of progress: a defeat whose losses will one day be redeemed by a definitive triumph, the establishment of a just regime that will fulfill the promise of the 1789 Revolution. (This is roughly what the creators of the musical point to by concluding with a stirring reprise of "Do You Hear the People Sing," offering an idealized and dehistoricized version of Hugo's narrative of progress.) Given the novel's revised first four parts, then, a Marius who would honor the memory of his friends by taking up the causes of social justice and the republic through other means, probably (though no longer necessarily) more peaceful and less revolutionary, would have been a logical figure for part 5.

On the other hand, however, the Hugo of 1860–62 did not fail to register the discouraging and disturbing lessons of June 1848. After reinforcing a progressive and even revolutionary horizon of expectations through his revision of parts 1 through 4, and affirming that horizon of expectations once again at the beginning of part 5, Hugo lets it slip away following the defeat of the barricade — through Marius's failure to remember or commemorate his dead comrades and through the subsequent disappearance of politics from his life. The absence of commemoration of the dead of the barricade goes hand in glove with the complete depoliticization of Marius, who never rededicates himself to their struggle. It thus illuminates a side of Les Misérables that is closer than one might expect to the melancholic post-1848 disillusionment typically associated with Baudelaire, Flaubert, and Nerval (whom Hugo explicitly takes to task in part 5 for confusing the halt in progress with the death of God [2: 621; 1236 (pt. 5, bk. 1, ch. 20)]). The contrast with the Romantic memorialization of the dead in the musical thus provides an effective entry into some of the novel's most fascinating internal tensions, which are related to its status as a work of belated Romanticism that attempts to affirm an idealized vision of progress at a time when the historical conditions that had sustained such visions had shattered.

I conclude by trying to answer two questions about this approach. First, Is this material actually teachable? Second, Why is it worth teaching?

Historical reference is undoubtedly a "hard sell" with students, even majors and minors with some background in French culture. Entire lectures on nineteenth-century French political history, even when the teacher feels comfortable giving them, are probably not a good idea. Fortunately, small doses of (external) historical instruction suffice, because Hugo himself sets out to teach the relevant history to his readers.[3] The French Revolution is covered in the bishop's conversation with the dying revolutionary; Waterloo has its own book; the Bourbon Restoration is explicated apropos of Tholomyès and Gillenormand; the July Monarchy in the first book of part 4; and so on. In my experience it is important to use students' goodwill toward the novel itself and the energy of Hugo's writing to encourage them to engage the political and historical material from the very beginning — in the bishop's dialogue with G., to be sure, but even before that in the first pages describing Msgr. Myriel's life and career. If the interest of such passages can be established or at least strongly suggested at this early stage, later (and admittedly longer and more digressive) ones will seem less strange. In general, Hugo's historical discussions can be made accessible to an adequate extent with fairly brief presentations of external information.

To be sure, Hugo's discussions are not scholarly or comprehensive histories, but history largely matters in Les Misérables insofar as it provides a political vocabulary to those who are assumed to remember it or to be able to partake in a collective memory that stretches somewhat beyond the limits of an individual's. History, in the novel, is close to memory. The successive regimes of nineteenth-century France signify, in other words, in ways comparable to the political-historical role played by decades or governments associated with particular dominant tendencies in recent times: "the sixties," "the Reagan (or Thatcher) years." Such comparisons, while always inexact, can give students a way of identifying with the time intervals between the historical events Hugo discusses and the times at which he is writing or publishing his novel. To be sure, the ideological and symbolic distance between nineteenth-century French regimes is far greater than anything experienced in postwar western democracies, but this very difference argues in favor of the interest and importance of Hugo's way of discussing politics through history.

As for the value of teaching the historical material, there is first its obvious importance to the author and in the economy of the novel: Hugo believed that the story of the *misérables* needed to be told in conjunction with that of modern attempts to create a more just and inclusive society. His story's true title, he writes, is "le Progrès" 'Progress' (2: 628; 1242 [pt. 5, bk. 1, ch. 20]). Yet he wrote this (and similar) ringing affirmations after two disillusioning blows to progressive hopes and narratives: the suppression of the June 1848 workers' uprising and the coup d'état of 2 December 1851. Complicit in the former and staunchly, famously opposed to the latter, Hugo's public persona was deeply marked by these calamities. Twelve years is a long time to drop one's greatest novel, to be uncertain if one will ever return to it! The significance of the novel's failure to conclude in its own progressive mode goes beyond politics. The shadow cast by 1848 over the final part of *Les Misérables* is a powerful reminder that even great works are beset with internal contradictions, that what are now the most famous and seemingly inescapable stories were once fragile works in progress, subject to the vicissitudes of history, part of the improvisational performances that made up their authors' lives. The novel's text teaches this lesson in a way that none of its modern adaptations have even attempted.

NOTES

[1] There is actually a third such modification, more punctual and less germane to the present argument: he refers several times to his own exile and his opposition to the Second Empire of Napoleon III.

[2] Most of these additions (but not those of "Les Amis de l'ABC" and "Quelques pages d'histoire") are signaled by notes in the Gohin edition cited here. English translations, even annotated ones, do not in general provide this information. For more comprehensive information on the composition history of the novel, see the 1985 edition by Guy-Rosa and Annette Rosa, especially pp. 1220–48, and the remarkable Web edition of the novel, directed by Guy Rosa (on the site *Groupe Hugo*) which provides three versions: the first draft, the state of the text as of February 1848, and the published text (groupugo .div.jussieu.fr/Miserables/).

[3] A seriously annotated edition or translation is helpful. Among the most useful works in English for students interested in studying the historical situation are Doyle and Fortescue.

But I Digress:
Teaching *Les Misérables* through the Historical and Philosophical Digressions

Mary Anne O'Neil

In his summary of the criticism leveled at Hugo at the time of the publication of *Les Misérables* in 1862, biographer Graham Robb notes that the "biggest supposed fault is Hugo's notorious tendency to go charging off on vast 'digressions'"(382). Much like today's students, who are accustomed to commercial literature's focus on the narrative, early reviewers were perplexed at the number of pages devoted to monasticism, warfare, and civil engineering, issues not apparently related to the plotline. It did not help that Hugo himself seemed to discount the relevance of his digressions. In the second paragraph of the novel, for example, he tells the reader that the life of Msgr. Myriel, the subject of the long digression that opens the novel, "ne touche en aucune manière au fond même de ce que nous avons à raconter" 'in no way concerns our story' (1: 35; 1 [pt. 1, bk. 1, ch. 1]). Jean Gaudon reports Flaubert's reaction to *Les Misérables*: "Et les digressions! Y'en-a-t-il! Y'en a-t-il!" 'And the digressions! So many of them! So many!' (qtd. in Gaudon ii; my trans.)

Critics in the second half of the twentieth century would view the digressions more favorably. The novelist Michel Butor claims that, through the digressions, Hugo departs from the dominant eighteenth- and nineteenth-century novelistic convention of concentrating on the life of a single character, as if the novel were a fictional biography. Hugo constantly "coupe le fil" 'cuts the thread' of his narration, so that the reader is encouraged not to reduce the novel to the adventures of Jean Valjean (61; my trans.). For Butor, the digressions are Hugo's way of situating the novel's many characters in contemporary history—not only in the context of current events but also in nineteenth-century intellectual and social history (62). The digressions allow Hugo to address enigmas that fascinate him by their poetic power, such as the redemption of a criminal or the power of prayer (64). For Gaudon, the tradition that Hugo subverts is that of equating the novel with Aristotelian tragedy and expecting every element of the narration to lead ineluctably to a dénouement (iv–v). Hugo breaks with this model through the digressions, exposing his philosophy of history and his aesthetics (ix). By doing so, he creates the polycentric novel, the forerunner of the twentieth century's nontraditional novel practiced by Proust, the surrealists, and the new novelists (xvi–ii). In his comments on the structure of the novel, Laurence Porter notes that "Hugo's historical and cultural digressions set the stage for the characters, explain the limits of their possibilities, and often hint at, foreshadow, or symbolize what he sees as an overarching spiritual odyssey of Fall and Redemption" (138). Victor Brombert, in *Victor Hugo and the Visionary Novel*, explains that Hugo uses the digressions to illustrate the plot's many parallels, such as the comparison between prisons and convents (128).

The length of *Les Misérables*, read without the digressions, already poses a problem for a teacher who has only a few class periods to devote to the novel. Yet leaving out the digressions makes it extremely difficult to come up with a coherent explanation for how Jean Valjean transforms himself from a criminal to a savior and why Hugo presents the failed June 1832 insurrection as a victory, not to mention why we should give any consideration to secondary characters like Gavroche. Among the novel's many digressions, I have found that the following are the most helpful in making sense of the novel's complex themes and events:

Pt. 1, bk. 1: "Un juste" 'An Upright Man'
Pt. 2, bk. 1: "Waterloo"
Pt. 2, bk. 7: "Parenthèse" 'A Parenthesis'
Pt. 3, bk. 7: "Patron-Minette"
Pt. 4, bk. 7: "L'argot" 'Argot'
Pt. 5, bk. 2: "L'intestin de Léviathan" 'The Intestine of Leviathan'

The first fifty pages of "Un juste" present in great detail the past, daily activities, and social interactions of the Bishop of Digne. They can easily be summarized as the description of an upright priest. However, the two final chapters of the digression—"Ce qu'il croyait" 'What He Believed' and "Ce qu'il pensait" 'What He Thought'—turn to the beliefs that inspire the bishop's charitable behavior. Hugo insists that Monseigneur Myriel, or Bienvenu as he is called by his parishioners, is not bound by church dogma. Motivated by "un excès d'amour" 'an excess of love' (1: 98; 52 [pt. 1, bk. 1, ch. 13]), he accepts as his unique doctrine Christ's command to love one another (1: 104; 57 [pt. 1, bk. 1, ch. 14]). Neither is he a mystic. He expresses his faith by giving alms and consoling the afflicted through self-sacrifice but also work (1: 100; 54 [pt. 1, bk. 1, ch. 13]). He communicates with the deity through nonrational means. The words "meditation," "contemplation," "reverie," and "prayer" recur throughout these chapters, and the bishop is pictured several times meditating on the stars. Hugo also tells us that the bishop's love is not a matter of temperament. He was not always a saintly man:

> Monseigneur Bienvenu avait été jadis . . . un homme passionné, peut-être violent. Sa mansuétude universelle était moins un instinct de nature que le résultat d'une grande conviction filtrée dans son cœur à travers la vie et lentement tombée en lui, pensée à pensée.   (1: 99 [pt. 1, bk. 1, ch. 13])

> Monseigneur Bienvenu had formerly been a passionate, even violent man. His universal tenderness was less an instinct of nature than the result of a strong conviction filtered through life into his heart, slowly dropping into him, thought by thought.   (53)

The transformation the bishop has already experienced will serve as a model for that of Jean Valjean.

One way to open a discussion of the protagonist's resemblance to Bienvenu is to ask how Jean Valjean's conscience is awakened and subsequently develops. We discover that he, like the bishop, perceives truth through suprarational avenues. He initially grasps his moral degradation during the Petit Gervais episode when, in a hallucinatory state, he hears a bodiless voice presenting the choice between salvation and damnation. A dream that follows the sleepless night in "Une tempête sous un crâne" 'A Tempest within a Brain' sets him on the road to Arras, where he ultimately saves Champmathieu. He perceives the nuns' chant as "un hymne qui sortait des ténèbres, un éblouissement de prière et d'harmonie dans l'obscur et effrayant silence de la nuit" 'a hymn emerging from the darkness, a bewildering mingling of prayer and harmony in the fearful, shadowy silence of the night' when he enters the Petit Picpus Convent (1: 595; 461 [pt. 2, bk. 5, ch. 6]). This pattern continues to the novel's conclusion. Jean Valjean navigates the maze of the Paris sewers "ne voyant rien, ne sachant rien, plongé dans le hasard, c'est-à-dire englouti dans la providence" 'seeing nothing, knowing nothing, plunged into chance, that is to say, swallowed up in Providence' (2: 672; 1280 [pt. 5, bk. 3, ch. 1]). He spends "La nuit blanche" 'The White Night' that precedes his decision to reveal his identity to Marius in a "rêverie vertigineuse" 'whirling reverie' (2: 798; 1388 [pt. 5, bk. 6, ch. 4]) in which he communicates with "Le On qui est dans les ténèbres" 'The One Who Is in the Darkness' (2: 799; 1388).

Another way to connect Valjean to Bienvenu is to ask how closely his life after the Petit Gervais episode resembles that of the bishop. Students will easily note that in Montreuil-sur-Mer Valjean uses the money gained from his theft to build a factory that employs and brings prosperity to the community. He works as a gardener in the Petit Picpus Convent. He opens his purse to the poor on his daily walks through Paris with Cosette. His self-sacrifice goes further than that of Bienvenu, since he risks his life in the Parisian sewers to save Marius and ultimately relinquishes the only person he has loved, Cosette. Such extraordinary acts of self-denial justify the comparisons between Jean Valjean and Christ that Hugo makes with increasing frequency in part 5.

When we reach the novel's conclusion, I ask students to read the death scene in the light of the chapters of "Un juste" that we have studied. Such a comparison makes the novel's final pages appear much less sentimental. When the dying hero tells Cosette and Marius "Aimez-vous bien toujours. Il n'y a guère autre chose que cela dans le monde: s'aimer" 'Love each other dearly always. There is scarcely anything else in the world but that: to love one another,' he is repeating the bishop's words (2: 886; 1461 [pt. 5, bk. 9, ch. 5]). In imitation of Bienvenu's contemplative pose in the garden, Valjean dies gazing at the heavens. Both the language and imagery of this scene remind us of the crucial role the bishop plays in Valjean's transformation from criminal to upright man.

The remaining five digressions are more closely related to Hugo's account of nineteenth-century French history, which merges with the story of the convict turned savior in the course of the novel. Writing from exile, at a time when

France had been ruled for over a half century by monarchs, Hugo sought to reassure his readers that the values of 1789—liberty, equality, and fraternity—still exerted an irresistible influence over human events. This is the message of part 4, "L'idylle rue Plumet et l'épopée rue Saint-Denis" 'Saint-Denis and Idyll of the Rue Plumet,' and the beginning of part 5, "Jean Valjean," on the unsuccessful June 1832 insurrection, which Hugo interprets as a revolutionary event that furthers the cause of democracy. He prepares the reader to accept his belief that the values of the French Revolution have not been extinguished, beginning in part 2, "Cosette," through the digressions "Waterloo" and "Parenthèse."

Brombert calls "Waterloo" "the most provocative digression in all of Hugo's fiction" because of its length and tenuous connection to the plot (*Victor Hugo* 86). Only students of military history will be interested in the detailed analyses of geography or the protracted descriptions of the battle that crushed Napoleon's imperialist ambitions. The link to the plot comes in the final chapter (pt. 2, bk. 1, ch. 19), where Thénardier, who has already appeared in part 1, accidentally saves the wounded Colonel Pontmercy, the father of the novel's younger hero, Marius. Teachers may wish to read the last pages of this chapter for their relevance to the plot or they may simply summarize the story. Two brief chapters, "L'inattendu" 'The Unexpected' and "Faut-il trouver bon Waterloo?" 'Should We Approve of Waterloo?,' present Hugo's interpretation of the historical importance of Waterloo and should be read in their entirety.

In "L'inattendu," after describing the French cavalry's tumble into an unexpected ravine—the event that initiated the imperial army's defeat—Hugo asks if Napoleon could have won the battle under different circumstances. He answers: "Bonaparte vainqueur à Waterloo, ceci n'était plus dans la loi du dix-neuvième siècle. . . . Cet individu comptait à lui seul plus que le groupe universel" 'For Bonaparte to be conqueror at Waterloo was no longer within the law of the nineteenth century. . . . This individual alone counted for more than the whole of mankind' (1: 436–37; 329 [pt. 2, bk. 1, ch. 9]). After the revolution, history would not tolerate the supremacy of a single individual. To those who might point out that Napoleon's defeat ushered in the reign of Louis XVIII, Hugo replies, in "Faut-il trouver bon Waterloo?," that neither the Restoration kings nor Louis-Philippe were absolute monarchs but rather leaders bound by law to respect the rights of their citizens (2: 460; 349 [pt. 2, bk. 1, ch. 27]). The cause of liberty had advanced. More important, in this chapter Hugo equates progress with revolution but also with the future:

> Voulez-vous vous rendre compte de ce que c'est que la révolution, appelez-le Progrès; et voulez-vous vous rendre compte de ce que c'est que le progrès, appelez-le Demain. Demain fait irrésistiblement son œuvre. . . . Il arrive toujours à son but étrangement.   (1: 460 [pt. 2, bk. 1, ch. 27])

> If you wish to understand what Revolution is, call it Progress; and if you wish to understand what Progress is, call it Tomorrow. Tomorrow performs

its work irresistibly. . . . It always accomplishes its aim through unexpected
means.   (349)

Here Hugo tells us that revolution is inevitable. Since we do not understand the
mysterious workings of progress as he does, he will demonstrate how to interpret all events in French history since 1789 as steps toward democracy.

"Parenthèse," the penultimate book of part 2, is as much about the author's spiritual convictions as about French history. Brombert and others have
pointed out that Hugo was specifically concerned with countering the rise of
atheism and materialism among political liberals and social reformers in Second Empire France (Albouy 122–23; Brombert, *Victor Hugo* 118–19; Leuilliot,
"Philosophie(s)" 60–61). The digression indeed begins with the statement: "Ce
livre est un drame dont le premier personage est l'infini" 'This book is a drama
whose first character is the infinite' (1: 653; 509 [pt. 2, bk. 7, ch. 1]). In these
pages, however, Hugo not only declares his faith in an infinite being but ex-
tends the argument he presented in "Waterloo" to find the seeds of democracy
in France's past. He presents the convent as an early revolutionary community.
While he condemns the fanaticism of the cloister, he sees the nuns as precursors
to 1789: "Là où il y a la communauté, il y a la commune; là où il y a la commune,
il y a le droit. Le monastère est le produit de la formule: Égalité, Fraternité. . . .
la Liberté suffit à transformer le monastère en république" 'Where community
exists, there likewise exists the true body politic, and where the latter is, there too
is justice. The monastery is the product of the formula "Equality, Fraternity." . . .
Liberty is enough to transform the monastery into a republic!' (1: 661; 516
[pt. 2, bk. 7, ch. 4]). Readers have no difficulty in divining Hugo's message: the ir-
repressible impulse toward democracy is found throughout human history.

In parts 3 and 4, two digressions keep the focus on revolution even as the plot
becomes more complicated. "Les mines et les mineurs" 'Mines and Miners,'
the brief opening chapter of "Patron-Minette" (pt. 3, bk. 7), is placed between
the story of Marius's intellectual evolution and the ambush of Jean Valjean by
Thénardier's criminal gang. Here, the author presents society as a mine, where
writers, philosophers, politicians, and religious thinkers throughout history are
constantly eroding the foundations of established order until revolution erupts
to propel humanity forward. His claim that all these workers, "depuis le plus
sage jusqu'au plus fou, ont une similitude . . . : le désintéressement" 'from the
wisest to the craziest, have one thing in common . . . disinterestedness' serves a
practical purpose (1: 904; 719–20 [pt. 3, bk. 7, ch. 1]). The notion of disinterestedness prepares us for Jean Valjean's involvement in the insurrection, his pardon of Javert, and the rescue of Marius. It also anticipates the willingness of the
young friends of the ABC to die for a lost cause. Hugo uses this short digression
to remind his readers—and France's rulers—that his writings undermine the
Second Empire just as the *philosophes'* books weakened the old regime.

"L'argot," (pt. 4, bk. 7) is a philological *tour de force* in which Hugo gives the
entire history of French slang. We need only read the digression's final chapter,

"Les deux devoirs: veiller et espérer" 'The Two Duties: To Watch and to Hope,' where Hugo recognizes the people as the force that will bring the revolution to fruition in the nineteenth century: "Oui, le Peuple, ébauché par le dix-huitième siècle, sera achevé par le dix-neuvième. Idiot qui en douterait! L'éclosion future, l'éclosion prochaine du bien-être universel, est un phénomène divinement fatal" 'Yes, the people, rough-hewn by the eighteenth century, shall be completed by the nineteenth. An idiot is any who doubts it! The future birth, the speedy birth of universal well-being, is a divinely inevitable phenomenon' (2: 338; 1000 [pt. 4, bk. 7, ch. 4]). By their appropriation of the French language, the poor and orphaned who populate the novel continue 1789's revolt against oppression.

The four digressions we have just examined give the theory of history that Hugo brings to life in the story of the barricades. The length of this episode—it begins in the second half of part 4 and concludes only in the first book of part 5—makes it difficult to read in its entirety. If possible, students should read chapters 15–24 of the first book, "La guerre entre quatre murs" 'War Between Four Walls,' which recount the heroic actions and deaths of many of the novel's secondary characters and bring together the novel's two protagonists, Jean Valjean and Marius. It is impossible to miss the allusions to the French Revolution in these pages. The insurgents address each other as "Citoyen" 'Citizen.' Grantaire and Enjolras die as the former cries "Vive la République!"(2: 640; 1252 [pt. 5, bk. 1, ch. 23]). Hugo's message is clear: June 1832 continued the work of 1789.

However, to paraphrase our author, "Should we approve of the insurrection?" A look back at the digressions in parts 2, 3, and 4 tells us yes. Unlike Napoleon, who fought for personal glory, the insurgents of 1832—in Hugo's view, at least—fight for the whole of mankind. They exemplify the republican values of equality and fraternity as they struggle for liberty. The participants are of every age, from the elderly Mabeuf to the child Gavroche. They are retirees, students, lawyers, parents, bachelors, thinkers, workers, and beggars. Hugo has composed his gathering of troops to create the impression of a truly democratic action. The inclusion of Gavroche and Éponine, representatives of the lowest classes—the poor and illiterate—harks back to "Mines and Miners," where Hugo warns his readers that forces from below (Brombert, *Victor Hugo* 113) have undermined political and social systems since the beginning of history and will continue to do so in the nineteenth century. The final chapter of "Argot," "The Two Duties: To Watch and to Hope," has prepared the reader to accept the people as the new agents of progress.

The final digression, book 2 of part 5, "L'intestin de Léviathan," marks the end of the insurrection and the return to Jean Valjean's story. Three chapters, "L'histoire ancienne de l'égout" 'The Ancient History of the Sewer,' "Progrès actuel" 'Present Progress,' and "Progrès futur" 'Future Progress,' prepare us for this change in the plot but also maintain our attention to history. In "Progrès actuel" Hugo calls the renovation of the Parisian sewers in the nineteenth century a revolution in hygiene (2: 660–62; 1269–70 [pt. 5, bk. 2, ch. 5]). However, this revolution, like that of 1789, is incomplete. The chapter on the future speaks of the quicksand traps that threaten those daring to explore the sewers, as well as of the fetid air that escapes from the entrances to threaten the health of the entire population. The sewers, like democracy, are a work in progress. June 1832 leaves its mark, nevertheless, on the tome of France's history inscribed in Paris's debris: the sewer is "[une] sentine redoutée qui a la trace des révolutions du globe comme des révolutions des hommes, et où l'on trouve des vestiges de tous les cataclysmes depuis le coquillage du déluge jusqu'au haillon de Marat" '[an] awful sink, bearing the traces of the revolutions of the globe as well as of the revolutions of men, and in which we find vestiges of all the cataclysms from the shellfish of the deluge down to Marat's rag' (2: 667; 1275 [pt. 5, bk. 2, ch. 6]). The chapter on the ancient sewers claims that they have functioned throughout history as the conscience of a city: "Tout y converge et s'y confronte" 'All things converge into it and are confronted with one another' (2: 651; 1261 [pt. 5, bk. 2, ch. 2]). This brief sentence is an apt description of the many threads of Jean Valjean's story that converge in the conclusion. It prepares us for the final confrontations with self-interest and the acts of renunciation that mark Valjean's transformation from criminal to saint. This sentence also supports an idea that Hugo has implied throughout the novel: the history of France has always been linked to the fortunes of its capital, the site of social upheavals that brought about change in the past and promise to do so in the future.

One obvious consequence of eliminating the major digressions of *Les Misérables* is a failure to engage with Hugo's views on religion and spirituality. Another is to misunderstand why Hugo places such faith in the triumph of social justice and the liberation of his country when it is under the thumb of Napoleon III. By including, in any study of *Les Misérables*, the digressions in the order that they appear in the novel, either partially or in whole, we ensure that our students have a richer experience of the novel and one closer to the author's intentions.

No Expectations:
An Aspect of Misery in *Les Misérables*

Timothy Raser

In one of the early scenes of Hugo's *Ruy Blas*, Don Salluste requires his servant Ruy Blas to write a note in which he acknowledges that he is his master's servant and that his duty is to obey. Ruy Blas *is* his servant, his duty *is* to obey, and at this point he has no choice: he writes and signs. Students wonder, however, why a fact so obvious must be consigned to paper, and they wonder also what Salluste's purpose is in telling Ruy Blas to do this. They expect the letter to make another appearance—and it does, to Ruy Blas's and the queen's dismay, in the last act of the play. The writing of the letter in the first act gives Salluste the letter he will use in the last act; put differently, the meaning of the letter becomes clear only later on. This delayed revealing of meaning often goes by the name of motivation: the early event motivates the later one; an early event whose meaning is conspicuously absent creates the expectation that the meaning it hides will be revealed. As Gérard Genette put it,

> C'est cette logique paradoxale de la fiction qui oblige à définir tout élément, toute unité du récit par son caractère fonctionnel, c'est-à-dire entre autres par sa corrélation avec une autre unité, et à rendre compte de la première (dans l'ordre de la temporalité narrative) par la seconde, et ainsi de suite—d'où il découle que la dernière est celle qui commande toutes les autres et que rien ne commande . . .   ("Vraisemblance" 94)

> The paradoxical logic of fiction requires that we define each component part of a narrative by its function, that is, among other things, by its correlation with another component, and to account for the first (in the sequence of the narrative) by the second, and so forth—as a consequence the last part is what dominates all the others, and that nothing dominates . . .
> ("Plausibility" 182)

In the theater, where the time between an early mention and a later event doesn't often exceed three hours, expectations and their fulfillment are easily associated: we need only ask our students about the latest horror movie to confirm how well they understand the device. Such association is much more difficult, however, in novels, especially in *Les Misérables*, where the sheer length of the work is compounded by Hugo's use of digression—that is, mentions that lead nowhere. The task of recalling what was mentioned several hundred pages earlier is a daunting one, and establishing associations is often frustrating. Frustration in turn makes reading less rewarding, and readers less attentive.

Technology is of great use here: when a student has a digital copy of the work it takes only a few seconds to determine whether what one is reading now was announced—albeit discreetly—many pages earlier.[1] Thus, for example, students can be asked to find the name of the comte Anglès, which recurs six times in the novel: three times in the context of poor police work, and twice in that of Inspector Javert and his protector, Chabouillet. Through this repeated association Hugo tells the students, and none too subtly, that the kind of dogged pursuit incarnated by the inspector is hardly beneficial to society.

But if we ask students to compare the results of their search, they find that the sixth instance is different: here, Jean Valjean has escaped from prison in Toulon and is now back in Paris, on his way to find Cosette, when the king, taking his afternoon ride in his carriage, passes. The duc d'Havré notices him:

> Il dit à Sa Majesté: "Voilà un homme d'assez mauvaise mine." Des gens de police, qui éclairaient le passage du roi, le remarquèrent également, et l'un d'eux reçut l'ordre de le suivre. Mais l'homme s'enfonça dans les petites rues solitaires du faubourg, et comme le jour commençait à baisser, l'agent perdit sa trace, ainsi que cela est constaté par un rapport adressé le soir même à M. le comte Anglès, ministre d'État, préfet de police.
>
> (1: 513 [pt. 2, bk. 3, ch. 6])

> He said to His Majesty, "There is a man with a rather unsavory look." Some policemen, who were clearing the way for the king, also noticed him. But the man plunged into the little empty streets of the Faubourg, and as night was coming on the officer lost track of him, as is stated in a report addressed on the same evening to the Comte Anglès, Minister of the State, Prefect of Police. (393)

The designation of a single agent who follows but loses Valjean's trace all but compels us to apply a name: Javert. This is, for all intents and purposes, a definition of the character; it is what Javert does. But whereas in the theater expectations generally lead to some resolution, that is not the case here: the agent never finds the "homme d'assez mauvaise mine" and never even gets named. Difficulties with examples such as this one often arise, for the logic of motivation tells students that something should come of this brush with the law, but nothing ever does: motivation is as much a tease as it is an announcement of things to come.

This paradigm recurs often in *Les Misérables*—so often, in fact, that one wonders whether Hugo is not recasting the function of motivation. If the generators of expectations—indications of blood relations, separations, chance encounters—are indeed present, they tend not to produce the satisfactions to which they are conventionally tied. Such is the case when grandfather Gillenormand concludes that Marius's absences subsequent to his father's death indicate that he is having an affair: worried that his grandson isn't the ladies' man that his elder thinks he was himself, he mistakes Marius's secretive interest in his father for an amourette, and the family delegates cousin Théodule to find out just whom

Marius has been honoring with his visits. Here, students can be usefully asked how the signs that Marius is sending are interpreted by different groups, and why these interpretations vary. Speculation runs to young women, to balls, to gifts of flowers and conversations: a sequence of activities leading up—in the conventional narrative that his family uses to interpret Marius's actions—to sexual conquest and subsequent disclosure. Théodule thus takes the coach that Marius has booked for Vernon in hopes of identifying the lucky lady, only to find Marius weeping at a grave. The events that lead Gillenormand to expect a woman in a boudoir lead instead to a cemetery and a father's tomb. Worse, Théodule's discovery fails to resolve the quid pro quo because he doesn't find it sufficiently interesting to reveal to his aunt, and when Marius does return home, Gillenormand tellingly exclaims, "Victoire! nous allons pénétrer le mystère! nous allons savoir le fin du fin! nous allons palper les libertinages de notre sournois! nous voici à même le roman" 'Victory! We are about to penetrate the mystery, unravel the wanton ways of our rascal! Here we are right to the core of the romance' (1: 811; 642 [pt. 3, bk. 3, ch. 8]). But while Gillenormand expects the "romance" to eventually fulfill expectations, Hugo's novel is at its heart a machine for creating and deflecting expectations, a reflexive structure hinting that the pleasure of reading is no longer as simple as it once was.

Here we can ask students to list the anticipations that seem to plague the Gillenormand household. The servant Magnon presents M. Gillenormand with two babies in two successive years, babies whom he refuses to acknowledge as his but whom he nonetheless funds. Hugo, however, kills off Gillenormand's putative sons and has Mme Thénardier rent out her two youngest to Magnon so Magnon can continue to receive child support. But misfortune descends yet again on Magnon: caught in a police sweep that sends her to prison, she is separated from her "sons," whom she sends "back" to Gillenormand clutching a scribbled address to help them find their way. It's winter, though; hands are cold and the wind is blowing, and the piece of paper blows away, simultaneously depriving the boys of destination and point of departure. Providence in the form of Gavroche intervenes, and with it expectations of a reunion with their "family": he is, after all, their elder brother. He offers them food, shelter, and lessons in street slang, giving them what his own mother denied him. But he never learns that they are related to him by blood.

Two more moments of frustrated expectations concern Gavroche; the first occurs when Montparnasse summons him to rescue a prisoner who has become trapped on top of the prison's wall while making his escape and who, when dawn comes, will surely be discovered and shot. Gavroche suddenly sees whom he is supposed to rescue: "Tiens! dit-il, c'est mon père! . . . Oh!, cela n'empêche pas" '"Wait a minute!" he said, "that's my father!—Well, never mind!"' (2: 311; 977 [pt. 4, bk. 6, ch. 3]. For his part, Thénardier is even more blasé: when Babet says, "Il me semble que c'est ton fils.—Bah! dit Thénardier, crois-tu? Et il s'en alla" '"It seems to me it's your son." "What?" said Thénardier. "You think so?" And he left' (312; 978).

Useful questions arise from such reversals of expectations: Who is saving whom? How do their attitudes differ? What does that tell us about Thénardier and his son? Given the stakes, shouldn't such an occasion entail some sort of reunion of the broken family?

Gavroche makes a final, albeit implicit, appearance when a bourgeois tells his sated son to throw his uneaten brioche to the swans in the basin of the Luxembourg gardens: "—Jette-le à ces palmipèdes. . . .—Sois humain. Il faut avoir pitié des animaux" 'Throw it to those palmipeds. . . . Be humane. We must take pity on the animals' (2: 607; 1224 [pt. 5, bk. 1, ch. 16]). At that moment, Gavroche's two brothers race the swans for the food, managing to retrieve it only in the nick of time. Again, questions concerning expectations arise: Why doesn't Hugo have the bourgeois or his son turn around to see the struggle behind them? Why do children have to fight animals for food? When they get the brioche, why does the elder reuse Gavroche's slang phrase, "Colle-toi ça dans le fusil" 'Poke that in your gun' (608; 1226)? What can students deduce from the contrast between what he is doing and what he is saying? And what just happened a few hours earlier, across town at the "barricade de Corinthe"?

Here we can ask for a provisional conclusion: Why are the feelings of plenitude and dramatic satisfaction arising from an expectation fulfilled so markedly absent? Has Hugo tantalized his readers only to deny them a pleasure they have been led to expect?

Immersed as they are in the plot, students often have difficulty seeing motivation as a device rather than a realistic sequence of events. The distinction becomes apparent when we stop their reading midway and ask them questions about their expectations: initially, it seems that Hugo has devised situations where it should be possible to fulfill anticipations. When we continue reading, however, students learn that these situations tend not to resolve into clarity or understanding. Since expectation is a narrative device, one that propels a story forward, one could say that these failed satisfactions and missed opportunities cause the narrative to slow down under the weight of questions asked, never to be answered. Certainly, the narrative does not unfold as they expect it to, and when anticipation leads nowhere, they wonder why the earlier, motivating structures were put into place.

Here it is useful to point out an observation by Hugo's early critics. In his review of the very first volume of *Les Misérables*, Jules Barbey d'Aurevilly wrote that readers would recall images and scenes: "Ces phrases seraient charmantes, j'en conviens, si on ne les avait jamais vues, mais on les connaît. On les a déjà admirées en vers et en prose dans les *Œuvres complètes* de M. Hugo" 'These words would be charming, I agree, if they hadn't been seen before, but they are known. They have already been admired in the verse and prose of the *Complete Works* of Mr. Hugo' (23). Barbey accuses Hugo of recycling used material and asserts that acute readers will detect these passages and the author's laziness.

The strongest echo of earlier texts arises when Théodule tracks Marius to Pontmercy's tomb. As they have seen, the aunt, M. Gillenormand, and Théodule are all convinced that the only explanation for Marius's trips and absences must be a woman. Each step Marius takes implies a rendezvous with a lover—an interpretation that, when superimposed on the reality of Marius's trip, either endows love for one's father with an erotic dimension or invests the erotic with a death wish.

Instructors may point out that, as Barbey said, this love affair with the dead is familiar to Hugo's readers: the passage echoes Hugo's much-anthologized "Demain, dès l'aube" ("Tomorrow, at Dawn") from book 4 of *Les Contemplations*. There, the poet announces his intention to take a trip to his beloved, using direct address and attributing anticipation to that person: "Vois-tu, je sais que tu m'attends" 'You see, I know you're waiting for me' (*Contemplations* [1973] 226), the implication being that a lover awaits. At the end of the poem, however, the poet's destination turns out to be a tomb, and if Hugo is speaking personally, that of his dead daughter Léopoldine conveniently fills the bill. Here the conflation of desire and death is quite familiar to students: it just might be necessary to shift their focus away from great literature to popular culture and horror films, where the association is so frequent that it could be called causal. In any case, the loss of narrative movement sets up a moment of introspection, where one could call Marius's weeping "lyric," even if the lyric poem in question is found only in the registers of the reader's memory.

Without this reference, students often have difficulty understanding that the poem still can be read. Here, teachers can point out its uncanny effect: something like anticipating seeing a long-lost friend at a high school reunion, only to learn on arriving that he died many years previously. If there was no future for that expectation, just what was its object? In the weeks before the reunion, was one thinking of the past or the future? Was the friend a person or a ghost? Can one ever expect to meet a specter? This kind of paradox can't easily be resolved in narratives, but it does lend itself to poetry, and Hugo's propensity to turn from narrative to lyric has brought good fortune to efforts to recast *Les Misérables* as a musical.

The moment is also referential: earlier in the collection—between poems 2 and 3 of book 4, *Pauca meæ*—a line of dots crosses the page, underscoring a date: "4 SEPTEMBRE 1843" (*Contemplations* 209); only readers who have detailed knowledge of Hugo's life would know that this was the date when Léopoldine drowned in the Seine, and yet all would know it hid a meaning. "Demain, dès l'aube," which carries the date of "3 septembre 1847," refers to the fourth anniversary of the death, and thus exists in a system of echoes, where some readers will respond by understanding the date ("So that's what happened on that date!") and others will interpret the poem's date of 3 September 1847 as the eve of the four-year anniversary of some unspecified catastrophe: the date between poems 2 and 3 explains the meaning of the date of "Demain, dès l'aube." Regardless, students need to be reminded that the echo of "Demain" in the story of Marius's mourning pulls the reader out of the novel's temporality into something else, a moment where narrative time has stopped, simultaneously enabling lyricism and reference.

In both the chapter from *Les Misérables* and "Demain, dès l'aube" Hugo substitutes a tomb for the beloved expected by the reader. But the extension given to the quid pro quo in the novel entails significant differences. In the poem, it is the reader's interpretation that changes, while in the novel, Hugo's use of Théodule as an intermediary makes him bear the burden of the episode's surprise ending. As a result, the novel's readers can step back and laugh at Théodule for his gullibility because we knew all along that Marius was venerating his father. The contrast between the two possible objects of Marius's affection is sharp here and has a comic effect. In the poem, by contrast, the tone slowly shifts from optimism to sadness; images of the exterior world are replaced by images of interiority, affirmations by negations: it is hard to say when exactly one understands that the poet is not traveling to a tryst and thus where, precisely, the difference between the anticipation of a tryst and the contemplation of death lies.

Hugo's deployment of the metaphor in a comic mode allows enjoyment of Théodule's disappointment, especially given that all along he has been the butt of criticism. Asked why, students often point to his foppery, his flirtations with girls, his eye on an inheritance from Gillenormand. That he slept soundly in the coach while Marius braved the weather outside makes him more ridiculous and structures his surprise at seeing a tomb as a deserved comeuppance.

The question of who, exactly, "les misérables" are is a good one to ask, and students' responses can be compared with those of Baudelaire, who, in his early review of *Les Misérables*, wrote:

> *Les Misérables* sont donc un livre de charité, un étourdissant rappel à l'ordre d'une société trop amoureuse d'elle-même et trop peu soucieuse de l'immortelle loi de fraternité; un plaidoyer pour les *misérables* (ceux qui *souffrent* de la misère et que la misère *déshonore*).
>
> ("*Les Misérables*" 224)

> *Les Misérables* is thus a work of charity, a stunning recall to order to a society too much in love with itself and too little preoccupied with the immortal law of fraternity; a plea for the *wretched* (those who *suffer* from misery and those whom misery *dishonors*).

A few lines later, he writes:

> N'est-il pas utile que de temps à autre le poète, le philosophe, prennent un peu le Bonheur égoïste aux cheveux, et lui disent, en lui secouant le mufle dans le sang et l'ordure: "Vois ton œuvre et bois ton œuvre?"

> Isn't it useful that, from time to time, the poet, the philosopher, takes egotistical Happiness by its hair and says to it, pushing its snout into the blood and mud: "Look at your work and drink it up?"

For Baudelaire, one cannot show misery without indicating its cause, for it is because people are unaware in their happiness of the suffering of others that suffering grows. Certainly, the complacent Mme Victurnien oppresses Fantine with her blinkered morality, and she embodies the concepts of egotistical satisfaction and self-love that Baudelaire denounces. Students readily understand that a critical aspect of *les misérables* — the people, not the novel — is that they are not seen. To take Jean Valjean as an example: for years, he is a number, not a name, and not even the same number at that. Later, when he has power and influence, he is M. Madeleine; to Marius, he is M. Leblanc, and then, M. Fauchelevent; to Cosette, he is "Père." Even to Monseigneur Bienvenu, he is a potential good man: Is he ever thus Jean Valjean, or does that name refer only to someone who existed before the novel began? If one looks at *les misérables* as a class, they are unknown, underground, invisible, and yet they exist in plain sight, a sort of social unconscious, not seen because they are repressed rather than hard to see.

But what name should we give this blindness and the corresponding failure to be seen? One under which the terrible back-and-forth of unspoken judgments and dismissals could be grouped? Students' answers are often surprising and display a sympathy not often shown among professional readers. In fact, Hugo has supplied just such a figure: her name is Éponine.[2] She shows up on the novel's pages just after Cosette's appearance and stays there until Jean Valjean's rescue of Marius. She lives to arouse expectations: that she will help Marius, that she will betray him, that she will love him, that she will help her father rob Jean Valjean. Almost all these expectations are frustrated, as are her own hopes to be seen or loved by Marius. She exists to be ignored, and thus to let expectations die. This is one of the social messages of the novel: like the sewage we unwisely allow to flow to the sea, where it is lost, the *misérables* are to be put out of mind until they disappear. In both cases, a terrible waste occurs: of a resource, of human potential. Éponine is wasted, and Marius goes on with his life unaware of the cost of his happiness. Éponine is just one example of the many names and words in *Les Misérables* that wait for the attentive reader to develop the potential they offer.

NOTES

[1] Guy Rosa's (in conjunction with the Groupe Hugo) digital editions—of *Les Misérables*, *Les Misères*, and the novel's first drafts—are an invaluable resource here (see groupugo .div.jussieu.fr/Miserables/).

[2] Her name comes from the Latin Epponina, who was the wife of the Gaul Julius Sabinus and who, in the first century AD, hid her husband from Vespasian's soldiers through several years and two pregnancies, only to be put to death for her efforts.

Type Transformed:
Character and Characterization in *Les Misérables*

Isabel K. Roche

This essay addresses Hugo's conception of character and character making from a critical perspective, asserting the original—and ultimately very modern—aspects of his conceptual, nonpsychological creations through analysis of the characters of *Les Misérables*. It provides a framework for addressing a question of central importance for the undergraduate literature classroom and for the study of nineteenth-century fiction: why do authors create characters in the ways they do? The essay also shows how the introduction and application of major theoretical approaches to character can sharpen students' understanding of both Hugo's conception of character and the novel.

While the enduring appeal of *Les Misérables* has much to do with its unforgettable characters, character making was long a discounted and devalued aspect of Hugo's novel. From Jean Valjean to Fantine, Cosette, and Javert, the characters of *Les Misérables*, much like Hugo's earlier creations, were met by his contemporaries with critical disapproval, ranging from disparagement to denigration. Gustave Flaubert, for one, vehemently expressed his exasperation with the novel in general and its characters in particular:

> Et des types tout d'une pièce, comme dans les tragédies! Où y a-t-il des prostituées comme Fantine, des forçats comme Valjean, et des hommes politiques comme les stupides cocos de l'A, B, C ? Pas une fois on ne les voit *souffrir* dans le fond de leur âme. Ce sont des mannequins, des bonshommes en sucre . . .   (*Œuvres complètes illustrées* 510)

> And theatrical types, just as in tragedies! Where are there prostitutes like Fantine, convicts like Jean Valjean, and politicians like the stupid blokes of the A, B, C? Not once do you see them *suffer*, in the depths of their souls. They are puppets, figures made out of sugar . . .[1]

Flaubert's view illustrates how the realist movement had taken firm hold in nineteenth-century France and had become the dominant aesthetic by 1862. Within the framework of this dominant model, psychologically based characters had become the standard by which to judge all others—hence Flaubert's criticism of the implausibility and perceived lack of depth of Hugo's characters. The reference to "types," too, is telling, as Flaubert's repugnance points to a shift whereby function, foregrounded in the monolithic characters of the stage, gives way to recognizable (social) generalization. While the extended arguments in the press subsequent to the novel's publication debated the significance and impact of its political, moral, social, and religious dimensions, the novel's literary merits were no less discussed, with consensus only on what these dimensions lacked: a logic that would justify the novel's outsize ambition and seemingly disparate narrative elements (see Bach; Hovasse, *Victor Hugo: Pendant* 695–725). Nearly uniform resistance to the composition of its characters confirms the pervasiveness of the realist hold to the detriment of virtually all other models, and particularly of characters derived from romance or melodramatic traditions—deemed clumsy, naive, and unsophisticated by comparison.

Yet Hugo, from his earliest reflections on the novel, imagined the possibilities of the genre differently from other novelists (see Roche). In his 1823 review of Walter Scott's *Quentin Durward*, Hugo, then twenty-one, called for a "new" novel in which universal truths were to be both condensed and amplified:

> Après le roman pittoresque mais prosaïque de Walter Scott, il restera un autre roman à créer, plus beau et plus complet encore selon nous. C'est le roman, à la fois drame et épopée, pittoresque mais poétique, réel, mais idéal, vrai mais grand, qui enchâssera Walter Scott dans Homère.
>
> (*Œuvres complètes: Critique* 149)

> After the picturesque but prosaic novel of Walter Scott, there remains another novel to be created, more beautiful and still more complete. This novel is at once drama and epic, is picturesque but also poetic, is real, but also ideal, is true, but also grand—it will enshrine Walter Scott in Homer.

This conception of a totalizing art veered significantly from the direction taken by other Scott admirers, such as Balzac, who turned inward to chronicle social truths and was further elucidated by Hugo in the preface to *Cromwell* (1827). The purpose of art in all its forms, he contends, is to place the struggles of the human condition on center stage for all to experience in a distilled form: "le but multiple de l'art . . . est d'ouvrir au spectateur un double horizon, d'illuminer à la fois l'intérieur et l'extérieur des hommes . . . de croiser, en un mot, dans le même tableau, le drame de la vie et le drame de la conscience" 'the multiple objective of art . . . is to open for the viewer a double horizon, to illuminate at the same time the interior and the exterior of man . . . to bring together, in a word, in the same scene the drama of life and the drama of conscience' (*Œuvres complètes: Critique* 26).

The kind of character central to this concentrated vision, and to Hugo's fictional enterprise in particular, is one whose foundation—and strength—lies not in its social and historical believability and grounding but rather in its ability to project a discourse on history and society and to convey through it the universal truths each novel seeks to tell. It is no surprise, then, that Hugo's first jottings on the novel that would become *Les Misérables* present its characters in general rather than in social terms: "Story of a saint, story of a man, story of a woman, story of a doll" (Hugo, *Œuvres complètes* [1967–69] 11: 49)—saint rather than bishop, man instead of convict, woman as opposed to prostitute, doll in place of socially vulnerable young girl and woman: the historical and social truths of Myriel, Valjean, Fantine, and Cosette are told within what is first and foremost a universal frame. The novel's epigraph, as well, presents the impact of the century's gravest social problems categorically, in relation to their impact on man, woman, and child: "la dégradation de l'homme par le prolétariat, la déchéance de la femme par la faim, l'atrophie de l'enfant par la nuit" 'the degradation of man by the exploitation of his labor, the ruin of woman by starvation, and the atrophy of childhood by physical and spiritual night.'

What Is a Literary Character?

When I teach a course on *Les Misérables*, I prepare students for understanding Hugo's characters by asking them early on to collectively produce a definition of a literary character — a task they find surprisingly difficult and whose outcome is most often deemed unsatisfying. They can typically reach consensus only around some version of "a person in a story" and feel the limitations of this articulation strongly. The questions raised and debated along the way (Do characters have lives that extend beyond the text? a past that is not recounted? or what could be called a future? How is a character different from us? Can a character be something other than the representation of a human being?) point them immediately to some of the central theoretical tensions around character.

A working definition created by the class can then serve as a valuable baseline for sustained reflection throughout the course on the ways in which characters in literature can be said to "exist" as well as on the connection between a character's being (compositional, constituting features) and doing (textual itinerary and narrative functions), exposing students to different approaches, from narratological to semiotic to psychoanalytic to those of reader-response criticism. The primary theoretical opposition, which sorts most approaches, involves two alternative views of character in narrative fiction: a textual one, which maintains that a character does not exist other than as the sum of the parts that compose it (a motif among motifs in a closed system) and a dynamic one, which asserts that a character is both embedded in the text and detachable from it, opening the door to the application of theories of psychology and psychoanalysis that enlarge the scope of inquiry. [2]

In privileging the functional, the first approach allows for the classification or grouping of characters based on the roles that they fulfill (as in Vladimir Propp's typology of the fairy tale, A. J. Greimas's actantial model, Philippe Hamon's semiotic model, etc.). Asking students to use any of these models to map the characters of *Les Misérables* is a worthwhile exercise and draws their attention to how the distribution of roles contributes to the overall construction and to the movement of the narrative. For many students, even those who are already strong critical readers, considering character from this angle provides a different and better opportunity for understanding the inner workings of narrative, and also lets them directly experience what is ultimately unsatisfying about these textual approaches, which fail, even in their most complex forms, to address the essence of character.

The second approach to character, set forth and argued by critics such as W. J. Harvey and Baruch Hochman, privileges essence, insisting that characters acquire an independent status and can be extracted from their context and maintaining that this is not a sentimental misunderstanding of the nature of literature but a valid means of inquiry. Probing—among other things—the unconscious motivations of character helps better comprehend the human stakes of narrative, stakes that lie necessarily beyond the boundaries of the text. In the case of *Les Misérables*, the application of this type of lens is a beneficial tool for establishing the primacy of characters' universal core.

While mutually exclusive from a theoretical perspective, these opposing views are pedagogically useful. Their examination sets the stage for the introduction of a third view, which privileges the role of the reader, showing how character can be seen simultaneously as a textual element and in relation to what it represents. This effort, not so much a reconciliation of the two approaches but an attempt to hold them in constructive tension, has been compellingly advanced in reader-response criticism, positing character as both a construction of the text and a reconstruction of the reader.[3] Building on the semiotic notion that a character functions as a semantic blank, introduced and then filled in progressively by all the textual indications attributed to it, the reader-response approach asserts that it is only through the act of reading that a character fully comes to life, springs forth from the page—a product of the interaction of the reader with the text, which codes and shapes our construction without programming it entirely. The possibility of (controlled) variance from one reader's reconstruction to another's, based on narrative, emotional, and cultural understanding, is not only acknowledged but desired, assuring the dynamic and rich nature of reading and interpretation. How construction and reconstruction work in concert can be effectively illustrated for students studying *Les Misérables* through, for example, close readings of the first appearance of the novel's main characters, which substantiate how a reading is programmed by the text and how it is necessarily individualized by the reader. In analyzing the elements used to introduce the characters, such as physical portrait, psychological and social portrait, onomastics, and reference to their immediate or more distant past (backstory), we see how the distribution among these elements (skewed by external focalization toward dominant physical and social characteristics) sets the foundation for their progressive textual reconstruction, in which meaning is never built through psychological resonance but through the distillation and confrontation of universal realities.

Archetype, Type, and Prototype

This preparatory critical reflection on the question of character allows students to better understand character making in *Les Misérables* and the ways in which

Hugo reached back in his fiction and his character making to core elements of the romance tradition of medieval courtly literature. In this model, characters are minimally drawn, referenced most often in relation to the larger category to which they belong, and devoid of personal psychology. In addition, a mythical pattern is grafted onto the world of human experience, depicted through the trials and ultimate exaltation of the archetypal hero who grows in self-knowledge in triumphing over a series of obstacles.

The characters of *Les Misérables* are thus highly stylized, and the entirety of Jean Valjean's textual itinerary takes the form of a quest, where his soul is the prize in a battle waged between good and evil, light and dark, right and wrong. Valjean's transformation from sinner to saint, initiated by Myriel, thus serves as the novel's central narrative thread: starting with his immediate regression in stealing from Petit Gervais; through his reincarnation as the benevolent Madeleine, the avowal of his true identity in the Champmathieu affair, his arrest and return to prison, the rescue of Cosette from the Thénardier family, his burial and resurrection as Ultime Fauchelevant, the repeated testing of his paternal love; and up to his ultimate sacrifice: saving Marius at the barricades and returning Marius to life and a future with Cosette.

Yet if Valjean emerges victorious from these successive moments of crisis, his reward is not an earthly one, nor does the quest's completion result in the reestablishment of social order, as in the romance tradition. On the contrary, Hugo makes use of these elements to challenge the very truths the romance tradition reinforced and to establish the foundation for a broader discourse on the nature and limits of social and historical progress. Just as in Hugo's earlier novels, the hero's recompense comes only through death and individual, anonymous ascendancy and salvation. Valjean, once discharged of his obligation to Cosette, wills himself to die at the conclusion of *Les Misérables*, actively seeking the exit that will allow transcendence of a social world that cannot recognize or accept him, as underscored in the long exchange with Marius in which he reveals the painful secrets of his past: "Est-ce que j'ai le droit d'être heureux? Je suis hors de la vie, monsieur" 'Do I have the right to be happy? I am outside of life, monsieur' (2: 809; 1397 [pt. 5, bk. 7, ch. 1]).

This subversion of the romance model is further effectuated through the hero's basic duality, a duality that cannot be fused; his two sides, the sinner and the saint, remain equally evident and irreconcilable throughout his itinerary, his tenuous and all-demanding moral progress completed only in death: "avec la conscience, on n'a jamais fini" 'We are never done with conscience' (pt. 5, bk. 6, ch. 4; vol. 2, 797; 1387). This double nature is additionally complicated in the novel by the doubling of characters, through the multiplication of the romance schema's participants and through the transmutation of opposing characters into each other. The clear-cut roles of hero, heroine, and villain are muddied and reinvested: there is a secondary hero, Marius, whose trajectory echoes but differs significantly from Valjean's; the role of the heroine is played at different moments by Fantine, Cosette, and Éponine. The character of the villain—critical to the romance genre—is split into two distinct roles: that of the adversary (Javert) and of the true villain (Thénardier). The adversary is connected to the hero in important ways: Javert and Jean Valjean are linked to each other through their social precariousness: "Javert était né dans une prison d'une tireuse de cartes dont le mari était aux galères" 'Javert was born in a prison. His mother was a fortune-teller whose husband was in the galleys' (1: 240; 170 [pt. 1, bk. 5, ch. 5]). And he does not die at the hand of the hero. The villain, defined by an irremediable moral decay, goes unpunished, setting sail at the novel's end to the New World.

This reorientation is also reinforced by the use—and similar inversion—of codes and structures of melodrama, which had taken root in France at the beginning of the nineteenth century as a stage form in which moral imperatives were emphasized through the polarized representation of good and evil. In *Les Misérables*, Hugo rewrites in particular the conflict between the hero and the villain—deflating the villain's role as an obstacle in the hero's path—and the identity mystery. While Thénardier and Valjean intersect at multiple points in the novel, Thénardier never truly gets the upper hand, and he does not even recognize Valjean in their final encounter in the sewers. In this way, Hugo transfers the melodramatic impulse inward so that the interplay of opposing forces of good and evil within Valjean is much more significant than an externally generated and sustained conflict. Whereas in melodrama the restoration of a character's true identity typically serves to restore a lost social status and thus strengthen social order, the discovery of Valjean's true identity is and remains undesirable throughout. It is, in fact, his decision to reveal his true name, first to Javert and then to Marius, that brings about Valjean's subsequent and ultimate dispossession of self. His true name thus disallows a social existence: "Fauchelevent a eu beau me prêter son nom, je n'ai pas le droit de m'en servir . . . Un nom c'est un moi." 'Fauchelevent lent me his name, I have no right to use it . . . A name is a Me' (2: 811; 1398 [pt. 5, bk. 7, ch. 1]). But it ensures, through the moral beauty it has earned, his salvation.

Reaching back to the compositional features of character and motifs of the romance and melodramatic traditions and transforming them to suit his novelistic ends, Hugo effectively creates an alternative model to the dominant psychological mode, one that serves as a primary support for his totalizing vision of the novel and of art and, again, one that underscores his divergence from his contemporaries.[4] Although Hugo never formally entered the theoretical debate around type, his reflections on authors from Homer to Shakespeare in the unwieldy (and unfavorably received) *William Shakespeare* (1864) provide a useful window into the convergences of his conception of character and his views on the nature of type. At the center of each is the common human core—the duality with which his characters are instilled as a manifestation of the fundamental characteristics of the *homo duplex*—from whom all are derived and in whom good and evil, sublime and grotesque, freely intermingle: "Ils sont de l'idéal, réel. Le bien et le mal de l'homme sont dans ces figures. De chacun d'eux découle, au regard du penseur, une humanité" 'They are the ideal, realized. The good and evil of man are in these figures. From each of them flows, in the eyes of the thinker, a humanity' (*Œuvres complètes: Critique* 356). Moreover, this central core is intentionally magnified to better render its generalized truths: "un type ne reproduit aucun homme en particulier; il ne se superpose exactement à aucun individu; il résume et concentre" 'a type does not reproduce any man in particular; it cannot be superimposed exactly on any one individual; it summarizes and concentrates' (355).

The characters in all Hugo's novels are indeed compact and compressed versions of man's essence, with the central duality most fully explored through the itinerary of the hero, whose external struggles form the narrative spine and whose internal struggles propel a metaphysical and ideological questioning of individual moral and social progress. This central duality is importantly also on display in the character of the hero's adversary, in whom both sides are rigidly and fatally set, provoking a dilemma that tests these extremes and results most often in an inability to reconcile them. Around these two characters gather a host of others in whom one pole of the duality is strongly emphasized, establishing their symbolic importance. On the oversize canvas of *Les Misérables* all three of these categories of Hugolian type character—the redefined hero, the discordant double, and the symbolic type—are composed in ways that reinforce the universal core within the historically and socially determined, and determining, world of the novel. To do so, Hugo draws heavily here, as elsewhere in his fiction, on the characterization techniques typical of romance and melodrama, such as insertion into larger categorical frames and regular reference to dominant traits instead of more complete physical, social, or psychological portraits. Deliberate selective lapses in omniscience, in which the strong and authoritative narrator points to what cannot be known about the characters (and Valjean and Javert in particular) counters oversimplification by creating the illusion of mystery and sanctity.

The symbolic type, wherever it is situated on the scale of sublime to grotesque, has a limited or intermittent narrative presence and can be either static or dynamic (transformed). Its actions and motivations are presented by the narrator through a fully omniscient lens, allowing the reader to see and know all about it. At the top of the scale of symbolic-type characters is the saintly Myriel, whose story opens the novel. From his decision to change his residence from the episcopal palace to the adjoining hospital to create more room for the sick, to his strict management of his income to maximize contributions to those in need, to his visit to a small community in the mountains near an area inhabited by bandits and to the dying *conventionnel*—everything that we learn about Myriel is designed to highlight his goodness and prefigure its continuation in his intersection with Valjean in the exchange that forms the novel's central arc. The directness with which Myriel's interiority is rendered leaves no doubt as to what motivates him, while the absence of physical description or other concrete details focuses the reader's attention on this internal makeup and thus his emblematic importance: "Ce qui éclairait cet homme, c'était le cœur" 'What enlightened this man was the heart' (1: 102; 56 [pt. 1, bk. 1, ch. 14]). Other symbolic-type characters in the novel are similarly constructed around a single fixed positive quality: for Cosette (child), it is her innocence; for Gavroche, it is his generosity of spirit; for Cosette (young woman), it is physical purity; for Enjolras and Mabeuf, it is moral purity. At the other end of the scale, the negative pole is represented specifically by the base and immovable moral ugliness of M. and Mme Thénardier, and more generally by examples of *le mauvais pauvre* (the bad pauper), such as the members of Patron-Minette. Thénardier's portrait, as sketched, externalizes this moral makeup: "Le Thénardier était un homme petit, maigre, blême, anguleux, osseux, chétif, qui avait l'air malade et qui se portait à merveille, sa fourberie commençait là" 'Thénardier was a little man, skinny, pale, angular, bony, and puny, who looked sick but was healthy; that was where his skullduggery began' (1: 495; 378 [pt. 2, bk. 3, ch. 2]). The turpitude of Mme Thénardier is similarly manifest in the description of her physical makeup.

In the economy of *Les Misérables*, salvation is guaranteed to both the symbolic characters who are situated on the pole of the sublime and never waver and to those who are transfigured and attain sublimation through personal sacrifice: Fantine, redeemed by her maternity and Éponine, redeemed by her love for Marius. The same is denied, or its possibility cut off, to the symbolic characters whose moral deterioration is such that their only motivations are self-interest and hatred, whose moral progression is explicitly described, in the case of M. and Mme Thénardier, as a regression: "des âmes écrevisses *reculant* continuellement vers les ténèbres, *rétrogradant* dans la vie plutôt qu'elles n'y *avancent*, employant l'expérience à augmenter leur difformité, empirant sans cesse et s'empreignant de plus en plus de noirceur croissante" 'souls that, crablike, crawl continually toward darkness, going backward in life rather than advancing, using their experience to increase their deformity, growing continually worse, and becoming steeped more and more thoroughly in an intensifying viciousness' (1: 220; 153 [pt. 1, bk. 4, ch. 2]; emphasis added).

As for Javert and Valjean, dynamically composed characters in whom both sides of the *homo duplex* are clearly present and at odds, salvation is the very stake of their textual itineraries. If the multiple crises and corresponding conversions that punctuate Valjean's movement through the novel prepare for the reconciliation of the oppositions that inhabit him and his moral ascendancy, the crisis that Javert faces crystallizes the rigidity of his extremes and his permanent discordance. As the personification of "la justice, la lumière et la vérité dans leur fonction céleste d'écrasement du mal" 'justice, light, and truth, in their celestial functions of destroyers of evil,' Javert is unable to integrate Valjean's act of benevolence toward him into his strictly encoded value system (1: 388; 290 [pt. 1, bk. 8, ch. 3]). Death by suicide is the only outlet for the terrifying uncertainty that overcomes him. The ongoing and ultimate juxtaposition of Javert's and Valjean's itineraries and outcomes contributes not only to the metaphysical logic of the novel but also importantly illustrates how Hugo reimagines the dimensionality of character, eschewing psychological depth in favor of a conceptual breadth that transports the novel's meaning.

In *Les Misérables*, character serves first and foremost a conceptual purpose, as a point of intersection and support for an inquiry that probes a specific historical and social world—nineteenth-century France—and the foundation of time and history and their relation to progress of all kinds (personal, moral, social, historical). In this, the semiotic process through which characters progressively take on meaning through the filling in and out of their names through description and actions is paralleled by a thematic process of discharge and reduction, which drains and effaces most of them from a world in which human and moral imperatives are subordinated to social ones. That completion for Valjean and resolution for a host of others (Fantine, Éponine, Gavroche, Enjolras, Mabeuf) can take place only beyond the boundaries of the depicted world, be realized only through their absorption, in death, into a radiant cosmic whole (alternately called "le cosmos" and "l'infini"), underscores the limitations and failures of the social world, in which the primacy of human progress is not recognized.

The universal compositional core of Hugo's characters, as a principal anchor of this inquiry, is then neither simplistic nor indicative of clumsy character making but a feature of a larger system, one in which character has a reimagined and surprisingly modern function. Indeed, long before the twentieth-century declaration of "the death of the subject," Hugo decentralizes and destabilizes the notion of character as representation and as generator of meaning through psychological depth alone. In this way, the Hugolian character, larger than life by design and not by flaw, can be viewed as a prototype, a reimagined means of transmission. It also explains its staying power, since what has been a persistent criticism of Hugo's characters—their lack of psychological depth—is exactly what has allowed them to remain adaptable and detachable from the finite boundaries of the text, to become part of collective consciousness in a way that other nineteenth-century fictional characters have not.

NOTES

[1] Translation of all quotations other than from *Les Misérables* are my own.

[2] For a useful overview of these positions, see Montalbetti's introduction to *Le Personnage*.

[3] See, in particular, Jouve.

[4] As noted earlier relative to Flaubert's assessment of *Les Misérables*, views of type in literature shifted considerably over the course of the nineteenth century, and the novel proved a fertile new ground for the debate, in which Romantic writers, in the tradition of Madame de Staël, argued exemplarity while realist ones focused on generalizing social features.

NOTES ON CONTRIBUTORS

Rachel G. Fuchs was Regents' Professor and Distinguished Foundation Professor of History at Arizona State University. She was a social historian of nineteenth- and twentieth-century France, working primarily on issues related to gender, the family, and the state. *Les Misérables* was an inspiration for her scholarly work during her entire career, from *Abandoned Children in Nineteenth-Century France*, inspired by Gavroche and Cosette, to *Poor and Pregnant in Paris: Strategies for Survival in the Nineteenth Century* and *Contested Paternity: Constructing Families in Modern France*, which include the story of Fantine. She died in 2016.

Michal P. Ginsburg is professor emerita of French and comparative literature at Northwestern University. Her main research areas are the nineteenth-century European novel (especially in France and England), narrative theory, and Israeli fiction. She is the author of *Flaubert Writing: A Study in Narrative Strategies*, *Economies of Change: Form and Transformation in the Nineteenth-Century Novel*, and *Portrait Stories*; coauthor of *Shattered Vessels: Memory, Identity, and Creation in the work of David Shahar*; and editor of *Approaches to Teaching Balzac's* Old Goriot.

Andrea Goulet is professor and graduate chair of French and Francophone studies at the University of Pennsylvania. She is the author of *Optiques: The Science of the Eye and the Birth of Modern French Fiction* and *Legacies of the Rue Morgue: Space and Science in French Crime Fiction*; she is the coeditor of the forthcoming volume *Orphan Black: Performance, Gender, Biopolitics*. She has coedited an issue of *Contemporary French Civilization* (on visual culture) and an issue of *Yale French Studies* (on crime fictions) and currently serves as cochair of the Nineteenth-Century French Studies Association.

Kathryn M. Grossman is professor emerita of French at Pennsylvania State University. Her research centers on nineteenth-century French literature, especially Victor Hugo's novels and other visionary prose fiction. She is the author of two books on *Les Misérables* — Les Misérables: *Conversion, Redemption, Revolution* and *Figuring Transcendence in* Les Misérables: *Hugo's Romantic Sublime* — as well as of two further studies of Hugo's early prose fiction and later novels. With Bradley Stephens, she has recently coedited Les Misérables *and Its Afterlives: Between Page, Stage, and Screen*.

Cary Hollinshead-Strick is associate professor of comparative literature and English at the American University of Paris, where she teaches classes on literature and on media history. Many of her courses rely on the city of Paris as an extended classroom. She publishes on nineteenth-century popular theater and the press, theories of spectatorship, and the epistemology of print metaphors. A book, tentatively titled *Staging Publicity: The Fourth Estate at the Fourth Wall in July Monarchy France*, is forthcoming from Northwestern UP.

André Iliev started his teaching career at the National Institute of Labor and Social Studies, (University of Carthage) and the Higher Institute of Documentation (Manouba University), where he taught literature, grammar, and language and techniques of expression. He joined the team at the École Franco-Américaine de Chicago in 2007. He is the author of a number of articles on nineteenth- and twentieth-century French novels, poems, and songs. His most recent research addresses the promotion of critical thinking through literary commentaries.

Dorothy Kelly is professor of French at Boston University. Her research centers on gender and nineteenth-century French narrative viewed through psychoanalysis, sociology, and gender theory. She is the author of *Fictional Genders: Role and Representation in Nineteenth-Century French Literature, Telling Glances: Voyeurism in the French Novel*, and *Reconstructing Woman: From Fiction to Reality in the Nineteenth-Century Novel*. She is now writing a book on the metaphor of the living dead in Balzac, Zola, and Baudelaire.

Bettina R. Lerner is assistant professor of French and comparative literature at the City College and the Graduate Center of the City University of New York. Her research focuses on popular culture and literature in nineteenth-century France. She is the author of *Inventing the Popular: Literature and Culture in Nineteenth-Century Paris*. Her more recent research addresses the rise of intellectual property laws in nineteenth-century France.

Joseph Mai is associate professor of French at Clemson University, where he also teaches in the world cinema program. He is the author of *Jean-Pierre and Luc Dardenne* and of *Robert Guédiguian* and has published a number of essays related to ethics and aesthetics in French film, literature, and world cinema. He is currently preparing a volume on the Franco-Cambodian filmmaker Rithy Panh.

Brian Martin is professor of French and comparative literature at Williams College, where he teaches courses on nineteenth- and twentieth-century French literature and film. He is the author of *Napoleonic Friendship: Military Fraternity, Intimacy, and Sexuality in Nineteenth-Century France*. Nominated for a Lambda Literary Award in 2012, *Napoleonic Friendship* was awarded the Laurence Wylie Prize in French Cultural Studies in 2013. Martin's work focuses broadly on gender and sexuality in France and on Nordic masculinities from Scandinavia to Québec.

Philippe Moisan is professor of French at Grinnell College. His research and teaching interests include the nineteenth-century novel, particularly Chateaubriand, Hugo, and Flaubert, as well as cultural studies and the French New Wave in cinema. He is the author of Les Natchez *de Chateaubriand: L'utopie, l'abîme et le feu*. He is currently working on Victor Hugo's last novels, written while the author was in exile in Guernsey.

Dean de la Motte is professor of French and comparative literature at Salve Regina University. He is the coeditor of *Making the News: Modernity and the Mass Press in Nineteenth-Century France* and of *Approaches to Teaching Stendhal's* The Red and the Black. In addition to publishing articles that explore nineteenth-century narrative and the idea of progress, he has contributed to the MLA Approaches to Teaching volumes on *Madame Bovary, Old Goriot*, and *Wuthering Heights*.

Mary Anne O'Neil is professor emerita of foreign languages and literatures at Whitman College, where she taught French language and nineteenth- and twentieth-century French literature for thirty-three years. She is the author of *Conversations with Native Speakers: La France et la Francophonie* and *From Babel to Pentecost: The Poetry of Pierre Emmanuel*. She has published articles on Victor Hugo's novels and Chateaubriand's *Atala* and *Mémoires d'Outre-Tombe*.

Anne O'Neil-Henry is assistant professor of French at Georgetown University. She is the author of *Mastering the Marketplace: Popular Literature in Nineteenth-Century France* and coeditor of *French Cultural Studies for the Twenty-First Century*. Her research interests include popular literature and culture in nineteenth-century France, in particular the World's Fairs in Paris, and she has published articles on these topics.

William Paulson is the Edward Lorraine Walter Collegiate Professor of Romance Languages and Literatures at the University of Michigan, where he introduced a course on *Les Misérables*. His books include *The Noise of Culture: Literary Texts in a World of Information* and *Literary Culture in a World Transformed: A Future for the Humanities*. He has also published numerous articles on nineteenth-century French literature and a book on Flaubert's *Sentimental Education*.

Anne-Marie Picard, formerly an associate professor at Western University, Canada, is currently a professor of French and comparative literature at the American University of Paris. She teaches psychoanalysis, linguistics, and French and English literatures. Her forthcoming publication is *From Illiteracy to Literature: Psychoanalysis and Reading*. She has published numerous articles in scholarly journals and books on French authors, notably Colette, Sartre, Cixous, Duras, and Houellebecq.

Laurence M. Porter currently serves as an affiliate scholar in comparative literature at Oberlin College. He previously taught French, comparative literature, and humanities at Michigan State University, where he received the Distinguished Faculty Award and was also an NEH Senior Fellow and an Andrew W. Mellon Distinguished Professor of Comparative Literature at the University of Pittsburgh. He has published on every period of French literature, and especially on Baudelaire, Flaubert, and Hugo; in comparative literature; and in francophone studies.

Timothy Raser is professor of French at the University of Georgia, where he has taught since 1985. He has written extensively on Baudelaire's art criticism, and his most recent is *Baudelaire and Photography*. The problem of reference in Hugo's works is the subject of his 2004 book *The Simplest of Signs: Victor Hugo and the Language of Images in France, 1850–1950*. His current project concerns Hugo's poetry. He is the editor of *Peripheries of Nineteenth-Century French Studies: Views from the Edge*.

Isabel K. Roche is provost and dean of the college and a faculty member in French at Bennington College. She is the author of *Character and Meaning in the Novels of Victor Hugo* and has published articles in *The French Review* and *French Forum*. She wrote the introduction and notes to Hugo's *The Hunchback of Notre-Dame* and Leroux's *The Phantom of the Opera*. Roche's research interests include the nineteenth-century French novel and French Romanticism.

Daniel Sipe is associate professor of French studies in the Department of Romance Languages and Literatures at the University of Missouri, Columbia. His book, *Text, Image and the Problem with Perfection in Nineteenth-Century France*, is an interdisciplinary study of the many utopian discourses that circulated in French society in the decades after the revolution. He is currently working on a project dealing with the rise of gastronomic culture in postrevolutionary France.

Bradley Stephens is senior lecturer in French at the University of Bristol. His research focuses on the reception and adaptation of French Romantic fiction, with a particular interest in Victor Hugo. He is the author of numerous studies and articles in this field, including *Victor Hugo, Jean-Paul Sartre, and the Liability of Liberty* and a new introduction to Hugo's *The Hunchback of Notre-Dame*, and has coedited several collections, most recently Les Misérables *and Its Afterlives: Between Page, Stage, and Screen*. He is currently working on a critical biography of Hugo.

Pauline de Tholozany is assistant professor of French at Clemson University. She specializes in nineteenth-century French literature and culture, in particular the relations between civility and the novel. Her first book, *L'école de la maladresse*, is a history of clumsiness in the eighteenth and nineteenth centuries. She is working on her second book, which explores the concept of impatience in nineteenth-century novels.

Julia Douthwaite Viglione is professor emerita of French at the University of Notre Dame. She is the author of *The Frankenstein of 1790 and Other Lost Chapters from Revolutionary France* and *The Wild Girl, Natural Man, and the Monster*. She has edited several collections of essays, most recently *Rousseau and Dignity: Art in the Service of Humanity*, which has forty-two contributors aged seven to ninety-two. She is coediting a forthcoming book in the MLA's Options for Teaching series entitled *Teaching Representations of the French Revolution*.

SURVEY RESPONDENTS

Listed below are the names and affiliations of the scholars and teachers who generously agreed to participate in the survey of approaches to teaching *Les Misérables*. The information they provided was invaluable in preparing this volume.

Marva A. Barnett, *University of Virginia*
Masha Belenky, *George Washington University*
David Bellos, *Princeton University*
Mary Claypool, *University of Wisconsin, Madison*
Fiona Cox, *University of Exeter*
Andrea Goulet, *University of Pennsylvania*
Kathryn M. Grossman, *Penn State University*
Cary Hollinshead-Strick, *American University of Paris*
Sarah Hurlburt, *Whitman College*
Page R. Laws, *Norfolk State University*
Bettina R. Lerner, *City University of New York, City College*
Briana Lewis, *Allegheny College*
Rosemary Lloyd, *Indiana University*
Louise Lyle, *University of London, Institute in Paris*
Joseph Mai, *Clemson University*
Brian Martin, *Williams College*
Philippe Moisan, *Grinnell College*
Dean de la Motte, *Salve Regina University*
Marshall Olds, *Michigan State University*
Mary Anne O'Neil, *Whitman College*
Anne O'Neil-Henry, *Georgetown University*
Anne-Marie Picard, *American University of Paris*
Timothy Raser, *University of Georgia*
Isabel K. Roche, *Bennington College*
Maurice Samuels, *Yale University*
Daniel Sipe, *University of Missouri, Columbia*
Eloise Sureau-Hale, *Butler University*
Pauline de Tholozany, *Clemson University*
Maris Verna, *Università Cattolica, Milan*
Julia Douthwaite Viglione, *University of Notre Dame*
Marta Wilkinson, *Wilmington College of Ohio*

WORKS CITED

Works by Hugo

Hugo, Victor. *Actes et paroles I. Œuvres complètes.* Edited by Jacques Seebacher and Guy Rosa, Laffont, 1985.

———. *Actes et paroles II. Œuvres complètes*, vol. 44, Hetzel, 1883.

———. *Les Châtiments. Les Contemplations.* Gallimard, 1967. Bibliothèque de la Pléiade.

———. *Choses vues: Nouvelle Série.* Calmann Lévy, 1900.

———. *Claude Gueux.* Edited by Etienne Kern, GF Flammarion, 2010.

———. *Les Contemplations.* Michel Lévy Frères, 1856. 2 vols.

———. *Les Contemplations.* Edited by Pierre Albouy, Gallimard, 1973. Gallimard Poésie.

———. *Le Dernier Jour d'un condamné.* Gallimard, 1970.

———. "Discours à l'Assemblée législative 1849–1851. La misère." *Wikisource*, fr.wikisource.org/wiki/Discours_à_l'Assemblée_législative_1849–1851.

———. "Discours sur la misère, 9 Juillet 1849 à la tribune de l'assemblée nationale, notre père, Hugo." *Wikisource: La bibliothèque libre*, fr.wikisource.org/wiki/ Discours_%C3%A0_l%E2%80%99Assembl%C3%A9e_l%C3%A9gislative_ 1849–1851.

———. *Littérature et philosophie mêlées.* Hetzel, 1882.

———. Les Misérables: *Roman épique et historique.* Edited by Alexandre Gefen, Éditions Larousse, 2007.

———. *Les Misérables.* Edited by Yves Gohin. Gallimard, 1999. 2 vols.

———. *Les Misérables.* Translated by Lee Fahnestock and Norman MacAfee, Signet Classics, 1987.

———. *Les Misérables.* Edited by Guy Rosa and Annette Rosa, *Œuvres complètes: Roman II*, Laffont, 1985.

———. *Les Misérables. The Works of Victor Hugo.* Vols. 2 and 3, Nottingham Society, 1907. 10 vols.

———. *Les Misérables.* Edited by Guy Rosa, *Groupe Hugo*, Université Paris-Diderot, groupugo.div.jussieu.fr/Miserables.

———. *Œuvres complètes.* Edited by Jean Massin, Le Club Français du Livre, 1967–69. 18 vols.

———. *Œuvres complètes: Critique.* Edited by Jean-Pierre Reynaud, Laffont, 1985.

———. *Œuvres complètes: Politique.* Edited by Jean-Claude Fizaine, Laffont, 1985.

———. *Œuvres poétiques.* Edited by Pierre Albouy, Gallimard, 1964–78. 3 vols. Bibliothèque de la Pléiade.

————. "Préface." *Les Rayons et les ombres*. *Œuvres poétiques*, edited by Pierre Albouy, vol. 1, Gallimard, 1964. pp. 1017–22. Bibliothèque de la Pléiade.

Adaptations Cited

ArmJoe. Takase, 1998. Video Game.

August, Bille, director. *Les Misérables*. Mandalay Entertainment / Columbia Pictures, 1998. DVD.

Avens, Sally, and Jeremy Mortimer, directors. *Les Misérables*. BBC Radio, 2001, www .bbc.co.uk/programmes/b00f9g1j.

Bellorini, Jean, director. *Tempête sous un crâne*. Bel Air Media, 2011. DVD.

Bernard, Raymond, director. *Les Misérables*. Pathé-Natan, 1934. DVD.

Blackton, J. Stuart, director. *Les Misérables*. Vitagraph Company of America, 1909. Film.

Bluwal, Marcel, director. *Les Misérables*. France 2 (and CNC), 1972. DVD.

Boleslawski, Richard, director. *Les Misérables*. Twentieth Century, 1935. DVD.

Boublil, Alain, and Claude-Michel Schönberg. *Les Misérables*. Palais des Sports, Paris, 1980. Performance.

————. *Les Misérables*. Lyrics by Herbert Kretzmer, Music Theater International, New York City, 1987. Performance.

Capellani, Albert, director. *Le Chemineau*. Pathé Frères. 1905.

————, director. *Les Misérables*. Pathé, 1912/1913. Film.

Cham. "Les Misérables." *Le Journal amusant*, 6 Sept. 1862–4 Apr. 1863. 10 parts, PDF file.

Christophe, François, director. *Les Misérables*. France Culture Radio, 2012. Web.

Colcord, Ray, director. "One Term More!" Uploaded by Christina Saffran Ashford, 13 Aug. 2012. *YouTube*, www.youtube.com/watch?v=0WHw32bv9BQ.

Dayan, Josée, director. *Les Misérables*. TF1 Vidéo, 2000. DVD.

"Dream and Shout." Uploaded by Teddiefilms, 2 Apr. 2013. *YouTube*, www.youtube .com/watch?v=P3fjFtlSz3Q.

Fescourt, Henri, director. *Les Misérables*. Société des Cinéromans, 1925. Film.

Glassborow, Philip, director. *Les Misérables*. Focus on the Family Radio, 2001. CD.

Hooper, Tom, director. *Les Misérables*. Working Title / Universal Pictures, 2012. DVD.

Hossein, Robert, director. *Les Misérables*. G.E.F. / Société Française de Production, 1982. DVD.

Jordan, Glenn, director. *Les Misérables*. ITC, 1978. DVD.

Kim, Kyungsin Pablo, producer, and Dahoon Chung, director. "*Les Miserables* ROK Air Force Parody Les Militaribles." *YouTube*, 5 Feb. 2013, www.youtube.com/ watch?v=lZunEARBb6I.

Le Chanois, Jean-Paul, director. *Les Misérables*. Deutsche Film (DEFA), 1958. Film.

Lelouch, Claude, director. *Les Misérables*. Canal+ / Les Films 13 / TF1, 1995. DVD.

Les Misérables: Jean Valjean. Anuman Interactive, 2014. Video Game.

Lukashevich, Tatyana, director. *Gavrosh*. Mosfilm, 1937. Film.

Neville, Henry. *The Yellow Passport*. London, 1868. PDF file.

Nunn, Trevor, and John Caird, directors. *Les Misérables*. Lyrics by Herbert Kretzmer. RSC Barbican Theatre, London, 1985.

McKinnel, Norman. *The Bishop's Candlesticks: A Play in One Act*. 1908. Reprinted by Kessinger Publishing, 2007.

Milestone, Lewis, director. *Les Misérables*. Twentieth-Century Fox, 1952. DVD.

Porter, Edwin S., director. *Les Misérables*. Edison Manufacturing, 1909. Film.

Silvermoon, Crystal, and SunNeko Lee. *Les Misérables*. UDON Manga Classics, 2014.

Sundel, Alfred, and Norman Nodel. *Les Misérables*. *Classics Illustrated*, no. 9, 1961.

Ultimate Improv. "Les Misbarack." Uploaded by NatHeadquartersObama, 4 Sept. 2008. *YouTube*, www.youtube.com/watch?v=W3ijYVyhnn0.

Welles, Orson, director. *Les Misérables*. Mercury Theater, Mutual Network, 23 July–3 Sept. 1937. Radio program.

Other Primary and Secondary Works

Adkin, Mark. *The Waterloo Companion*. Aurum Press, 2001.

Albouy, Pierre. *Mythographies*. Corti, 1976.

Allen, James Smith. *Popular French Romanticism: Authors, Readers, and Books in the Nineteenth Century*. Syracuse UP, 1981.

"Amusements." *The New York Times*, 1 Apr. 1863, p. 7.

Ariès, Philippe. "La découverte de l'enfance." *L'enfant et la vie familiale sous l'Ancien Régime*, Seuil, 1973, pp. 53–74.

———. "The Discovery of Childhood." *Centuries of Childhood*. Translated by Robert Baldick, Vintage Books, 1962, pp. 33–49.

Armstrong, Tim. *Modernism: A Cultural History*. Polity, 2005.

Aron, Paul. "Le banquet des *Misérables* vu à travers la presse: La presse française." Despy-Meyer et al., pp. 41–47.

"Art, Advertising and Gaul." *The Fort Worth Telegram*, vol. 26, no. 151, 14 June 1908, p. 151.

Ashburn-Miller, Mary. *A Natural History of Revolution: Violence and Nature in the French Revolutionary Imagination, 1789–1794*. Cornell UP, 2011.

Auerbach, Erich. *Mimesis: The Representation of Reality in Western Literature*. Translated by Willard R. Trusk, Doubleday, 1953.

Bach, Max. "Critique et politique: La réception des *Misérables* en 1862." *PMLA*, vol. 77, 1962, pp. 595–608.

Bakhtin, Mikhail. *Rabelais and His World*. Translated by Helene Iswolsky, MIT P, 1968.

Balzac, Honoré de. *L'Auberge rouge*. Edited by Adrien Goetz, Gallimard, 1994.

———. "Un épisode sous la Terreur." *Scènes de la vie politique*, edited by Armand Olivier, Carrousel, 1999, pp. 15–41.

———. *Le père Goriot*. Edited by Thierry Bodin, Gallimard, 1971. Collection Folio classique.

Barbéris, Pierre, and Claude Duchet, editors. *Manuel d'histoire littéraire de la France, 1789–1848*. Éditions Sociales, vol. 4, 1972.

Barbey d'Aurevilly, Jules-Amédée. Les Misérables *de M. V. Hugo*. Chez tous les libraires, 1862. *Gallica*, gallica.bnf.fr/ark:/12148/bpt6k141726j.r=.langEN.

Barnett, Marva A., editor. *Victor Hugo on Things That Matter: A Reader*. Yale UP, 2010.

Barrère, Jean-Bertrand. *Victor Hugo, l'homme et l'œuvre*. Éditions CDU, 1984.

Barthes, Roland. "L'effet de réel." *Le bruissement de la langue*, Seuil, 1984, pp. 179–87.

———. "The Reality Effect." *The Rustle of Language*. Translated by Richard Howard, Hill and Wang, 1986, pp. 141–48.

Baudelaire, Charles. "Journaux intimes. Mon Cœur mis à nu." Baudelaire, *Œuvres complètes* [Pichois], vol. 1, pp. 676–708.

———. "*Les Misérables* par Victor Hugo." Baudelaire, *Œuvres complètes* [Pichois], vol. 2, pp. 217–24.

———. *Œuvres complètes*. Laffont, 1980. Collection Bouquins.

———. *Œuvres complètes*. Edited by Claude Pichois, Gallimard, 1975–76. 2 vols. Bibliothèque de la Pléiade.

———. *The Parisian Prowler: Le Spleen de Paris. Petits poèmes en prose*. Translated by Edward K. Kaplan, U of Georgia P, 1989.

———. *Selected Poems*. Translated by Carol Clark, Penguin, 2004.

Bell, David A. *The First Total War: Napoleon's Europe and the Birth of Warfare as We Know It*. Houghton Mifflin, 2007.

[Bellanger, C.]. *Le Falot du people, ou Entretiens de Madame Saumon, marchande de marée, sur le procès de Louis XVI*. 1793.

Bellos, David. *The Novel of the Century: The Amazing Adventures of* Les Misérables. Penguin, 2017.

Bellosta, Marie-Christine. "Victor Hugo: Les Rues des *Misérables*." *Magazine littéraire*, no. 332, 1995, pp. 36–39.

Bénichou, Paul. *Les Mages romantiques*. Gallimard, 1988.

Berlanstein, Lenard. *The Working People of Paris, 1871–1914*. Johns Hopkins UP, 1984.

Berlin, Isaiah. *The Roots of Romanticism*. Princeton UP, 1999.

Bernheimer, Charles. *Figures of Ill Repute: Representing Prostitution in Nineteenth-Century France*. Harvard UP, 1989.

Berquin, Arnaud. *L'Ami des enfants: Contes et historiettes*. E. Ardant et C. Thibaut, 1871. *Gallica*, gallica.bnf.fr/ark:/12148/bpt6k54938004.r=berquin+ami+des+enfants.langEN.

Bersani, Leo. *Balzac to Beckett: Center and Circumference in French Fiction*. Oxford UP, 1970.

Bettelheim, Bruno. "Little Red Riding Hood." *The Uses of Enchantment: The Meaning and Importance of Fairy Tales*, by Bettelheim, Vintage Books, 1989, pp. 166–82.

Blond, Georges. *La Grande Armée*. Translated by Marshall May, Arms and Armour, 1995.

Bouchardon, Pierre. *Le Banquier de Pontoise et les vrais mystères de Paris*. Éditions des Portiques, 1929.

Bouchet, Thomas. "La barricade des *Misérables*." Corbin and Mayeur, pp. 125–35.

———. *Le roi et les barricades: Une histoire des 5 et 6 juin 1832*. Seli Arslan, 2000.

Bourdieu, Pierre. *Masculine Domination*. Translated by Richard Nice. Stanford UP, 2001.

Bowman, Frank Paul. *French Romanticism: Intertextual and Interdisciplinary Readings*. Johns Hopkins UP, 1990.

Bressant, Marc. *Les Funérailles de Victor Hugo*. Maule, 2012.

Brombert, Victor. *The Hidden Reader: Stendhal, Balzac, Hugo, Baudelaire, Flaubert*. Harvard UP, 1988.

———. *Victor Hugo and the Visionary Novel*. Harvard UP, 1984.

Bronner, Stephen. *Modernism at the Barricades: Aesthetics, Politics, Utopia*. Columbia UP, 2012.

Brooker, Peter, et al., editors. *The Oxford Handbook of Modernisms*. Oxford UP, 2010.

Brooks, Peter. *The Melodramatic Imagination*. Yale UP, 1976.

———. *Realist Vision*. Yale UP, 2005.

Brosman, Catharine Savage. *Visions of War in France*. Louisiana State UP, 1999.

Brunel, Pierre, editor. *Hugo: Les Misérables*. Éditions InterUniversitaires, 1994.

Burgwinkle, William, et al., editors. *The Cambridge History of French Literature*. Cambridge UP, 2011.

Burke, Edmund. *Reflections on the Revolution in France*. Edited by Frank M. Turner, Yale UP, 2003.

Burnham, Catharine C. "The Street Boy and His Future: The Berkshire Industrial Farm Solves the Problem for Those It Can Reach." *New York Observer and Chronicle*, vol. 89, no. 19, 11 May 1911, p. 593.

Butler, Judith. *Bodies That Matter: On the Discursive Limits of Sex*. Routledge, 1993.

Butler, Marilyn. *Romantics, Rebels, and Reactionaries: English Literature and Its Background, 1760–1830*. Oxford UP, 1982.

Butor, Michel, "Victor Hugo romancier." *Tel Quel*, no. 16, 1964, pp. 60–77.

Calvet, C. "8e période" and "9e période." *Histoire de France: Cours moyen*, Bibliothèque d'Éducation, 1902, pp. 159–210.

Carlyle, Thomas. *The French Revolution*. 1837. *Project Gutenberg*, www.gutenberg.org/ebooks/1301.

Cartmell, Deborah, and Imelda Whelehan, editors. *The Cambridge Companion to Literature on Screen*. Cambridge UP, 2007.

————, editors. *Teaching Adaptations*. Palgrave Macmillan, 2014.

Castex, Pierre-Georges. *Horizons romantiques*. Corti, 1983.

Chamarat, Gabrielle, editor. Les Misérables: *nommer l'innommable*. Paradigme, 1994.

Charle, Christophe. "Le Champ de la production littéraire." Martin et al., pp. 127–57.

Charles, David. "Le trognon et l'omnibus: faire 'de sa misère sa barricade.'" Corbin and Mayeur, pp. 137–49.

"Charles Hugo; *Les Misérables*; Victoria Theatre." *Alexandria Gazette*, 12 Jan. 1863, p. 3.

Charlton, David G. *The French Romantics*. Cambridge UP, 1984.

Chartier, Roger. "De la fête du cour au public citadin." *Culture écrite et société: L'ordre des livres (XIVe–XVIIIe siècle)*, by Chartier, Albin Michel, 1996, pp. 155–204.

Chenet, Françoise. "Du Champs de l'Alouette au champ de l'Étoile: toponymie et métaphore." *Groupe Hugo*, groupugo.div.jussieu.fr/Groupugo/DOC/05-02-12Chenet.pdf.

Chevalier, Louis. *Laboring Classes and Dangerous Classes in Paris during the First Half of the Nineteenth Century*. Translated by Frank Jellinek, Howard Fertig, 1973.

Cohen, Margaret. *The Sentimental Education of the Novel*. Princeton UP, 1999.

Collier, Peter, and Judy Davies, editors. *Modernism and the European Unconscious*. St. Martin's Press, 1990.

Combes, Charlotte. *Paris dans* Les Misérables. CID éditions, 1981.

Condorcet, Marie Jean Antoine Nicolas de Caritat, Marquis de. *Esquisse d'un tableau historique des progrès de l'esprit humain*. Masson et fils, 1822.

Cooley, Arthur. "On the Trail of Jean Valjean." *French Review*, no. 3, 1930, pp. 355–64.

Corbin, Alain, and Jean-Marie Mayeur. *La barricade*. Publications de la Sorbonne, 1997.

Cragin, Thomas. *Murder in Parisian Streets: Manufacturing Crime and Justice in the Popular Press, 1830–1900*. Bucknell UP, 2006.

Crouzet, Michel. *Essai sur la génése du romantisme*. Flammarion, 1983.

Curmer, Léon, editor. *Les Français peints par eux-mêmes: Encyclopédie morale du XIXe siècle, 1840–42*. Preface and notes by Pierre Bouttier, Omnibus, 2003, 2 vols.

Cutchins, Dennis, et al. "Introduction." Cutchins, Dennis, et al., *Pedagogy*, pp. xi–xix.

————, editors. *The Pedagogy of Adaptation*. Scarecrow Press, 2010.

Dällenbach, Lucien, and Laurent Jenny, editors. *Hugo dans les marges*. Zoé, 1985.

Davidson, A. F. *Victor Hugo: His Life and Work*. E. Nash, 1912.

Decaux, Alain. *Victor Hugo*. Perrin, 1984.

Decker, Michel de. *Hugo: Victor pour ces dames*. Belfond, 2002.

Démier, Francis. *La France du XIXe siècle: 1814–1914*. Seuil, 2000.

"The Depravity of Prison Life." *Daily Picayune*, 19 Nov. 1897, p. 4.

Descotes, Maurice. *La Légende de Napoléon et les écrivains français du 19e siècle*. Minard Lettres Modernes, 1967.

————. *Victor Hugo et Waterloo*. Lettres Modernes, 1984.

Desjardins, François. "Le prix payé pour nous habiller." *Le Devoir*, 5 May 2013, p. A1.

Desné, Roland. "Histoire, épopée et roman: *Les Misérables* à Waterloo. *Revue d'Histoire littéraire de la France*, vol. 75, no. 2–3, 1975, pp. 321–28.

Despy-Meyer, Andrée. "Le banquet des *Misérables* vu à travers la presse: La presse belge." Despy-Meyer et al., pp. 33–40.

Despy-Meyer, Andrée, et al. *Les editeurs belges de Victor Hugo et le banquet des "Misérables."* Crédit Communal, 1986.

Diaz, José-Luis, editor. *Victor Hugo,* Les Misérables: *La preuve par les abîmes.* SEDES, 1994.

Dickens, Charles. *A Tale of Two Cities*. Edited by Richard Maxwell, Penguin, 2000.

"Dixon Fellows Program." Clemson University, 2018, www.clemson.edu/cuhonors/dixon-fellows/index.html.

Douthwaite, Julia V. *The Frankenstein of 1790 and Other Lost Chapters from Revolutionary France*. U of Chicago P, 2012.

Doyle, William. *The French Revolution: A Very Short Introduction*. Oxford UP, 2001.

"The Drama." *The Independent*, vol. 62, no. 303, 31 Jan. 1907, p. 263.

Drouet, Guillaume. "Cosette retournepeau." *Littérature*, no. 143, 2006, pp. 94–113.

Dubois, Jacques. "L'affreux Javert." Dällenbach and Jenny, pp. 9–34.

Elias, Norbet. *The Court Society*. Translated by Edmund Jephcott, Pantheon Books, 1983.

Espagne, Michel. *Les Transferts culturels franco-allemands*. PUF, 1999.

Ewing, Annie, editor. "Victor Hugo et la revolution." Transcript by Patrick Garcia and Jean-Yves Mollier. PICS and U of Iowa, 1991.

Eysteinsson, Astradur, and Vivian Liska, editors. *Modernism*. John Benjamins Publishing Company, 2007.

Ferber, Michael. *Romanticism: A Very Short Introduction*. Oxford UP, 2010.

———, editor. *A Companion to European Romanticism*. Blackwell, 2005.

Ferguson, Priscilla Parkhurst. *Paris as Revolution: Writing the Nineteenth-Century City*. U of California P, 1994.

Fillipetti, Sandrine. *Victor Hugo*. Folio, 2011.

Flaubert, Gustave. *Correspondance: 1973–91*. Edited by Jean Bruneau, Gallimard, 1973. Collection La Pléiade, 3 vols.

———. *Madame Bovary*. Edited by Bernard Ajac. Garnier-Flammarion, 1986.

———. *Œuvres complètes illustrées: Correspondance*. Vol. 2, Librairie de France, 1923.

"Forced to Sell Her Hair." *Hopkinsville Kentuckyan*, 21 Oct. 1916, p. 6.

Fortescue, William. *France and 1848: The End of Monarchy*. Routledge, 2005.

Foucault, Michel. *Discipline and Punish: The Birth of the Prison*. Translated by Alan Sheridan, Vintage Books, 1977.

———. *Surveiller et punir: Naissance de la prison*. Gallimard, 1975.

Fourier, Charles. "System of Passionate Attraction." *French Utopias: An Anthology of Ideal Societies*, edited by Frank E. Manuel and Fritzie P. Manuel, The Free Press, 1966.

Frégier, H.-A. *Des Classes dangereuses de la population dans les grandes villes, et des moyens de les rendre meilleures*. J.-B. Baillière, 1840. 2 vols.

Freud, Sigmund. "On Transformations in Instinct as Exemplified in Anal Eroticism." *On Sexuality: Three Essays on the Theory of Sexuality and Other Works*, edited by James Strachey and Angela Richards, Penguin, 1991, pp. 295–302.

Frey, John Andrew. *A Victor Hugo Encyclopedia*. Greenwood Press, 1999.

Fuchs, Rachel G. *Abandoned Children: Foundlings and Child Welfare in Nineteenth-Century France*. State U of New York P, 1984.

———. *Contested Paternity: Constructing Families in Modern France*. Johns Hopkins UP, 2008.

——— . *Poor and Pregnant in Paris: Strategies for Survival in the Nineteenth Century*. Rutgers UP, 1992.

Gaillard, Jeanne. *Paris, La Ville (1852–1870)*. L'Harmattan, 1997.

Gallo, Max. *Victor Hugo I: "Je suis une force qui va!": 1802–43*. XO Éditions, 2001.

———. *Victor Hugo II: "Je serai celui-là!": 1844–85*. XO Éditions, 2001.

Gamel, Mireille, and Michel Serceau, editors. *Le Victor Hugo des cinéastes*. Corlet Éditions Diffusion, 2006.

Garcia, Patrick, and Jean Leduc. *L'Enseignement de l'histoire de France de l'ancienrégime à nos jours*. A. Colin, 2003.

Garval, Michael D. *A Dream of Stone: Fame, Vision, and Monumentality in Nineteenth-Century French Literary Culture*. U of Delaware P, 2004.

Gaudon, Jean. "Digressions hugoliennes." Hugo, *Œuvres complètes* [Massin], vol. 14, 1967, pp. i–xvii.

Gautier, Théophile. *Émaux et camées*. Edited by Claudine Gothot-Mersch, Gallimard, 1981.

———. "Préface." *Mademoiselle de Maupin*, edited by Alvah Cecil Bessie and S. Guy Endore, Garnier-Flammarion, 1966.

Genette, Gérard. "Plausibility and Motivation." The Princess of Clèves: *Contemporary Reactions, Criticism*, edited and translated by John D. Lyons, W. W. Norton, 1994, pp. 178–85.

———. "Vraisemblance et motivation." *Figures*, Seuil, 1966, pp. 71–99.

Genlis, Stéphanie-Félicité du Crest. *Les Veillées du château, ou Cours de morale à l'usage des enfants*. Vol. 1, Lambert et Baudouin, 1884. *Gallica*, gallica.bnf .fr/ark:/12148/bpt6k6272524c.r=veillees+du+chateau.langEN.

Gettleman, Jeffrey. "An Ebola Orphan's Plea: 'Do You Want Me?'" *The New York Times*, 14 Dec. 2014, pp. 1, 18.

Gildea, Robert. *Children of the Revolution: The French, 1799–1914*. Penguin, 2009.

Gohin, Yves. "Les Réalités du crime et de la justice pour Hugo avant 1829." Hugo, *Œuvres complètes* [Massin], vol. 3, 1967, pp. i–xxvi.

———. *Victor Hugo*. PUF, 1987.

Grant, Elliott M. *The Career of Victor Hugo*. Harvard UP, 1945.

Grant, Richard B. *The Perilous Quest: Image, Myth, and Prophecy in the Narratives of Victor Hugo*. Duke UP, 1968.

Greimas, A. J. *Sémantique structurale*. Larousse, 1966.

Griffith, D. W. [David Wark]. *Orphans of the Storm*. D. W. Griffith, 1921.

Griffiths, Kate, et al. "Introduction: Multimedia Adaptation and the Pull of Nineteenth-Century France." *Dix-Neuf*, vol. 18, no. 2, 2014, pp. 126–33. *Taylor and Francis Online*, www.tandfonline.com/doi/full/10.1179/1478731814Z.00000000048.

Grossiord, Sophie. *Victor Hugo: Et s'il n'en reste qu'un . . .* Gallimard, 1998.

Grossman, Kathryn M. *Figuring Transcendence in* Les Misérables: *Hugo's Romantic Sublime*. Southern Illinois UP, 1994.

———. "The Making of a Classic: *Les Misérables* Takes the States, 1860–1922." Grossman and Stephens, pp. 113–28.

———. Les Misérables: *Conversion, Revolution, Redemption*. Twayne Publishers / Macmillan, 1996. Masterwork Studies.

Grossman, Kathryn M., and Bradley Stephens, editors. Les Misérables *and Its Afterlives: Between Page, Stage, and Screen*. Routledge, 2015.

"Grover's Theatre." *Daily National Intelligencer*, vol. 51, no. 15,732, 1 Jan. 1863, p. 1.

Guéroult, Constant. *L'Affaire de la rue du Temple*. Hachette Livre BNF, 2013. 2 vols.

Guyaux, André. *Baudelaire: Un demi-siècle de lectures des* Fleurs du Mal, *1855–1905*. PU de Paris-Sorbonne, 2007.

Hamilton, Paul, editor. *The Oxford Handbook of European Romanticism*. Oxford UP, 2016.

Hamon, Philippe. "Pour un statut sémiologique du personnage." *Poétique du récit*, Seuil, 1972, pp. 115–80.

Harsin, Jill. *Barricades: The War of the Streets in Revolutionary Paris, 1830–1848*. Palgrave, 2002.

Harvey, David. *Paris: Capital of Modernity*. Routledge, 2003.

Harvey, W. J. *Character and the Novel*. Cornell UP, 1965.

Heinzen, Jasper. "A Negotiated Truce: The Battle of Waterloo in European Memory since the Second World War." *History and Memory*, vol. 26, no. 1, 2014, pp. 39–74.

Hemmings, F. W. J. *Culture and Society in France, 1789–1848*. Leicester UP, 1987.

Heywood, Colin. *Childhood in Nineteenth-Century France: Work, Health, and Education among the "Classes Populaires."* Cambridge UP, 2002.

Hiddleston, J. A. *Victor Hugo, romancier de l'abîme*. Legenda, 2002.

Hine, Lewis W. "The American Gamin: As Foreshadowed by Victor Hugo in *Les Misérables* and Described by Quotations from That Masterpiece." *The Outlook*, 6 June 1917, p. 224.

L'Histoire véritable de Gingigolo, roi du Mano-Emugi. Circa 1789.

Hobsbawm, Eric J. *The Age of Revolution: Europe, 1789–1848*. Mentor, 1962.

Hochman, Baruch. *Character in Literature*. Cornell UP, 1985.

Hofschröer, Peter. *1815: The Waterloo Campaign*. Greenhill Books, 1999.

Hollier, Denis, editor. *A New History of French Literature*. Harvard UP, 1989.

Houston, John Porter. *Victor Hugo*. Twayne Publishing, 1974.

Hovasse, Jean-Marc. *Victor Hugo: Avant l'exil, 1802–1851*. Fayard, 2001.

———. *Victor Hugo: Pendant l'exil, 1851–1864*. Fayard, 2008.

Hudelet, Ariane. "Avoiding 'Compare and Contrast.'" Cartmell and Whelehan, *Teaching Adaptations*, pp. 41–55.

Hugo, Adèle. *Victor Hugo raconté par un témoin de sa vie*. Lacroix et Verboeckhoven, 1863.

Hutcheon, Linda. *A Theory of Adaptation*. With the assistance of Siobhan O'Flynn, 2nd ed., Routledge, 2013.

Itard, Jean. "Mémoire sur les premiers développements de Victor de l'Aveyron (1800)." *Les Enfants sauvages*, edited by Lucien Malson, Éditions 10/18, 1964, pp. 127–89.

———. "Rapport sur les nouveaux développements de Victor de l'Aveyron (1806)." *Les Enfants sauvages*, edited by Lucien Malson, Éditions 10/18, 1964, pp. 190–247.

Jameson, Fredric. *The Antinomies of Realism*. Verso, 2013.

Janin, Jules. "Le Gamin de Paris." Curmer, vol. 2, pp. 161–73.

Jeanne, Charles. *À cinq heures nous serons tous morts! Sur la barricade de Saint-Merry, 5–6 juin 1832*. Edited by Thomas Bouchet, Éditions Vendémiaire, 2011.

Jones, Colin. *Paris: Biography of a City*. Allen Lane, 2004.

Jouhaud, Christian. *Mazarinades: La fronde des mots*. Aubier, 1985.

Le Journal amusant: journal illustré, journal d'images, journal comique, critique, satirique. *Gallica*, gallica.bnf.fr/ark:/12148/bpt6k894143q/f1.image.

Jouve, Vincent. *L'Effet-Personnage dans le roman*. PUF, 1992.

Juin, Hubert. *Victor Hugo*. Flammarion, 1980–86. 3 vols.

Kahn, Jean-François. *L'extraordinaire métamorphose: Ou 5 ans de la vie de Victor Hugo, 1847–1851*. Seuil, 1984.

Kalifa, Dominique. *Les Bas-fonds: Histoire d'un imaginaire*. Seuil, 2013.

———. "Crime Scenes: Criminal Topography and Social Imaginary in Nineteenth-Century Paris." *French Historical Studies*, vol. 27, no. 1, Winter 2004, pp. 175–94.

Kern, Stephen. *The Culture of Time and Space, 1880–1918*. Harvard UP, 2003.

Kidder, Tracy. *Strength in What Remains*. Random House, 2009.

Koresky, Michael. "Eclipse Series 4: Raymond Bernard." *The Criterion Collection*, 23 July 2007, www.criterion.com/current/posts/587–eclipse–series–4–raymond–bernard.

Krebs, Katja. "Introduction: Collisions, Diversions, and Meeting Points." *Translation and Adaptation in Theatre and Film*, edited by Krebs, Routledge, 2014, pp. 1–12.

Kristof, Nicholas. "Is Hard Life Inherited?" *The New York Times*, 10 Aug. 2014, pp. SR 1, 11.

Lafayette, Madame de. *The Princesse de Clèves, The Princesse De Montpensier, The Comtesse De Tende*. Translated by Terence Cave, Oxford UP, 2008.

La Fontaine, Jean de. *Selected Fables*. Translated by Christopher Wood, Oxford UP, 1995.

Lamartine, Alphonse de. *Correspondance: 1830–1867*. Vol. 1, Champion, 2000.

Larousse, Pierre. *Grand dictionnaire universel du XIXe siècle*. Deuxième supplément, Administration du Grand Dictionnaire Universel, 1890.

———. "Le Progrès." *Grand dictionnaire universel du XIXe siècle*, vol. 13, Administration du Grand Dictionnaire Universel, 1875, pp. 224–26.

Latrobe, John H. B. *Colonization: A Notice of Victor Hugo's Views of Slavery in the United States, in a Letter from John H. B. Latrobe, of Baltimore, to Thomas Suffern, of New York*. John T. Toy, 1851.

Lefebvre, Georges. *Napoleon: From Tilsit to Waterloo, 1807–1815*. Translated by J. E. Anderson, Columbia UP, 1969.

Lehan, Richard. *Realism and Naturalism: The Novel in the Age of Transition*. U of Wisconsin P, 2005.

Leuilliot, Bernard. "Les barricades mystérieuses." *Europe*, vol. 63, no. 2, 1985, pp. 127–36.

———. "Philosophie(s): Commencement d'un livre." Rosa and Ubersfeld, pp. 59–75.

———. *Victor Hugo publie* Les Misérables. Klincksieck, 1970.

Levinas, Emmanuel. *Totality and Infinity*. Translated by Alphonso Lingis, Duquesne UP, 1969.

Lévi-Strauss, Claude. *The Savage Mind*. Translated by George Weidenfeld, Weidenfeld and Nicolson, 1966.

Livesey, James. *Making Democracy in the French Revolution*. Harvard UP, 2001.

Lough, John, and Muriel Lough. *An Introduction to Nineteenth-Century France*. Longman, 1978.

Lukács, György. *Studies in European Realism*. Translated by Edith Bone, Hillway, 1950.

Lyons, Martyn. "Les best-sellers." Martin et al., pp. 368–401.

———. *Readers and Society in Nineteenth-Century France: Workers, Women, Peasants*. Palgrave Macmillan, 2001.

Mahias, J. Untitled essay. *La Presse*, 14 May 1862, p. 3.

Mahuzier, Brigitte. "Forget Waterloo." *South Central Review*, vol. 29, no. 3, 2012, pp. 5–19.

Marin, Louis. *Utopiques: Jeux d'espaces*. Minuit, 1973.

Martin, Brian Joseph. *Napoleonic Friendship: Military Fraternity, Intimacy, and Sexuality in Nineteenth-Century France*. U of New Hampshire P, 2011.

Martin, Henri-Jean, and Odelie Martin. "Le Monde des éditeurs." Martin et al., pp. 159–215.

Martin, Henri-Jean, et al. *Histoire de l'édition française*. Vol. 3, Promodis, 1985.

Marx, Karl. *The Eighteenth Brumaire of Louis Bonaparte.* Translated by Saul K. Padover, Progress Publishers, 1937.

Matlock, Jann. "Ghostly Politics." *Diacritics*, vol. 30, no. 3, 2000, pp. 53–71.

———. *Scenes of Seduction: Prostitution, Hysteria, and Reading Difference in Nineteenth-Century France.* Columbia UP, 1994.

Merriman, John M. *Police Stories: Building the French State, 1815–1851.* Oxford UP, 2006.

Meschonnic, Henri. *Pour la poétique, IV: Écrire Hugo.* Gallimard, 1977. Collection Le Chemin.

Mettra, Claude. Postface. *Waterloo*, by Victor Hugo, Éditions Bernard Couta, 1992, pp. 75–80.

Millet, Claude, editor. *Hugo et la guerre.* Maisonneuve et Larose, 2002.

———. *Le Romantisme: Du bouleversement des lettres dans la France postrévolutionnaire.* Librairie générale française, 2007.

Milner, Max. *Le Romantisme, 1820–1843.* Vol. 1. Arthaud, 1973.

"*Les Misérables* in Real Life: Hugo's Characters, Thénardier, Fantine and Cosette, Figure in a Local Case: Woman Slaved to Pay Her Daughter's Board." *Duluth News Tribune*, vol. 44, no. 296, 2 Feb. 1913, p. 16.

Molière. *Le bourgeois gentilhomme.* Translated by Nick Dear, Absolute Classics, 1992.

Molinari, Danielle, editor. Les Misérables: *Un roman inconnu?* Paris Musées, 2008.

Montalbetti, Christine. *Le Personnage.* Flammarion, 2003.

"Morgan's Escape." *National Tribune*, 23 Feb. 1899, p. 8.

"Mrs. Bough's Paper Feature at Fort Nightly." *The Grand Forks Daily Herald*, vol. 33, no. 317, 28 Oct. 1914, p. 10.

Musée Carnavalet. *Le Peuple de Paris au XIXe siècle.* Paris Musées, 2011.

Neefs, Jacques. "Penser par la fiction." Seebacher and Ubersfeld, pp. 98–107.

The New Catholic Encyclopedia. 2nd ed., Thomson-Gale, 2003.

Nicholls, Peter. *Modernisms: A Literary Guide.* Palgrave Macmillan, 1995.

Nightingale, Benedict, and Martyn Palmer. Les Misérables: *From Stage to Screen.* Carlton, 2013.

Nord, Philip. *The Republican Moment: Struggles for Democracy in Nineteenth-Century France.* Harvard UP, 1995.

"Number 13: Revolution." *The Beatles 100 Greatest Songs: Special Collectors' Edition*, edited by John Dioso, Rolling Stone Publications, 2010, p. 38.

Nye, Robert. *Crime, Madness, and Politics in Modern France.* Princeton UP, 1984.

Ozouf, Mona. *Les Aveux du roman: Le XIXe siècle entre Ancien Régime et révolution.* Fayard, 2001.

Parent-Duchâtelet, Alexandre. *La Prostitution à Paris au XIXe siècle*, edited by Alain Corbin, Seuil, 2008. Originally published as *De la Prostitution dans la Ville de Paris, considérée sous le rapport de l'hygiène publique, de la morale et de l'administration*, 1836.

Pasco, Allan H. *Sick Heroes: French Society and Literature in the Romantic Age, 1750–1850.* U of Exeter P, 1997.

Pena-Ruiz, Henri, and Jean-Paul Scot. *Un Poète en politique: Les combats de Victor Hugo*. Flammarion, 2002.

Perrault, Charles. *Contes*. Illustrated by Gustave Doré, Hetzel, 1867. *Gallica*, gallica .bnf.fr/ark:/12148/bpt6k54186157.r=perrault+charles+gustave+Dore.langFR.

Perrot, Michelle. *Les Ombres de l'histoire: Crime et châtiment au 19e siècle*. Flammarion, 2001.

Petrey, Sandy. *In the Court of the Pear King: French Culture and the Rise of Realism*. Cornell UP, 2005.

Pigaillem, Henri. *Les Hugo*. Pygmalion, 2013.

Piroué, Georges. *Victor Hugo romancier: Ou Les dessus de l'inconnu*. Denoël, 1964.

Porter, Laurence M. *Victor Hugo*. Twayne Publishers, 1999.

Porter, Roy, and Mikulás Teich, editors. *Romanticism in National Context*. Cambridge UP, 1988.

Prendergast, Christopher. *The Order of Mimesis: Balzac, Stendhal, Nerval, Flaubert*. Cambridge UP, 1986.

———. *Paris and the Nineteenth Century*. Blackwell, 1992.

Propp, Vladimir. *Morphologie du conte*. Seuil, 1970.

Rabelais, François. *The Complete Works of François Rabelais*. Translated by Donald M. Frame, U of California P, 1991.

Régnier, Philippe. "Victor Hugo et le pacifisme d'inspiration saint-siméonienne." *Millet*, Hugo, pp. 267–81.

Reid, Donald. *Paris Sewers and Sewermen: Realities and Representations*. Harvard UP, 1991.

Richard, Jean-Pierre. *Études sur le romantisme*. Seuil, 1970.

Richardson, Joanna. *Victor Hugo*. Weidenfeld and Nicolson, 1976.

Rimbaud, Arthur. *Collected Poems*. Translated by Martin Sorrell, Oxford UP, 2001.

Riot-Sarcey, Michèle. *Le Réel de l'utopie: Essai sur le politique au XIXe siècle*. Albin Michel, 1998.

Robb, Graham. *Victor Hugo*. W. W. Norton / Picador, 1997.

Roche, Isabel. *Character and Meaning in the Novels of Victor Hugo*. Purdue UP, 2007.

Roman, Myriam. *Victor Hugo et le roman philosophique*. Champion, 1999.

Roman, Myriam, and Marie-Christine Bellosta. Les Misérables*: Roman pensif*. Belin, 1995.

Rosa, Guy. "Essais sur l'argot: Balzac et Hugo." Brunel, pp. 149–64.

———. "Histoire sociale et roman de la misère." Rosa, *Victor Hugo*, pp. 166–82.

———. "Jean Valjean: Réalisme et irréalisme des *Misérables*." Rosa and Ubersfeld, pp. 235–37.

———, editor. *Victor Hugo:* Les Misérables. Klincksieck, 1995.

Rosa, Guy, and Anne Ubersfeld, editors. *Lire* Les Misérables. Corti, 1985.

Rosen, Charles. *Romantic Poets, Critics, and Other Madmen*. Harvard UP, 1998.

Rousseau, Jean-Jacques. *Émile: Ou De l'éducation*. Gallimard, 1964.

Saminadayar-Perrin, Corinne. "Le Champ de Bataille de Waterloo: Usages polémiques du reportage." *Autour de Vallès*, no. 40, 2010, pp. 57–72.

Sartorius, Francis. "L'éditeur Albert Lacroix. " Despy-Meyer et al., pp. 9–29.

Sauvage, George M. "The Struggle for the Christian School in France." *The Catholic Education Review*, no. 1, Jan.–May 1911, pp. 231–38.

Savey-Casard, Paul. *Le crime et la peine dans l'œuvre de Victor Hugo*. PUF, 1956.

Savy, Nicole. "De Notre-Dame aux Bénédictines: L'Asile et l'exil." *Revue des lettres modernes: Histoire des idées et des littératures*, no. 1024–32, 1991, pp. 89–98.

———. "Victor Hugo féministe?" *La Pensée*, no. 245, 1985, pp. 5–18.

Sayre, Robert. *L'Insurrection des* Misérables: *Romantisme et révolution en 1832*. Lettres Modernes, 1992.

Schafer, Sylvia. *Children in Moral Danger and the Problem of Government in Third Republic France*. Princeton UP, 1997.

Schehr, Lawrence. *Rendering French Realism*. Stanford UP, 1997.

———. *Subversions of Verisimilitude: Reading Narrative from Balzac to Sartre*. Fordham UP, 2009.

Schom, Alan. *Napoleon Bonaparte*. HarperCollins, 1997.

Schwartz, Vanessa. *Spectacular Realities: Early Mass Culture in fin-de-siècle Paris*. U of California P, 1998.

Seebacher, Jacques. "Évêques et conventionnels: Ou La critique en présence d'une lumière inconnue." *Europe*, vol. 40, no. 394–95, 1962, pp. 79–91.

Seebacher, Jacques, and Anne Ubersfeld, editors. *Hugo le fabuleux*. Seghers, 1985.

Ségur, Sophie Rostopchine, Comtesse de. *Les Malheurs de Sophie*. Librio, 2005.

Serres, Michel. *Le Parasite*. Grasset, 1980.

Silberman, Neil Asher. "Reshaping Waterloo." *Archaeology*, vol. 60, no.1, 2007, pp. 53–58.

Sipe, Daniel. *Text, Image, and the Problem with Perfection in Nineteenth-Century France: Utopia and Its Afterlives*. Ashgate, 2013.

Sontag, Susan. *Regarding the Pain of Others*. Picador, 2003.

Spiquel, Agnès. "Éponine ou le salut au féminin." *Revue des lettres modernes: Histoire des idées et des littératures*, no. 1024–32, 1991, pp. 99–110.

"The Stage." *The Anaconda [MT] Standard*, vol. 17, no. 251, 20 May 1906, p. 2.

Stam, Robert. "The Theory and Practice of Adaptation." *Literature and Film: A Guide to the Theory and Practice of Film Adaptation*, edited by Robert Stam and Alessandra Raengo, Blackwell, 2005, pp. 1–52.

Stein, Marieke. *Victor Hugo*. Cavalier Bleu, 2007.

Stephens, Bradley. *Victor Hugo*. Reaktion Books, forthcoming.

———. *Victor Hugo, Jean-Paul Sartre, and the Liability of Liberty*. Legenda, 2011.

Stephens, Bradley, and Kathryn M. Grossman. "Introduction: *Les Misérables*: A Prodigious Legacy." Grossman and Stephens, pp. 1–16.

Stierle, Karlheinz. *Paris: Capitale des signes: Paris et son discours*. Éditions de la Maison des Sciences de l'Homme, 2001.

Sue, Eugène. *Les Mystères de Paris*. Edited by Judith Lyon-Caen, Gallimard, 2009.

Tackett, Timothy. "Interpreting the Terror." *French Historical Studies*, vol. 24, no. 4, Fall 2001, pp. 569–78.

Taylor, Jane H. M. *The Poetry of François Villon*. Cambridge UP, 2001.

Tew, Philip, and Alex Murray, editors. *The Modernism Handbook*. Continuum, 2009.

Thérenty, Marie-Eve, and Alain Vaillant, editors. *Presse et plumes: Journalisme et littérature au XIXe siècle*. Éditions du nouveau monde, 2004.

Thiesse, Anne-Marie. *Le Roman du quotidien: Lecteurs et lectures populaires à la Belle Époque*. Le Chemin Vert, 1984.

Thompson, C. W. *Victor Hugo and the Graphic Arts, 1820–1833*. Droz, 1970.

Tombs, Robert. *France, 1814–1914*. Longman, 1996.

Traugott, Mark. *The Insurgent Barricade*. U of California P, 2010.

Trousson, Raymond. "Victor Hugo chez les Belges." Despy-Meyer et al., pp. 9–13.

Truffaut, Serge. "*Les Misérables*: Drame au Bangladesh." *Le Devoir*, 27–28 Apr. 2013, p. B4.

———. "*Les Misérables*: Des millions de migrants." *Le Devoir*, 14 July 2014, p. A6.

Tuhabonye, Gilbert, and Gary Brozek. *This Voice in My Heart: A Runner's Memoir of Genocide, Faith, and Forgiveness*. Amistad/HarperCollins, 2006.

Ubersfeld, Anne. "Nommer la misère." *Revue des sciences humaines*, vol. 39. no. 156, 1974 pp. 581–96.

"Unsuccessful but Novel Attempt to Escape from the Alton Prison." *Big Blue Union*, vol. 2, no. 47, 20 Feb. 1864, p. 1.

Vaillant, Alain, editor. *Le Romantisme*. CNRS, 2012.

Valéry, Paul. *Lettres à quelques-uns*. Gallimard, 1952.

Vallès, Jules. "Le champ de bataille de Waterloo." *La Revue universelle*, no. 25, 22 June 1901, pp. 577–82.

Vargas Llosa, Mario. *The Temptation of the Impossible: Victor Hugo and* Les Misérables. Translated by John King, Princeton UP, 2007.

Vernier, France. "*Les Misérables*: Ce livre est dangereux." *L'Arc*, no. 57, 1974, pp. 33–39.

———. "*Les Misérables* ou: De la modernité." Rosa, *Victor Hugo*, pp. 46–62.

Vidocq, Eugène F. *Mémoires de Vidocq, chef de la police de Sûreté, jusqu'en 1827*. 1828–29.

Villon, François. *Selected Poems*. Translated by Peter Dale, Penguin Books, 1978.

Wajda, Andrzej. *Danton*. Gaumont and Les Films du Losange, 1983.

Wakefield, David. *French Romantics: Literature and the Visual Arts, 1800–1840*. Chaucer, 2007.

Waller, Margaret. *The Male Malady: Fiction of Impotence in the French Romantic Novel*. Rutgers UP, 1993.

"Western Jean Valjean, Too, Went Back to Prison." *Day Book* [Chicago], 7 Mar. 1914.

Whelehan, Imelda. "What Is Adaptation Studies?" *Adapt Blog*, 18 Apr. 2012, blogs.utas.edu.au/adapt/2012/04/18/what-is-adaptation-studies.

Whitworth, Michael. *Modernism*. Wiley, 2007.

Wildman, Stephanie M., and Adrienne D. Davis. "Making Systems of Privilege Visible." *White Privilege: Essential Readings on the Other Side of Racism*, edited by Paula S. Rothenberg, 4th ed., Worth Publishers, 2010, pp. 107–13.

Williams, Helen Maria. *Letters Written in France*. Edited by Niel Fraistat and Susan S. Lanser, Broadview Press, 2001.

Willms, Johannes. *Paris: Capital of Europe, from 1789 to the Belle Époque*. Holmes and Meier, 1997.

Wright, Gordon. *France in Modern Times: From the Enlightenment to the Present*. 5th ed., W. W. Norton, 1995.

INDEX